Page One

Billy Cunningham of the Philadelphia 76ers is right at home in the tangle of bodies and arms in the key. A good outside shooter, Cunningham nevertheless loves to drive into the middle, take whatever shoves and bumps his opponents dish out, then put in the lay-up anyway. An ex-University of North Carolina star, he got his early karate training on the hard playgrounds of Brooklyn.

Pages Two and Three

The shot has missed in a close game as the Seattle and San Diego players look up into the bright lights and hold out their hands as if they were flood victims being dropped a bundle of relief supplies.

Page Four

Jostling, elbowing, sometimes blatantly shoving, the giants of the game battle for position under the basket. That iron hoop is only 18 inches in diameter, and the many shots that carom off it and the backboard are fought for violently. Here, 6 foot-10 inch Willis Reed of the New York Knickerbockers and 6 foot-8 inch Westley Unseld of the Baltimore Bullets, two of the best centers in the NBA, duel violently as Reed tries for a three-point play.

Page Five

As purple-clad Los Angeles center Wilt Chamberlain is caught by surprise, Milwaukee's meal ticket, Lew Alcindor, fires a jump shot over him. The Lakers' Jerry West, a mere 6 feet 3 inches, watches helplessly. Lew is amazingly agile and quick for a 7-footer. Overnight he made the Bucks a championship contender—and, perhaps as important, he made the franchise a lucrative one.

Pages Six and Seven

Soaring high above the basket in a way that the sport's inventor, James Naismith, never envisioned, the University of Houston's 6 foot-9½ inch Elvin Hayes blocks a shot in the famous 1967 Astrodome game against UCLA. As a record crowd of 52,693 watched in the domed stadium, the Cougars upset the Bruins and Hayes completely outplayed UCLA's Lew Alcindor (left, being blocked out by one of Hayes' teammates). But Lew got his revenge later in the NCAA semifinals in Los Angeles. UCLA massacred Houston and went on to beat North Carolina for the national championship. Shot-blocking intimidators like Hayes and Alcindor were common in the late 1960s and early 1970s, leading some coaches and officials to call for a 12-foot-high basket (the present height is 10 feet). Even when a giant center fails to block a shot, the threat of his presence often throws off the opponents' shooting, and the big man's mates can play more daring defense because they know he is behind them, ready to swat shots into the third balcony or force a sloppy pass.

Page Eight

Basketball is supposed to be a noncontact sport, but when you put 10 large, fast men on a court, the resulting swirl of action—leaping for rebounds, fighting through picks, dribbling up the middle—has to result not only in contact, but in collision. One of the problems is that the big men want to be in the same area—under the basket—and there just isn't room. Referees are faced with the problem of keeping some semblance of order while not letting the game degenerate into a free-throw-shooting contest.

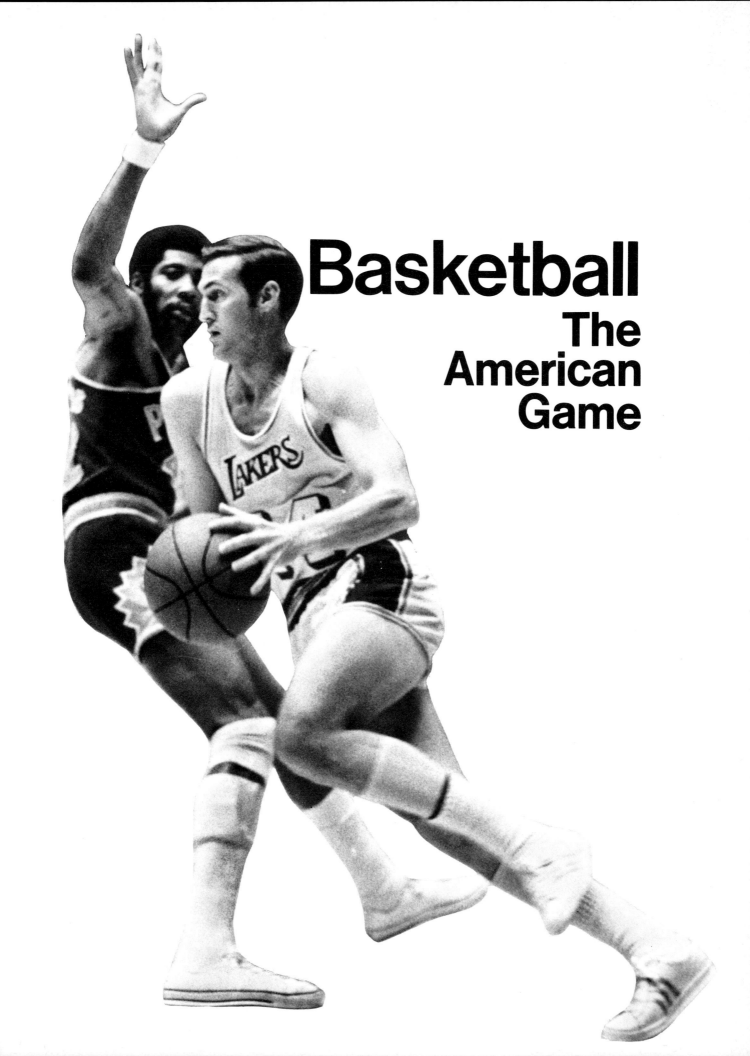

Basketball
The American Game

Basketball
The American Game

by Joe Jares

A Rutledge Book

Follett Publishing Company
Chicago

Fred R. Sammis	Publisher
John T. Sammis	Associate Publisher
Doris Townsend	Editor-in-Chief
Allan Mogel	Art Director
Marilyn Weber	Managing Editor
Myra Poznick	Art Associate
Jeanne Righter	Associate Editor
Arthur Gubernick	Production Manager
Diane Matheson	Production Associate
Suzy Jares	Photo Researcher

A Rutledge Book
ISBN 0–695–80203–8
Text copyright 1971 in all countries of the International Copyright
Union by Joe Jares
Photographs copyright 1971 in all countries of the International
Copyright Union by Rutledge Books, Inc.
Prepared and produced by Rutledge Books, Inc.
All rights reserved
This book is available at discounts in quantity lots
for industrial or sales-promotional use through
The Benjamin Company, Inc.
485 Madison Avenue
New York, New York 10022
Library of Congress Catalog Card Number: 73–146743
First Printing
Printed in Italy by Mondadori, Verona
Published by Follett Publishing Company
1010 West Washington Boulevard
Chicago, Illinois 60607

For Suzy

Contents

Introduction

Don't shoot from the corners

Sportswriter Dan Parker once called it "the silly business of throwing an inflated bag through a hoop." But there must be an almost unlimited supply of silly people in the U.S.A., for basketball is an immensely popular foolishness. Backboards and baskets are almost as much a part of the scene in the barnyards of America as weathervanes and those huge, faded barnside ads for Bull Durham chewing tobacco. A census-taker could drive up and down the avenues of some suburbs and tell which households had sons just by the baskets set up over garage doors. In the inner-cities kids shoot worn-out balls at bent hoops, and in the YMCAs paunchy businessmen relive old days in slow motion.

The Athletic Institute, a trade association of sporting-goods manufacturers, estimates that more than four million basketballs are sold in this country each year. An educated guess is that annual attendance at basketball games exceeds 150 million and that there are 16 million players—eight percent of the population.

There is something about the sport that inspires fanaticism. It is one of the few games that a kid can enjoy practicing by himself. All he needs is a ball, a basket and a little imagination. My own fantasyland was the playground at Palms Junior High School, two doors away from my house in Los Angeles. It was covered with asphalt and the backboards were mounted on top of iron poles. I used to climb the fence and practice shooting by the hour in my bare feet, toughened by whole California summers without shoes. When it got dark I would just move around to the side so I could see the rim outlined against the evening sky. A jump shot aimed at that rim was taken in the last seconds of the league-championship game; everything depended on me. Missed. Silence. Oh, well, this hook from the top of the key could win the *state* title. (We got there by fighting our way through the consolation bracket.) In! The imaginary cheers for that

T-shirted kid with the grimy feet filled the playground from the batting cage to the sand pit under the horizontal bar.

If there were other kids around, so much the better. Basketball is fun with any even number of players up to 12. One-on-one, two-on-two, full-court, halfcourt—it makes no difference. When we finally ran out of gas we'd play H-O-R-S-E. If the first kid made a left-handed fallaway jumper from the right corner, the second kid had to match it. Failure meant he had an H. If anybody had all five letters, he was eliminated. Nobody has ever explained to me why the game is called H-O-R-S-E and not S-N-A-K-E or C-U-R-S-E or C-R-A-Z-Y.

Of course, a playground is not absolutely necessary. I've seen games played in the street in northside Pittsburgh with the kids tossing a battered tin can through a sagging rim fastened to a telephone pole. A friend of mine who is a doctor of psychology grew up in the coal-mining town of Gallitzin, Pennsylvania. There was no place nearby to play basketball, so he walked two miles to the woods, cut down a tree, dragged it home and set it up in a hole dug in a field by his house. He made a "banking board" out of old lumber. He worked in a graveyard for a week to buy a ball, and covered it with tape to protect it from the elements and old rusty nails—until it weighed about 35 pounds.

"But we had some of the best times you could possibly imagine, slipping and sliding around on that field," he says. "There were about eight kids on the block and it was sheer joy for us."

An Indianapolis kid named Oscar Robertson had the same sort of devotion. He lived in a grim, tarpaper-roofed house on the west side of town and did his practicing two blocks away on an outdoor court known as "the dust bowl." He would come home every night and thoroughly wash his basketball with soap and water. However, the end result turned out better than for most of us fanatics.

After the rusty nails are cleared away, and after the mud
from the last rain has dried up, country boys from all over the
U.S. take to the courts. This is in Panguitch, Utah.

The height of what I call my "fullcourt career" was starting for the freshman team at the University of Southern California. There was one fellow on our team who had a basketball scholarship, and *he* never made the varsity—that's how mediocre we were. I was a slow 6 foot-2 inch forward with about as much aggression as a teddy bear. UCLA's frosh beat us four straight times.

The man playing behind me, Joe Braun, later transferred to San Jose State. I was reading the *Los Angeles Times* one morning and, lo and behold, Braun was leading the Spartan varsity in scoring. And here *I* was playing interfraternity ball and not even excelling at that! Jealous and frustrated, I wadded up the sports section and threw it at the wastebasket. It hit the back rim and bounced out.

Today my playing time is confined to lunch-hour halfcourt games at the West Side YMCA in New York. The first rule of Y basketball is: Don't shoot from the corners. At almost every Y in the country there is a running track encroaching on our air space overhanging each corner. Shoot with any arch at all and the ball comes right back in your face. The joggers on the track make their tedious way around and around. Some of them are so preoccupied with daydreams of winning the Boston Marathon they won't pause even for a second to kick down our ball when it gets lodged up there.

The second rule is: Get there early. With a little luck, two good teammates and a smidgen of high-school debating experience, you'll stay on the court the whole lunch hour.

The trouble with halfcourt games is that there are no referees. It is the responsibility of a man fouled to make the call himself, a system with obvious flaws. In a hotly contested game, some con men are going to try to win with their mouths (Trying to slay you with the jawbone of an ass?), making phony foul calls or, when they are accused

of fouling, loudly denying everything while wiping the blood off their sweat shirts. The cheating and arguing intensifies in direct proportion to the amount of time the losing team is going to have to wait before getting back on the court.

If an argument is a standoff, no one on the sidelines saw the play and one antagonist isn't significantly bigger and tougher than the other, the two debaters "choose it." They each put out one or two fingers at the same instant while one of them calls "odd" or "even." The winner gets the ball out of bounds.

Not only is a man hacked or shoved responsible for calling the foul, he must yell out the very second he is victimized (a small time lapse is allowed if he has been elbowed in the larynx). If a guy is creamed in the act of shooting, it is not cricket for him to wait and see if his shot is going to drop in before he sounds his complaint. It must be done right away. Often a man shoots and is fouled at the same time, calls the foul and sees the ball go in. Tough. He doesn't get the basket or a free throw. He merely gets the ball out of bounds.

Therefore, if an opponent gets around me and is sailing in for a lay-up, it pays to grab him. He loses his sure basket, I lose nothing.

There is an odd assortment of players at the West Side Y. We generally know each other by first name and style of game:

George: He's the managing editor of *Cosmopolitan*, a women's magazine, and it's great therapy for him to get away from all those women in his office and go work up a sweat with the boys. Has the spring and speed of a turtle but makes up for it by good positioning under the boards and a volatile debating style.

Kelly: Hooks with either hand. So easygoing and friendly that he lets physically weaker guys muscle him around. Once an All-America blocking back at Princeton, now an actor. Once saw him pull out his false teeth in a denture-cleaner commercial on TV. Presume he lost the teeth in football and not at the Y, but you never know.

The Midnight Cowboy: Fine physique and flowing blond hair but not very agile. Played against him one day and that night took my wife to see *The Boys in the Band,* an off-Broadway play about homosexuals. In the play the guest of honor at a fag party gets a birthday present, a husky male hustler, who turns out to be this fellow from the Y. "I hope this doesn't startle you," I whispered to my wife, "but I was in the shower with that guy this afternoon."

Then there is Rod, who used to run the hurdles for Penn State; Chuck, an ex-Penn player with a good hook, and actor Jim, who averaged 2.9 points a game in a brief NBA career (he does better than that against us). Ex-pro football player Frank Gifford and actor Elliott Gould used to play at the Y, but I haven't seen them there in at least a year. Unless they're inordinately busy in front of the cameras, I'm sure they're playing somewhere. Basketball is hard to get out of your system.

It is a sensual game to play—pleasurable to the senses of touch, sight and hearing. The nice sensation of fondling a new ball with its pebbly cover is sharpened if the manufacturer has spread a bit of stickum over the surface. I remember that my first leather ball was never allowed to touch anything but flesh, wood, hoop and net. One bounce of that sacrosanct leather on concrete would have jarred me inside. Owning it meant I no longer had to practice with one of those typical gymnasium monstrosities: smooth, peeling, dirt-darkened and heavy as a medicine ball. If there was a series of halfcourt games under way in the gym, I'd unobtrusively shoot around at one of the side baskets until it was my turn to get on. Then I'd offer to share my superior ball. But if my team was beaten and another group

was waiting to challenge, I was out of luck for a while. It was considered bad form to take the ball back until I was ready to go home.

Dribbling produces a reassuring thump-thump-thump, with different cadences for different players in different situations. Some highfalutin new surfaces, which have replaced wood at the University of Tennessee's fieldhouse and other places, are disturbing because the traditional staccato sound is considerably muffled. It's as if a ghost were dribbling, and it throws off visiting teams at first.

Shooting is an artistic, almost delicate action, requiring the hands of a surgeon or pianist to release the ball off the fingertips with a little backspin. Unless you're on defense, it's pleasant to see a shot arch up and go through the hoop, be held just a split second in the narrowed bottom of the net and then drop through with a sound that is more of a crisp *sschuu* than a swish. Making a shot through a hoop without a net is like pushing out the point of a ball-point pen and not hearing the click. Like stepping on peanut shells in Dodger Stadium and not hearing the crunch. Aesthetically disturbing.

That is not to say it is a garden party out there on the floor. It is a man's sport, especially under the basket, where most games are won. Scoffers should sit in the front row of the "end zone" seats at Madison Square Garden, almost close enough for the flying drops of sweat to land on their shoes. They would see how 235-pound Willis Reed of the New York Knicks and 245-pound Westley Unseld of Baltimore jostle and shove each other and try to block each other out. They would hear the grunts and growls and wince at the collisions. It looks as safe and sane as croquet from up high. From down close it is clearly mean and dangerous.

For the player it is exhilarating to leap high, grab the missed shot firmly with both hands and land with a WHOMP. Some prefer the one-handed method, *yanking* that ball down into the safety of the belly, protecting it from the clawing opponents. It is not so exhilarating to have a stray elbow loosen your front teeth. Or to have a higher jumping rival rip the ball out of your grasp from behind and wrench your back. Or to land on somebody else's foot and twist an ankle.

Basketball is a test: stopping and starting suddenly while the blisters rise on your feet, sprinting up and down the court until your lungs ache, making yourself run into that meat grinder under the basket to leap with the others. (How tempting to stand back after a shot goes up and assume it will go in.)

Maybe the biggest test is defense—"playing both ends of the court," in the lingo of the game. It is not as much fun as offense. It is not fun at all. New energy seems to surge through a player when his hands touch the ball. On defense nothing flows through the body except SOS messages to the brain from various weary parts. A defensive man must bend his knees, crouch, shuffle sideways like a crab, struggle to get through picks. He hears, "Don't let him beat you to the base line!" "Help out, help out!" "Keep your hands up!" "Bend those knees, they're the only springs in your body!" "You've got to talk to each other out there!" These are echoes from what seems like a thousand coaches in a thousand after-school practices in a thousand gloomy gyms, made gloomier still by the approaching dusk outside.

Playing defense is difficult, but playing it well results in victories and in a football lineman's sort of satisfaction from succeeding at a thankless task.

Basketball is not only fun to play, it is the best game in the world to watch. Soccer has more continuous action but, except for the goalies, soccer players don't use the most agile parts of their bodies. They kick the ball and even try to bang it off their heads into the goal—a look-ma-no-hands novelty act. Ice hockey players move up and down the playing area faster, but the puck is so small and the thrashing in front of the goal so violent that it is difficult to tell who scores (on television it is impossible). Besides, the armor packed on a hockey player is nearly as formidable and cumbersome as that of a knight entering a joust.

Basketball players, without the aid of skates, race up and down the court in the simplest of uniforms and, of course, use their hands to throw, catch, bounce and shoot the big, easy-to-see ball. The spectators are close and no buzzer, red light or siren is needed to tell them when a goal has been scored, even though the game is fast and clever. There are no goalies standing around inactive half the time.

Detractors claim that the sport is dominated by the referees, that it is simply one long parade back and forth between the free-throw lines. When I was growing up in Los Angeles, the sports editors of all four metropolitan newspapers seemingly hated basketball, and a well-known columnist, Braven Dyer of the *Times,* insisted on calling it "whistle-ball." But a stopwatch test will show that the most foul-filled basketball game has the ball in play for more minutes than any game of baseball or football. There is no huddle after every play, no relief pitchers ambling in from the bullpen, no interminable fouled-off pitches.

Another criticism is that basketball is dominated by freaks and goons. Is a 6 foot-10 inch center any more a freak than a 270-pound tackle? Wilt Chamberlain is 7 feet 1 inch, but in high school he ran the 440-yard dash and, without practice, triple-jumped 46 feet. At the University of Kansas, Olympic shotput champion Bill Nieder said that Wilt "is the only man I've ever hand-wrestled who I couldn't beat." Some goon. Bill Russell, agile and quick at 6 feet 9½ inches, high jumped 6 feet 7 inches in his first track meet. Some freak. *Time* once ran an article called: *The Graceful Giants.*

Crammed in among the tenements and small stores of the big cities are thousands of asphalt playgrounds, where kids shoot at bent hoops and dream of making high-school teams.

I have to confess that my arguments are weakened a little by some important dissenters in my own ranks. James Naismith, the man who invented basketball, once said he thought lacrosse was the best of games. I like to think that when he made that statement he was temporarily overcome with nostalgia for his McGill University days in Canada. John Wooden, UCLA coach and ex-Purdue guard, has openly said several times that baseball is his favorite sport, a shocking admission for a man from Indiana, where basketball is considered the most popular of the Protestant denominations.

Anyway, for those who like basketball—whistles and goons notwithstanding—I hope the words and photographs in this book capture so much of the game's flavor that it will be the next best thing to a spot in the starting five or a seat at courtside.

Joe Jares
RIVERDALE, N.Y.
JANUARY 1971

Chapter One / Beginnings

"Huh! Another new game!"

Shown here in his days as coach at the University of Kansas, James Naismith, a Canadian by birth, invented the game of basketball in Springfield, Massachusetts, when he was a young man just out of YMCA training school. OPPOSITE: An early demonstration of the sport before refs wore striped shirts.

One winter morning in 1891 a young Canadian named James Naismith walked down a hallway of the International YMCA Training School in Springfield, Massachusetts, with a soccer ball under his arm. The previous day he had thought up a new indoor game for his gym class, a group of would-be YMCA secretaries bored with calisthenics and Swedish gymnastics. He had already decided to use the soccer ball in his experimental diversion but had not found the boxes he wanted to use for goals.

"As I walked down the hall," Naismith wrote, "I met Mr. Stebbins, the superintendent of buildings. I asked him if he had two boxes about eighteen inches square. Stebbins thought a minute, and then said:

" 'No, I haven't any boxes, but I'll tell you what I do have. I have two old peach baskets in the storeroom.'

"I told him to bring them up, and a few minutes later he appeared with the two baskets under his arm. They were round and somewhat larger at the top than at the bottom. I found a hammer and some nails and tacked the baskets to the lower rail of the balcony, one at either end of the gym."

And that is how James Naismith almost invented boxball.

The Father of *Basket*ball was born November 6, 1861, in Almonte, Ontario, not far from Ottawa. His parents died when he was eight and he was reared by a bachelor uncle. He graduated from Montreal's McGill University in 1887 and then studied at a Presbyterian seminary for three years. During all seven years as a student he played on McGill's rugby team, a shocking activity that led some of his fellow theology students to meet and pray for his soul. He also played a bit for the Shamrocks, a professional lacrosse team in Montreal.

Before he completed his course at the seminary, Naismith decided he could better help people by being a physical education teacher. (He did get

Soon after a teacher from Buckingham Grade School formed the first girls' team, the idea evolved rapidly to sophisticated Wooden-type defenses, new uniforms and packed houses.

his degree, though, just in case.) At about the same time, a theology student at Yale—and an All-America end in 1889—came to the same conclusion. His name was Amos Alonzo Stagg. Naismith and Stagg met as students in the fall of 1890 at the YMCA Training School, later to become Springfield College.

Dr. Luther Halsey Gulick, the head of the school, was astute enough to recognize all this football talent and decided to field a team. He appointed Stagg captain and the team became known as "Stagg's Stubby Christians," starring Amos Alonzo at fullback and Naismith, all 160 pounds of him, at center. They played Harvard, Yale and the other top eastern teams of the day. In the old Madison Square Garden (there have been four Gardens in all), Naismith picked up a loose ball against Yale and ran almost the entire length of the field for a touchdown. To protect his cauliflower ears, he came up with what was probably the first football helmet. It was a cut-up rugby ball fitted over his head with flaps covering the tender ears.

Naismith was the jock-minister personified. He once preached a sermon at Springfield while sporting two black eyes from a football game. He asked Stagg why he had been placed at center. Answered the captain-coach:

"Jim, I play you at center because you can do the meanest things in the most gentlemanly manner."

Dr. Gulick, astute again, kept the two young men on as faculty members. Gulick was only in his early 30s at the time, but he made a big impression on Naismith, who described him as a tall man with "piercing blue" eyes and hair and whiskers that were "a peculiar shade of carroty red."

There was one particularly troublesome P.E. class at the school in 1891 and Gulick asked Naismith to take it over. Two teachers before him had failed to come up with anything to keep the class

interested for the whole period. Naismith tried to squirm out of the assignment, but Gulick was firm.

Naismith tried every indoor sport and activity he knew of to interest his new class. None generated much student enthusiasm. He tried to modify football for the indoors. A dismal failure. Then soccer, with the same sad result. Without much hope he tried lacrosse. It was far too rough in the confined space. Although dejected after the last experiment, he decided to try one more invention.

His basic idea was a game with a large ball because a little ball usually required a piece of "intermediate equipment" like a bat or stick. His second idea was to prevent the players from running with the ball.

"In my mind, I began to play a game and to visualize the movements of the players," he said. "Suppose that a player was running, and a teammate threw the ball to him. Realizing that it would be impossible for him to stop immediately, I made this exception: when a man is running and receives the ball, he must make an honest effort to stop or else pass the ball immediately. This was the second step of the game."

Step number three was probably the most important. What would he use for an objective? He visualized a goal at each end of the floor, à la football, soccer or lacrosse. The trouble with that was a hard-thrown ball would have a better chance of going in but "would lead to roughness, and I did not want that." Then Naismith remembered duck on the rock, a game he used to play behind a blacksmith's shop in Ontario.

A "duck" was a stone about as big as two clenched fists. There was also a large rock, on which the "guard" placed his duck. Another boy, from behind a line 20 feet away, would try to knock the guard's duck off the rock, retrieve his missile and get back behind the line before being tagged. Naismith remembered that it wasn't good strategy to throw the duck straight at the target. Whether or not a hard-thrown duck hit or missed, it went way past the big rock, making the chances slim for retrieval and getaway. It was much better to toss the duck in an arc because, if hit, the target usually fell on the far side of the rock and the thrown duck usually fell on the near side.

With this children's game in mind, Naismith visualized a horizontal goal, perhaps a box at each end of the floor. But how to keep the defensive players from simply gathering around the box? Well, he could place the goal above their heads. Eureka! It so happened that the lower rail of the balcony was ten feet above the floor, which is precisely the height of the hoop today.

After he put up the peach baskets, he spent less than an hour writing down thirteen rules on a scratch pad. Miss Lyons, the school stenographer, typed them on two sheets of paper and Naismith tacked them on a bulletin board just inside the gymnasium entrance.

Here are the original rules as they appeared a short time later—under the heading "A New Game" —in the school paper, the *Triangle*:

"The goals are a couple of baskets or boxes about fifteen inches diameter across the opening, and about fifteen inches deep. These are suspended, one at each end of the grounds, about ten feet from the floor. The object of the game is to put the ball into your opponent's goal. This may be done by throwing the ball from any part of the grounds, with one or both hands, under the following conditions and rules:

"The ball to be an ordinary Association football.

"1. The ball may be thrown in any direction with one or both hands.

"2. The ball may be batted in any direction with one or both hands (never with the fist).

"3. A player can not run with the ball. The

Although Naismith envisioned basketball as an indoor, winter sport, it quickly moved outdoors, too. Above, the equipment used in 1892 (from Amos Alonzo Stagg's lecture material). OPPOSITE: A player from 1909. Note size of the basketball.

player must throw it from the spot on which he catches it, allowance to be made for a man who catches the ball while running at a good speed if he tries to stop.

"4. The ball must be held in or between the hands. The arms or body must not be used for holding it.

"5. No shouldering, holding, pushing, tripping, or striking in any way the person of an opponent shall be allowed; the first infringement of this rule by any player shall count as a foul, the second shall disqualify him until the next goal is made, or, if there was evident intent to injure the person, for the whole of the game, no substitute allowed.

"6. A foul is striking at the ball with the fist, violation of Rules 3, 4, and such as described in Rule 5.

"7. If either side makes three consecutive fouls, it shall count a goal for the opponents (consecutive means without the opponents in the meantime making a foul).

"8. A goal shall be made when the ball is thrown or batted from the ground into the basket and stays there, providing those defending the goal do not touch or disturb the goal. If the ball rests on the edges and the opponents move the basket, it shall count as a goal.

"9. When the ball goes out of bounds it shall be thrown into the field of play by the person first touching it. In case of a dispute, the umpire shall throw it straight into the field. The thrower-in is allowed five seconds, if he holds it longer, it shall go to an opponent. If any side persists in delaying the game, the umpire shall call a foul on that side.

"10. The umpire shall be judge of the men and shall note the fouls and notify the referee when three consecutive fouls have been made. He shall have power to disqualify men according to Rule 5.

"11. The referee shall be judge of the ball and shall decide when the ball is in play, in bounds, to which side it belongs, and shall keep time. He shall decide when a goal has been made, and keep account of the goals with any other duties that are usually performed by a referee.

"12. The time shall be fifteen minute halves, with five minutes rest between.

"13. The side making the most goals in that time shall be declared the winner. In case of a draw, the game may, by agreement of the captains, be continued until another goal is made.

"The number composing a team depends largely on the size of the floor space, but it may range from three on a side to forty. The fewer players down to three, the more scientific it may be made, but the more players, the more fun. The men may be arranged according to the idea of the captain, but it has been found that a goal keeper, two guards, three center men, two wings, and a home man stationed in the above order from the goal is the best.

"It shall be the duty of the goal keeper and the two guards to prevent the opponents from scoring. The duty of the wing men and the home man is to put the ball into the opponent's goal, and the center men shall feed the ball forward to the man who has the best opportunity, thus nine men make the best number for a team."

The site of the first game was a former YMCA building at the northeast corner of State and Sherman streets in Springfield. The playing surface, 35 by 50 feet, was in the basement. A running track and gallery were on the street level above. The exact date is uncertain, but most likely it was sometime in mid-December. The first student who walked in, according to Naismith, uttered these historic words:

"Huh! Another new game!"

The world's first two basketball teams had nine on a side, only because eighteen men happened to show up for the class that morning. They were

ABOVE: Naismith (middle row in suit) poses with nine of the first eighteen players. The first game had nine on a side. LEFT: The site of the first game was the basement of this building, which has been torn down and replaced by a shopping center.

indeed men, not boys, and many of them sported beards or walrus mustaches. Their outfits consisted of long gym pants and long-sleeved jerseys. Eugene S. Libby of Redlands, California, and T. Duncan Patton of Montreal were appointed captains and they chose up sides. The first basket ever made was by William R. Chase of New Bedford, Massachusetts (he died August 30, 1951, at the age of 84), and according to Raymond Kaighn of Chapel Hill, North Carolina, the last surviving member of the team, it was the *only* basket scored that first game.

It was more of a melee than a game. There was no teamwork and everybody would converge on the man with the ball while Naismith, the first referee, stood there alternately blowing his whistle and yelling, "Pass it! Pass it!" Sometimes half a team would be standing in the penalty area on the sidelines.

"The forwards tried to make goals and the backs tried to keep the opponents from making them," wrote Naismith. "The team was large, and the floor was small. Any man on the field was close enough to the basket to throw for goal, and most of them were anxious to score. We tried, however, to develop teamwork by having the guards pass the ball to the forwards.

"The game was a success from the time the first ball was tossed up. The players were interested and seemed to enjoy the game. Word soon got around that they were having fun in Naismith's gym class, and only a few days after the first game we began to have a gallery."

The young instructor was forced to come up with another invention:

"Kids would sit on the balcony with their legs dangling between the bannisters and kick the ball away from the baskets," recalled Kaighn. "A few days later Jim erected some backboards and that was that."

Not long after the first game, Frank Mahan of North Carolina, another of the original eighteen, approached Naismith before class.

"You remember the rules that were put on the bulletin board?" he asked.

"Yes, I do," said Naismith.

"They disappeared," said Mahan.

"I know it."

"Well, I took them. I knew that this game would be a success, and I took them as a souvenir, but I think now that you should have them."

Mahan had stashed the two typewritten sheets in his trunk. He brought them in that afternoon and Naismith kept them as "one of my prized possessions."

The same Frank Mahan went to Naismith after a vacation period and asked him what he was going to call the game.

"I told him that I had not thought of the matter but was interested only in getting it started," wrote the founding father. "Frank insisted that it must have a name and suggested the name of Naismith ball. I laughed and told him that I thought that name would kill any game. Frank then said:

" 'Why not call it basket ball?' "

And that's what it was called from then on in the early days—two words, basket ball. It wasn't until about 1920 that it was regularly used as one word.

William C. Morgan, a YMCA instructor in another western Massachusetts town, Holyoke, invented a game in 1895 that also used a round ball and a net. He called it Minonette. The name didn't stick, but the game is one of the most popular in the world—volleyball.

The early years of basketball were—naturally—full of changes and "firsts." Teachers from Buckingham Grade School passed by the gym where Naismith's class was playing, looked at a few games and formed the first girls' team. It didn't take long for players to figure out that the dribble, originally intended as a defensive maneuver, was an offensive weapon as well. The double dribble was outlawed in 1898 and the rules makers also cracked down on the practice of running along juggling the ball.

The origin of the tipoff is obscured. Naismith wrote that he did not want the "mad scramble" that would result if he lined up the teams at either end of the court and threw the ball in the middle. Nor did he want the ball thrown in "between two lines of forward players" as in rugby. He finally decided to pick one player from each team and throw the ball up between them. However, he didn't mention the idea in his rules. Apparently many early referees did use the mad-scramble method until a center-jump provision was put in the rules in 1893.

Speaking of scrambles, Naismith's ninth rule—the first man to touch the ball after it had gone out of bounds could throw it back in without interference—led to desperate dives, fights and generally un-Christian behavior. When a ball landed in a balcony there would be logjams of bodies on the stairway, players elbowing and clawing each other in an early-day version of Roller Derby. Finally, in 1913, the rule book decreed that when a man knocked a ball out of bounds, or touched it last, a member of the other team should throw it back in.

The boundaries themselves often were poorly defined. Sometimes they were walls, which created great opportunities for players with billiards experience. By 1904, boundaries had to be straight lines. When backboards were placed flat against end walls, players could run up them for lay-ups. That gap in the rules was closed in 1916. Still, as late as 1953, Jefferson High School in Los Angeles had both backboards hung on the walls like pictures. The home team became adept at driving along the base line because anybody driving straight in toward the basket risked splattering himself against the bricks.

Some teams, usually professional, used chicken-wire or rope around the court. The Trenton, New Jersey, pro team is believed to have built the first "cage" for the 1896–97 season. Most were torn down by 1929–30, but basketball players are still called "cagers."

Naismith's original idea of "any number can play" didn't work. Ed Hitchcock Jr. of Cornell tried a game with about 50 on a side, with predictably chaotic results. After experiments with nine and seven and practically every other figure under 20, five-man teams were made mandatory in 1897. Free throws were introduced in 1894, first from 20 feet and then 15. Until 1924 a specialist on each team did all the foul shooting, which sounds pretty silly until you remember that football has place-kicking specialists to this day.

Why are basketball players called "cagers"? Cages, like the one above (at the Armory, Paterson, New Jersey), protected early spectators from players—or vice versa.

The original peach baskets didn't last long. In 1892 Lew Allen of Hartford, Connecticut, made cylindrical baskets of "heavy woven wire." The next year the Narragansett Machine Co. of Providence started manufacturing iron rims with braided-cord netting at fifteen dollars a pair. The referee pulled a chain attached to the bottom of the net and out rolled the ball—an enormous improvement (before, it was customary to have a man standing by with a stepladder or have the ball knocked out with an Indian club). The open-bottom net was approved for amateur championship play in 1912.

Backboards were made of many different materials, the most interesting being wire mesh. The mesh would develop dents known only to the home team. Plate-glass backboards were introduced in 1909.

Soccer and rugby balls, not really suitable for dribbling, were used in the early days, until—in 1894—the Overman Wheel Company, a maker of bicycles in Chicopee Falls, Massachusetts, manufactured the first basketball. Spalding replaced Overman in the late 1890s as the maker of the official ball. By 1905 the choice of brand was left up to each team or league. P. Goldsmith & Sons (which later became MacGregor) entered the field in 1903, Rawlings in 1905, Wilson in 1913 and Voit in the mid-1930s. The size of the ball has changed many times. It has been as big as 32 inches around, weighing 23 ounces. The official rules now decree its circumference should be no less than 29½ inches, no more than 30 inches; its weight not less than 20 ounces, not more than 22 ounces.

It was natural that the Young Men's Christian Association, with branches all over the country, should help popularize the new sport and sponsor some of the best teams. Perhaps the finest unit of the early years, certainly the longest lasting, was the Buffalo Germans, which played out of a YMCA on Genesee Street on that city's east side. Most of the people who used the facilities were of German extraction. The Germans played more than 30 years, disbanding in the mid- or late-1920s with a record of 792–86. In one stretch they won 111 straight games, the string ending when a team from Herkimer, New York, beat them in the middle of the 1910–11 season. They lost only six home games in 30 years, by a total of thirteen points. Two players, Al Heerdt and Eddie Miller, were with them from beginning to end.

The sport was introduced at the Buffalo Y in 1895 by Fred Burkhardt, who had learned the fundamentals from Naismith himself. Burkhardt organized a junior team that included Heerdt, Miller, Jay Bayliss, John Duerr and Alfred Haas (average age: fifteen) and it proceeded to clobber practically everybody.

In 1901 the Pan-American Exposition was held in Buffalo—and included a basketball tournament on a 40 by 60-foot grass court! The players had to wear cleats. The Germans, maturing young men by now and apparently unaffected by a grass-stained basketball, swept through seven straight games without a loss. The final scores of their preliminary-round games indicate what offensive thrillers they must have been: 10–6, 16–5, 10–5, 9–3, 10–4, 16–3.

For the final, against St. Joseph's of Paterson, New Jersey, three key Germans—Heerdt, Miller and Ed Reimann—were late. Buffalo had only three men on the court. For seven minutes the three controlled the ball as much as possible and played superlative defense to hold St. Joe's to a 1–1 tie. At that point, Miller pedaled up on his bicycle. Heerdt raced on the court after nine minutes had elapsed and played the rest of the half in his street clothes. Buffalo won 10–1.

An Olympic Games basketball demonstration tournament was held outdoors in St. Louis in the late summer of 1904. The Germans took that championship, too, winning four games against the strictly U.S. competition, losing none. They beat Xavier Athletic Association of New York 36–28, Missouri AA 97–8, Chicago Central YMCA 39–28 and the Turner Tigers of Los Angeles 77–6.* Buffalo finished that season with a 26 and 1 record, losing only to Allegheny College.

By 1905 the Germans had developed from a group of YMCA gym-rats into a formidable touring professional team. They received a five hundred dollar guarantee for playing a best-of-three series in Kansas City against the Kansas City Athletic Club. The club's star was guard-manager Forrest C. Allen, later to become a famous college coach. The Germans were billing themselves as "world champions," so it was quite an upset when Allen's team, after losing the first game, won the next two 30–28 and 45–15.

There is a perhaps apocryphal story that Buffalo originated the basketball doubleheader, playing both ends of it themselves. They once beat Dean Academy and the Carlisle Indian school on the same night. Before the Carlisle game the Germans watched the Indians warm up and took particular note of the famous football and track star Jim Thorpe. Then they gathered in a huddle to decide who was going to guard whom.

"How many points are you going to let Jim get tonight?" said Captain Heerdt in a loud voice.

"Well, two, maybe four," said Hank Faust. "No more."

Thorpe overheard, as he was meant to, and went out on the floor determined to show up the cocky Germans. But near the game's end Buffalo had the lead, as usual, and Jim had not scored. The action was under the Carlisle basket and Faust thrust the ball into Thorpe's hands.

"Here, shoot," he said. "If you don't get two points, I'll be a liar."

Some people around Buffalo claim the Germans played for 44 years, but there is almost no

mention of them after 1925. The German Y itself was shut down in 1927. The team did play an exhibition game in Tonawanda, New York, in 1931. Heerdt, Miller, Faust, George Schell and William Rohde, averaging 51 years of age, played in the game and won by one point.

Heerdt, who died February 4, 1958, just before his 77th birthday, remained in the sport for many years as a coach. In 1944, after CCNY had beaten Canisius by one point in Buffalo, the veteran CCNY coach invited Heerdt into the locker room. He told his players:

"I want you to meet the greatest basketball player of all time—Al Heerdt of the Buffalo Germans."

"No," Heerdt said. "Not Al Heerdt, the greatest basketball player. Al Heerdt of the Buffalo Germans, the greatest basketball team. Basketball is a team sport, not a one-man sport."

The YMCA also gave rise to professional and semipro teams in other parts of the East. The Ys in the Philadelphia area abandoned basketball as a competitive sport in the late 1890s because of rough play and lack of space. Some Y physical directors thought it was wrong to use such a large area for a ten-man activity. Teams then had to go out and hire halls and figure out a way to pay the rent. Charging admission was the obvious answer, and from there it was a small step for players to keep the surplus money, if any, for themselves.

Most historians agree that the first pro game probably was held in 1896 in a Trenton, New Jersey, Masonic hall. The Trenton players, some of whom had played for the local Y, received 15 dollars each, Captain Fred Cooper 16 dollars.

The first pro basketball league, the National, was formed in 1898 with six charter members: Trenton, Camden, New Jersey; Millville, Pennsylvania, the Pennsylvania Bicycle Club of Philadelphia,

* The records of the *Buffalo Evening News* show that the Germans played a fifth Olympic demonstration game, beating "St. Louis" 105–35. The *News* says the Xavier AA score was 38–28.

The Original Celtics, 1923. From left to right: Johnny Beckman, Johnny Whitty, Nat Holman, John Barry and Chris Leonard.

the Hancock Athletic Club and the Germantown Club. Trenton won the first two championships and the New York Wanderers (formerly of the Twenty-third Street YMCA) took the third. The league folded after the 1902–03 season.

To replace it, William J. Scheffer of the Philadelphia *Inquirer* organized the Philadelphia League, which soon expanded its horizons and renamed itself the Eastern League. The Central League, formed by a Pittsburgh newspaperman, started to play in 1906 and had such franchises as East Liverpool, Ohio, and South Side Pittsburgh. It ceased breathing in 1912. There were several others, just as ephemeral, most notably the Hudson River League, formed at Newburgh, New York, in 1909. The Troy, New York, Trojans dominated it to an unhealthy degree and quit after two seasons to go into the New York State League.

The Trojans began as an amateur team, Company E of Schenectady, New York, and beat the Kansas City Blue Diamonds for the national title in 1905. Representing Gloversville, New York, under the name of Company G, they beat the Buffalo Germans in an afternoon-evening doubleheader 51–33 and 56–13. Brothers Ed and Lew Wachter, William (Blondy) Hardman and James Williamson of Company E helped start the Trojans, who played

out of the medium-sized town of Troy, north of Albany where the Mohawk River flows into the Hudson.

Troy won the championship of the Hudson River League in 1909–10 and 1910–11 as Ed Wachter, Hardman and "Chief" Muller led the scoring. It switched to the New York State League and kept on winning titles, in 1911–12, 1912–13 and 1914–15. In 1915, six of the Trojans took a pioneering 39-day trip through the upper Midwest, following a rough schedule planned by Lew Wachter, who had to serve as both manager and sixth man. They played in Wisconsin, Minnesota, North Dakota, Illinois and as far west as Montana, winning 29, losing none.

The Trojans claimed to be the originators of several stratagems and rules changes, among them the fast break, the bounce pass and the idea that each player should take his own foul shots, rather than have a specialist on each team. The latter notion no doubt stemmed from the fact that all the Trojans were good free-throw shooters.

Good gymnasts, too. Trojan stars Jack Inglis and Andy Suils were playing with a team in Carbondale, Pennsylvania, when one of many touring outfits, Bill Manning's All-Stars, came through town. This was still in the era of the cages.

"I was guarding Inglis when he suddenly broke

downcourt," said one of the All-Stars. "I went right after him, hands high and flailing away to prevent any pass from coming over my head intended for Inglis. At that moment, Andy Suils threw a very high lead pass. Inglis leaped into the air on the left side of the basket, grasped the net enclosing the court and, flexing his left arm, raised his entire body higher into the air. He turned to his right, caught the pass from Suils with his right hand and with the same motion shot the ball cleanly through the basket."

Troy had many good players—Inglis, Suils, Dick Leary, Blondy Hardman—but 6 foot-6 inch Ed Wachter was considered the team's star and the greatest center of his day. He played on twelve championship teams from 1896 to 1924 and took part in about 1,200 amateur games and 1,800 pro games. Later he coached at Rensselaer, Albany State, Williams and, for thirteen years, Harvard (his record with the Crimson: 120 and 81). His brother Lew coached four years at Dartmouth and had a .694 winning percentage. Ed was one of the first three professional players elected to the Basketball Hall of Fame, along with Benny Borgmann and Barney Sedran.

Borgmann played in 2,500 pro games from 1918 to 1942, coached the game at two colleges, coached pro teams at Syracuse and Paterson, New Jersey, and worked as a big-league baseball scout. He played in at least three different leagues—in such cities as Paterson, Chicago, Newark and Kingston, New York—and led every one of them in scoring. He often averaged in double figures, quite a feat in those days. Sedran, who died in 1969 at the age of 77, played pro ball for fifteen seasons. He was considered too small to play basketball at New York City's DeWitt Clinton High School but, even though he was only 5 feet 4 inches and 118 pounds, he was able to survive in the elbow-swinging pro leagues. Playing for Utica, New York, in the 1913–14

season, he scored seventeen field goals in one game, without a backboard. In one three-game series, he suffered a two-stitch gash over his right eye the first night, a cut over his left eye the second and another cut over his right eye the third night.

"I kept playing," Sedran recalled a few years before his death. "You couldn't leave a game in those days. Once out, you weren't allowed back in."

Fouls were called only for assault with intent to kill, and players had to worry not only about their rough opponents but the fans and wire cages, too.

"Players were thrown against the wire," Sedran said. "Most of us were cut several times. The court was covered with blood.

"Ninety percent of the fellows I played with had broken noses. A good 50 years ago, it was more like hockey than basketball. If a fellow couldn't play defense, he couldn't draw a uniform. It was rough, maybe too rough."

John (Honey) Russell, who played more than 3,200 pro games with such teams as the Chicago Bruins, Rochester Centrals and Brooklyn Visitations, played with Sedran on the Northampton team in the Massachusetts League. He recalled the wild trips to Springfield, where the game was born:

". . . Springfield was always a fun-loving town. There was one night Barney went in for an easy lay-up and a front-row customer kicked him in the stomach. Marty Friedman, another teammate, ran over and yelled, 'Who did it?' All Barney could do was wave feebly in the direction of the crowd. Friedman charged out of the net cage, hauled a guy from a front seat and smashed him in the face. Unfortunately, it was the wrong guy. The riot lasted until 4 A.M.

"Every time we played in Springfield I wound up playing against Snooks Dowd. Snooks was a colorful one in every game he played—basketball, football or baseball. . . . Snooks was a cute one. He would maneuver me to the side on which his mother was sitting, right against the net and she'd jab me with her hatpin every chance she got."

Things were not as genteel in the Penn State League, where the coal miners would leave the pits and go directly to the games.

"The miners would always bring along handfuls of two-penny nails, which they would heat with their mining lamps before flicking them at the visiting team's foul-shooters," said Russell. "The local guys would practically invite you to chase a ball into a corner because the one who went after it there would always come out with a head ringing from fists full of nails."

Probably the best of the early-day pros, the Original Celtics, started as a New York City settlement-house team in 1914 and grew in prestige until they could demand as much as 5,000 dollars per game. Their star players made as much as 10,000 a year in the 1920s. They maintained a .900 winning percentage and between 1921 and 1928 their record was 720 and 75 (it was 204 and 11 one season).

"The stories you read about champions getting weary of winning are so much nonsense," said Nat Holman, captain of the team in its heyday. "No champion ever wins so many contests that he doesn't mind losing one."

The Celtics wandered all over the East, South and Midwest, seldom having a chance to rest and get their uniforms laundered, seldom having a home-court advantage and often playing in the most inhospitable gymnasiums America had to offer. Perhaps the worst place to visit was a dance hall in South Brooklyn. Its official name was Prospect Hall, but to the Celtics it was known as The Bucket of Blood.

"I used to wonder how they could get so many people into the place," recalled Celtic guard Henry (Dutch) Dehnert. "It seemed as though they

were hanging from the rafters. And the guys in the rafters thought nothing of shying a bottle at you when you were trying to shoot a foul. That was bad enough. But then the fellows sitting on the sidelines would trip you up when you were going down the court. Once a fellow stuck a lighted cigarette into the back of my leg as I was trying to pass a ball in from out of bounds. They were holy terrors."

Luckily the Celtics had a 6 foot-4 inch, 225-pound Pennsylvanian, George (Horse) Haggerty, to keep order on the court.

"Horse was my personal bodyguard," said Holman. "Any time I was hit, and I was hit a lot in those early days, Haggerty would go over to the fellow who fouled me, give him a robust nudge in the ribs and say, 'Now we're even.' They always knew what he meant, too."

In one of his books, *Holman on Basketball*, Nat, like Honey Russell and Barney Sedran, was able to reminisce almost fondly about cages and coal miners:

"Someone always came out of the wire cage with an infection because the darn things were always rusty. The game was so rough we used to wear hip pads and many a time I went to the foul line with tears in my eyes after two guys had whacked me. This was from a defensive maneuver we then called 'two men in.' Often it meant one man out.

"At a game in Scranton one night, Johnny Beckman, one of the greatest Celtics, was hit by a chunk of tobacco while he was at the foul line. Old Johnny rubbed his hand over the side of his face and hollered out, 'My God, I'm bleeding!' That was one of many funny incidents, but often we didn't know what those coal miners were going to throw at us. Many of them came to the games wearing their mining caps with carbide lamps attached and were pretty rough fellows."

John Whitty and Pete Barry were on the very first edition of the Celtics in 1914, when it was a team of kids from New York's West Side. World War I interrupted progress, but after peace returned, James and Thomas Furey reorganized the team and added the word "Original." That squad had Barry, Whitty, Ernie Reich (who died not long afterward, at the height of his career), Mike Smolick, Joe Trippe and Eddie White. Johnny Beckman and Dehnert joined up the next season.

In those days pros hopped back and forth from team to team, without contracts, getting 10 to 125 dollars an appearance and playing in 200 games or more a season. Joe Lapchick, who received his first basketball paycheck from the Yonkers Bantams in 1915 at the age of fifteen, played in four different leagues at once. Jim Furey didn't run the Celtics that way. He signed his players to exclusive contracts. Their success stabilized the game somewhat in the East and another good team arose, the New York Whirlwinds, featuring Barney Sedran, Chris Leonard and Holman (who also played for Germantown in the Eastern League).

In 1921 a three-game series between the Celtics and Whirlwinds was arranged. The first game drew 11,000 fans to the 71st Regiment Armory and the Whirlwinds won 40–27. The Celtics won the second 26–24 before 8,000 at the 69th Regiment Armory. The third game was never played and at the end of the season Furey lured Holman and Leonard over to the Celtics.

"He offered us, of all things, a seasonal contract," said Holman. "His offer amounted to more than we had ever dreamed of making playing ball and of course broke up the greatest team of all time [the Whirlwinds]."

At the end of the 1922–23 season, 6 foot-5 inch Joe Lapchick, the son of a Yonkers cop, jumped to the Celtics from the Visitations and replaced Horse Haggerty as the starting center. He played with the team for more than ten years, leaving it in 1936 to coach at St. John's University.

"The team had no time for alibis, excuses or explanations," he said. "The big asset was guts, and the only objective was to win basketball games.

"They were rough days and rough going. You carried your own uniform from game to game, night after night, with or without sleep and with no relief for aches and pains. There was no training season. You got in shape by playing. If you complained about anything, you were gutless. One thing you quickly learned—to keep your fingernails trimmed and check your opponent's hands to make sure his nails were cut.

"I believe the Celtics were 20 years ahead of their time. They introduced switching on defense, give-and-go and the pivot play; they were the first to operate as a unit with none of the members playing for other teams. . . ."

The pivot play was born during a southern swing. After performing in Florida, the Celtics went by train to Tennessee to play a local industrial team called the Chattanooga Railities. Nat Holman had to skip the trip and return to New York for business reasons, so the team picked up well-known pro Benny Borgmann to fill in. Dutch Dehnert remembered the details:

"Lapchick was a dandy at getting the tap. We had set plays from the tap, which no other club had ever heard of in those days. Beckie went in and took the first tap from Joe, passed over his head to me, and I went under and laid one up, coming up from guard position. Then Lapchick batted the next tap [the center jump was used after every basket] back to Barry, the other guard, and Pete dribbled in to score. We must have scored eight goals in two minutes, and we were in front 30–1 before there's a time out."

In the time out the Celtics discussed how to deal with Chattanooga's "standing guard," who was staying back on defense and causing trouble, although with that score the trouble must have been

slight. Dehnert suggested that he stand in front of the pest, receive passes from the other Celtics and give the ball back as they cut back and forth. It worked very well and in the next time-out huddle the Celtics were openly pleased with their innovation.

"Beckman was enthusiastic," said Dehnert, "and we knew if Beckie liked it we had something, because Johnny was the smartest man who ever played basketball.

"This was the pivot play, but we didn't even know it at the time. A couple of minutes later, however, the standing guard, in an effort to bat the ball out of my hands, moved around to my right side. All I had to do was pivot to my left, take one step and lay the ball up for a basket."

The Celtics were not above gimmicks, deceptions and pro-wrestling show biz to make money. One scheme was to allow a game to end in a tie and, since they had contracted to play only 40 minutes, walk off the court, while the local promoter hastily negotiated with their manager.

"If the promoter agreed to pay us extra for the overtime, we'd resume," said Lapchick. "If he refused, the game ended right there with no decision. . . . Besides, a tie was good for business. It left the fans talking and brought them out in droves when we returned there later that season or the following year."

The Celtics preferred to be independent, but they did play in two different leagues in the 1920s. They won the Eastern League pennant in 1921–22, beating Trenton in the playoffs. The next season they won thirteen straight games, then quit to return to the road. The American League, run by George Preston Marshall (better known for his pro football Washington Redskins) and Joe Carr (president of the National Football League), was a pioneer organization in that it banned the two-hand dribble and followed intercollegiate rules. The league had good teams in

Marshall's Washington Palace Five, the Chicago Bruins of George Halas, the Cleveland Rosenblums and Fort Wayne. The Celtics were not interested in joining up, but Carr forbade any of the A.L. teams to play them. That left the Celtics with the choice of joining or not having any top teams to compete against (and to draw customers).

They dominated the league, defeating Cleveland three straight in the 1926–27 playoffs 29–21, 28–20 and 35–32. They won again in 1927–28 and the cry went up to "Break up the Celtics!" They were, in fact, disbanded; the "cream"—Barry, Dehnert and Lapchick—went to the Rosenblums, who then won two straight titles. Holman went to Chicago and Haggerty landed with Washington.

In one tough Chicago–Washington game, the Palace Five was ahead by one point near the end and was stalling the time away. The ball was passed to Haggerty and all of a sudden Holman sprinted toward his own basket and yelled, "Here, George!" as loud as he could. Haggerty followed his old Celtic habit and threw a nice lead pass to Nat, who scored and won the game for Chicago.

After the Rosenblums won two championships, the Celtics regrouped and hit the road once more. In the spring of 1929 they played the New York Renaissance, a Harlem team run by West Indian native Bob Douglas, owner of the Renaissance Casino. This all-black team, which pre-dated the Harlem Globetrotters, had a load of stars in its 22 seasons (record: 2,318 wins, 381 losses), including Harold (Fats) Jenkins, 6 foot-5 inch "Wee Willie" Smith, Bill Yancey, William (Pop) Gates, Robert (Sonny) Wood, "Tarzan" Cooper and Eyre Saitch.

The first 1929 game was at the 71st Regiment Armory and Douglas put one of his best men, Cappy Ricks, on Holman. According to Nat, he scored fifteen points to Cappy's six. Also according to Nat, ". . . the Celtics never lost a series to any team during their entire playing period."

Knees better protected than feet, centers pose for center "jump." Joe Lapchick (left), a great star for the Original Celtics, is hardly taller than the referee.

Apparently he is only counting the seasons up to his retirement in 1930 because the *Converse Basketball Yearbook* says the Renaissance, or Rens, split a six-game series with the Celtics in 1926–27 and actually "trimmed a group of Celtic players in seven out of eight meetings" in 1933. On February 16, 1935, the tricky Rens controlled the ball for the last six minutes in a game in Kansas City and beat the Celtics by one point.

The Celtics of the 1930s toured in an old Pierce-Arrow and were sponsored for two winters by radio star Kate Smith. However, the '30s couldn't compare with the glory of the '20s, even though some of the names were familiar: Lapchick, Dehnert, Barry, Davey Banks, Nat Hickey, Pat Herlihy and Carl Husta. The Celtics' final appearance was on November 11, 1941, in Madison Square Garden, a 10-minute preliminary game against a group of New York Giants football players.

Despite the departure of the Celtics, the American League kept going, on and off, through 1951–52 with such clubs as the Brooklyn Jewels, Union City Reds, Hartford Hurricanes, Jersey City Atoms and Troy Haymakers. The dominant team through the 1930s and into the 1940s was the South Philadelphia Hebrew Association, known as the Philadelphia Sphas, managed and coached by The Mogul, Eddie Gottlieb.

Gottlieb, a native New Yorker who grew up in South Philly, helped organize the Sphas in 1917 when he was just out of high school. Earlier, the gang Eddie hung around with was asked to play basketball for a Young Men's Hebrew Association in North Philly. But the YMHA never came through with the promised carfare, so the next basketball season the boys accepted the sponsorship of a local Jewish social club in their neighborhood, the SPHA. It wasn't long before Eddie was running the outfit himself and it grew from amateur to semipro to pro. That was one of many things he promoted out of his hat, including pro wrestling, Negro baseball, semi-pro football.

For many years the team played home games on Saturday nights in the beautiful ballroom of the Broadwood Hotel, formerly an Elks Club. First, the ball game and the inevitable fistfights that went with it. ("The Sphas used to guarantee a fight every game," said Gottlieb. "Joe Sheehan and our Chickie Passon would start fighting right after they shook hands.") Then a nice dance. Gil Fitch, an ex-Temple star, used to play for the Sphas, then climb into a tuxedo and lead his dance band. Quite a bargain for nice Jewish girls bent on finding husbands and a little entertainment—they were charged only thirty-five cents and four or five Saturday nights a year they were admitted free. Gottlieb says it was common in those days for promoters to combine basketball and dancing, despite the resulting slippery floors. Some places had dancing at half time.

The Sphas dominated the Eastern League before switching, along with Trenton, to the American for the 1933–34 season. Trenton won the first half of the season, but CCNY star Moe Goldman joined the Sphas for the second half and they won all fourteen games, then beat Trenton in the playoff. They eventually won eight A.L. championships and The Mogul became one of the founding fathers of the National Basketball Association, in which games are seldom followed by anything more rhythmic than the clack-clack-clack of press-row typewriters.

The nation's high schools took an early interest in the sport, too. New Jersey, which produced the first pro team and had the dubious honor of introducing the cage, also had the first nationally celebrated high-school dynasty. The Passaic High "Wonder Teams" won 159 straight games from December 17, 1919, to February 6, 1925. The victory string started with a 44–11 win over Newark Junior College and ended five and a half seasons later with a 39–35 loss to Hackensack High.

For most of the way the coach was Ernest A. Blood, who taught basketball at many different places in his career, including four YMCAs and a Young Men's Hebrew Association. At most of his stops, losses were as rare as length-of-the-court field goals. Passaic's 100th win, 59–38 over St. Mary's Academy of Ogdensburg, New York, was broadcast by radio station WBAN in Paterson (something novel in those days), and the 150th win, according to basketball historian William Mokray—a graduate of Passaic High—was "the first high school cage affair ever filmed."

Blood's best players were John Roosma, a fine shooter who later led West Point to a 33-game winning streak and was elected to the Hall of Fame; Bobby Thompson, who scored more than 1,000 points in 1921–22, and Fritz Knothe, all-state for four years and later a weak-hitting infielder for the Boston Braves and Philadelphia Phillies. Knothe was one of two people who saw every one of the 159 wins.

Blood left Passaic near the end of the 1924–25 season and another coach handled the team in the final nine triumphs. Blood moved to St. Benedict's Prep in Newark and stayed for 24 years, compiling a 421 and 128 record and winning twelve state championships. After 52 years of coaching, he retired in 1949 with an amazing lifetime record (college, high school, YMCA and YMHA) of 1,268 wins, only 165 losses. He died in Florida in February of 1955 at age 82.

In the states that have season-ending, state-wide tournaments—Indiana, Illinois, Colorado and Ohio, for instance—there are almost always legends about some tiny, backward school in the boondocks (enrollment: 11 boys and three girls) that by a miracle once rose up and beat out the big-city powers for the championship. It won despite the handicap of having to practice outdoors with an old bundle of rags rather than a ball.

Of all the legendary boondock teams, none ever caught the public's fancy like that of Carr Creek, Kentucky, in the season of 1927–28. The wire services filed reams of copy about the skinny hill-billies, and Will Rogers wrote about them in his syndicated newspaper column. The team was made up of eight country boys, all related. Carr Creek is in mountainous Knott County in the southeastern part of the state, and even today it isn't what anyone would call a metropolis. In those days the team played most of its home games outdoors, which was probably OK as far as the visitors were concerned because the tiny indoor court was in a hall with a 13-foot ceiling. Shots in that place had about as much arch as a shot from Daniel Boone's rifle.

Carr Creek did well in the regular season and was invited to the regional at Richmond, so the local folks got together enough money to buy the players makeshift jerseys and shorts. Surprisingly, they played beautifully in Richmond and qualified for the state finals, to be held at the University of Kentucky's gymnasium in Lexington. The people in Richmond were so impressed that they bought the players eight new uniforms. To get to the big city, the boys had to travel to Jeff by log wagon, then to Sassafras by bus, then to Lexington by train. It was the first time any of them had been on a train.

Carr Creek surprised everybody again by reaching the championship game against Ashland, unbeaten in 37 games and captained by Ellis Johnson (later a star at Kentucky). The game went into four overtimes before Ashland pulled it out 13–11, Johnson dribbling around, in and out, to use up the final seconds. Ashland thus qualified for a national tournament being run at that time at the University of Chicago by Amos Alonzo Stagg. Carr Creek had attracted so much attention that it was invited along, too.

The mountain boys beat teams from New Mexico, Texas and Connecticut before losing to

Georgia 23–11. Ashland won the national champion-
ship by beating Naugatuck, Connecticut; Orego,
Missouri; Morris, Alabama; Vienna, Georgia and
Canton, Illinois.

The first three colleges to have basketball teams
(after the YMCA Training School in Springfield, of
course) were the University of Chicago, Geneva
College of Beaver Falls, Pennsylvania, and the University of Iowa, all in 1892–93. A few other pioneers
were Yale and Wesleyan in 1895–96, Pennsylvania
in 1896–97, Notre Dame, Dartmouth and Cornell in
1897–98, and Harvard, Columbia and Princeton in
1900–01. Some of the schools we associate with the
sport today were relative latecomers—Kentucky in
1904–05, Utah in 1908–09 and UCLA in 1919–20, a
real straggler. At that time UCLA was the poor little
stepbrother—the "Southern Branch"—of the University of California at Berkeley. The Bruins played
such opponents as Hollywood and Polytechnic high
schools.

The first intercollegiate game with five on a
side was played January 16, 1896, Iowa versus
Chicago at Close Hall in Iowa City. Chicago won
15–12. Two of Naismith's friends from Springfield,
Amos Alonzo Stagg and H. F. Kellenberg, had introduced the sport at the two Midwest schools. In
the East the first five-versus-five game was played
by Yale and Penn on March 30, 1897.

Yale was a leader in the sport. In 1896 the
Bulldogs played the Brooklyn Central YMCA at the
13th Regiment Armory and won 8–7, with the aid
of a referee who penalized the Y players several
times for rough and even dirty play. During the
Christmas season of 1899 an eight-man squad from
Yale went barnstorming across the country in what
was advertised as "the longest trip ever taken by a
United States college team."

The captain was Albert H. Sharpe, a versatile
fellow who rowed for the crew, pitched for the
baseball team (he once beat the New York Giants)

On December 29, 1934, sportswriter Ned Irish staged Madison Square
Garden's first college-basketball doubleheader. St. John's
met Westminster in one game. Here, NYU hosts Notre Dame.

and made the All-America team as a halfback. He later became a successful football and basketball coach at Cornell and other schools. Even with athletes of his caliber, the trip was not a completely joyous one for Yale. The Bulldogs won two games on the way to the Chicago area and two on the way back, but several games were canceled and they were forced to step down and play the Company E team of Fond du Lac, Wisconsin, three times in a crowded old armory and lost all three.

College basketball was not a big deal in those days, and this is proven by the fact that players whose names most people remember actually earned their fame in other fields: Stagg (football), "Greasy" Neale of West Virginia Wesleyan (football), Jim Thorpe of Carlisle (football and track), Christy Mathewson of Bucknell (baseball), coach Joseph Stilwell of West Point (the Army, as General "Vinegar Joe" Stilwell).

The names of the men who made their reputations essentially in basketball are buried in the back pages of college press guides and the fading memories of old-timers. Christian Steinmetz of Wisconsin, Class of 1905, once scored 50 points in a game, 60 years or so before Lew Alcindor. John Schommer of Chicago, a great defensive player of the early 1900s, scored an 80-foot field goal versus Pennsylvania. Victor Hanson, Syracuse '27, scored 25 of his team's 30 points against Penn. Charles Hyatt, Pittsburgh '30, led his team to a 60 and 7 record over three years and after that was an AAU All-America for nine seasons. Montana State had a 102 and 11 record the three seasons ending in 1929.

Even when a college basketball game was considered important, interest was usually confined to one region. Styles and strategy developed independently on both coasts and in the South and Midwest. Fans in New Haven, Connecticut, or New York City didn't know about, or much care about, teams and players in California or Kansas.

Interest on a nationwide basis really started in the late 1930s with the launching of the two big national tournaments, the National Invitation and the National Collegiate. The situation was helped over a 20-year period by the ending of the center jump after each basket, improved methods of travel and increased attention from the national media, notably the wire services, *Sports Illustrated*, *Sport* and *The Sporting News* (the first national polls appeared in 1929 in *College Humor*).

James Naismith, the man who started it all, did not drop out of sight, although he was seldom treated like a celebrity. He left Springfield and spent three years at Gross Medical College in Denver, paying his tuition by working as a gym instructor at the local YMCA. He received his doctorate in 1898 and, on the recommendation of Amos Alonzo Stagg, was hired by the University of Kansas, to be director of physical education and leader of prayers at chapel. Naturally, he introduced basketball.

KU's first official game was on Friday, February 3, 1899, versus the Kansas City YMCA. Naismith refereed before 150 people and KU lost 16–5. The university's student newspaper reported that a notorious fellow named Jesse James played "at times a very ungentlemanly game" for the Y. He had to be cautioned and punished.*

Naismith was at Kansas more than 40 years, with the exception of almost two years in France in World War I (for the YMCA) and a few months as chaplain with a Kansas regiment on the Mexican border in 1916. His way of keeping the soldiers on leave in the camp—instead of going into town and getting into trouble—was to stage boxing matches in the camp. ("Prize fights may sound like strange preaching," he said, "but they did work.") At Kansas he coached basketball—although he preferred the word "taught"—for nine years and had

* This player might indeed have been notorious and might even have been named Jesse James, but he was not the infamous outlaw. That Jesse was dead.

a losing record (53 and 56), which his successor, Forrest (Phog) Allen, called "a case of 'physician, heal thyself' if I ever heard one."

A 1947 book, *Coach Phog Allen's Sports Stories,* tells of Phog's start in coaching. Dr. Naismith had received a letter from Baker University saying it wanted to hire Allen. Later that day Naismith met Phog in old Snow Hall on the KU campus.

"I've got a good joke on you," said Naismith. "They want you to coach basketball down at Baker."

"What's so funny about that?" asked Phog.

"Why, you can't coach basketball. You just play it," Naismith told him.

"Well, you can certainly teach free-throwing. And you can teach the boys to pass at angles and run in curves."

In 1927 there was a move to outlaw dribbling by limiting a player to one bounce each time he had the ball. A small story in the April 10, 1927, *Des Moines Register* was headlined, "Cage Dribble Is Restricted to a Single Bound." The next day in Lawrence, Kansas, both Naismith and Allen spoke out against the change. On April 15 Phog spoke to a physical education convention in Iowa and asked for a hand vote on the rule; only one man was for it. Two weeks later at the Drake Relays, a big force of college basketball coaches showed up to protest. Thanks mostly to Phog, the dribble was reinstated.

A member of the current KU coaching staff was going through old game films recently and made a rare discovery, a silent, three-reel film directed by Phog in about 1936. Titled "Modern Basketball Fundamentals," it features some of the most god-awful, old-fashioned techniques imaginable. More importantly, it begins with Phog and Naismith standing side-by-side holding a ball and discussing the sport. Present KU coach Ted Owens said he was going to donate the movie to the Basketball Hall of Fame in Springfield.

After giving up control of the Kansas team in 1907, Naismith still went to see most of the Jayhawks' home games but never raised his voice or showed excitement. And rather than watch his protégé, Allen, run practices, he'd be off in a corner of the gymnasium teaching a small group of students how to fence. He was unhappy about some of the changes others had made in his invention, including the rule requiring the offense to cross the center line in a certain amount of time. He told a newspaper interviewer:

"From a pastime played all over the court, and which required a good degree of smart maneuvering, basketball now has evolved into one of speed, confusion and congestion, because all of the ball-handling and passing has to be done in one-half the court."

Nor did he approve of the elimination of the center jump after each score:

"They could have had rotating centers, where each member of the two teams are paired according to their height, and each pair asked to jump at center when their turn came. That way, no team would have any special advantage. . . ." He added, "Some of the game's cleverest and most thrilling plays came on premeditated moves around the center jump."

Two years after the center jump went out, on November 28, 1939, Dr. Naismith—an ordained Presbyterian minister, a professor with many degrees (including one in Greek), an athlete with cauliflower ears from wrestling and rugby—died, 78 years old.

A simple, modest man, he made hardly a penny from basketball. He once let Phog talk him into endorsing a certain brand of ball, but the royalties he got from that would have made a big-time professional athlete laugh. Charles Darrow, the man who invented Monopoly, the boxed play-money game, made millions of real dollars from his brainchild. The inventor of basketball died with his house still mortgaged.

Phog, the Baron and the India rubber man

Madison Square Garden Number Three, which was not on Madison Square or even Madison Avenue, had a seedy-looking marquee more suitable for advertising peepshow skin flicks than sporting events. In the busy forecourt the scalpers quite openly hustled their tickets. Next door, hungry people with good subway combat training elbowed their way up to the counters at Nedick's to fight for hamburgers. Inside, the tobacco smoke was so thick you couldn't see your hand in front of your face. The basketball floor was very old—one player insisted it was "made out of planks that were part of the *Mayflower's* deck."

Garden Number One stood 52 years and was torn down in 1889. Number Two, designed by Stanford White for a seventy-five thousand dollar fee and opened in 1890, had a 332-foot central tower, "graced at its pinnacle by a bronze statue of Diana, Greek Goddess of the Hunt." Number Three opened in 1925 and was replaced in 1968 by Number Four, perched atop Pennsylvania Station sixteen blocks south. Number Three is now a parking lot, but even though its grimy bricks have been disassembled and carted away, it will be remembered for giving college basketball its biggest boosts upward in the 1930s.

In 1934, Edward Simmons (Ned) Irish, who was making about forty-eight dollars a week as a sportswriter for the *New York World-Telegram*, came up with the idea of promoting college-basketball doubleheaders in the Garden. One of the sport's enduring legends is that Irish got his inspiration one night when he couldn't get into Manhattan College's jammed gymnasium to cover a game, had to crawl in through a window and in the process ripped his best pair of pants. The trousers no doubt did get torn, but the true inspiration probably was a pair of Garden tripleheaders Irish helped promote in 1931 for the Mayor's Unemployment Relief Fund. There had been pro doubleheaders long before at

various armories and on the stage of the New York Hippodrome.

The head of the Garden, General John Reed Kilpatrick, would not assume any of the risk and Irish had to pay a flat rental. He came out ahead on the deal. His first card, December 29, 1934, had St. John's versus Westminster and New York U. versus Notre Dame. It drew 16,138 fans. His eight programs that season attracted 99,955 people, an average of more than 12,000. Soon Ned was the Garden's basketball boss. Attendance at his promotions there the first six years was 1,014,000.

The sportswriting business also deserves credit for the start of the National Invitation Tournament (NIT), staged in the Garden at the end of every season. The Metropolitan Basketball Writers Association launched it in 1938. (Present Supreme Court Justice Byron White played for Colorado in the first one; the Buffaloes lost to Temple in the final 60–36.) The Eastern Collegiate Athletic Conference has been running the NIT since 1940.

"The writers found it too hot to handle and asked us to take it over," said Asa Bushnell of the ECAC. "People kept making snide remarks about the writers all driving new cars from the proceeds of the tournament and they figured they had better drop it because it was a conflict of interest."

At first only six teams were invited, then eight. In 1949 four New York schools, CCNY, Manhattan, NYU and St. John's, were competing for the last spot and couldn't be separated. The selection committee decided to take all four and add another team to make an even twelve. Today there are sixteen teams in the opening round.

The Garden became the proving ground of college basketball. Ignatz Glutz could average 60 points a game in Peoria or Laramie, but until he did something of note in the cigar-smoke haze of the Garden, he was just another unproven hotshot from the sticks (which, to many New Yorkers, meant any-

UCLA's Sidney Wicks frustrates a Wyoming scoring attempt. With Alcindor's departure, Wicks became the Bruins' big man, leading his team to a fifth consecutive NCAA title.

1923 champs, Kansas. Notables are Adolph Rupp, top left, Phog Allen and James Naismith, center in suits, and in the first row with ball, Paul Endacott, one of the greatest.

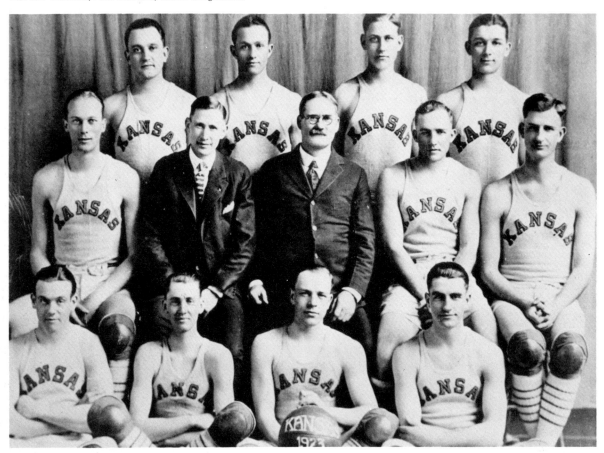

thing west of Hoboken, New Jersey. There were All-Americas who never had a bad game in their college careers but flopped before the big-town cognoscenti. One was Ken Sears of Santa Clara, who made up for it later by becoming a good player for the New York Knickerbockers.

"It was awful," he said of his debut. "The publicity people had been giving me a terrific buildup. Big West Coast star, and all that. So we came into the Garden to play St. John's and I'm the biggest bust in town. I was trying so hard to make good that I couldn't do anything right. They call it 'Gardenitis' in New York. Well, by the time I fouled out in the third period, I had scored exactly four foul shots. I couldn't sink one field goal."

Among those who passed the Garden test—in fact, the guy who probably made the best impression of any visiting college player ever—was Angelo Enrico Luisetti of Stanford, nicknamed Hank. In December of 1936, Stanford beat Temple 45–38 in

Philadelphia, then traveled north for a much more important game. The Indians were to play Long Island University, which had won 43 straight. The LIU Blackbirds were coached by Clair Bee and had a rosterful of eastern stars, including Jules Bender (Bee's first All-America), Ben Kramer and Art Hillhouse. Most of their home games were played at the Brooklyn College of Pharmacy, but this game was one of Irish's Garden specials and attracted 17,263 fans.

LIU scored first, but Stanford pulled ahead and had an eight-point lead at the half, which was a very substantial lead in those days. More startling than the potential upset was the way Luisetti was shooting. One-handed! OK, a lay-up or a short hook with one hand, but this guy was shooting from some distance! Stanford went on to win 45–31 and Luisetti scored fifteen points.

Today, thanks mostly to him, someone who uses a two-handed set shot is considered a throwback to the Pleistocene epoch, but in 1936 that was the only way to shoot. "I'd quit coaching before I'd teach a one-hand shot to win a game," said CCNY's Nat Holman. "Nobody can convince me a shot that is more a prayer than a shot is the proper way to play the game." Nat was overruled by practically everybody—but stayed in the business anyway.

"I'll never forget the look on Art Hillhouse's face when I took that first shot," said Hank. "He was about 6 feet 8 inches and he never expected a shot like that to be thrown. Guess he'd never seen one.

"When it hit I could just see him saying, 'Boy, is this guy lucky.' But that was the way we shot. That was what made it for us. Nobody but us believed we could win that night."

"It seemed Luisetti could do nothing wrong," said *The New York Times* the next morning. "Some of his shots would have been deemed foolhardy if attempted by anybody else, but with Luisetti shooting, these were accepted by the enchanted crowd."

Stanford went east again the next season, when Hank was a senior, and beat LIU by fifteen and CCNY by three. In the latter game he had only six points at half time, although he had played well. In the second half he scored thirteen straight points and put Stanford in front to stay. One reporter called it "a breathtaking exhibition of exquisite artistry." But it was the December LIU game in 1936 that created the Luisetti legend and popularized the one-hand shot. It was one of many examples, before and since, of a man's reputation being made in New York City.

"I guess we didn't really know what we were starting that night," said Luisetti. "We actually had no idea that we would bring on a revolution. You know, I've thought about that night many times over the years. I had no notion what that one game would mean to me. Getting all that publicity in New York changed my life, my whole life. It made me

Superbly conditioned, a relentless competitor, John Wooden was an idol at Purdue. Wooden today, face more lined, glowers at refs as he did at cameras forty years ago.

a national figure with stories about me in the *Saturday Evening Post* and *Colliers* and all that. I had just been a local kid up until then."

Local kid Luisetti was a star at San Francisco's Galileo High School, near Fisherman's Wharf. (The same school already had produced baseball star Joe DiMaggio and many years later was to graduate a football player named O. J. Simpson.) He started shooting with one hand at Spring Valley Playground at Broadway and Larkin (now Helen Wills Moody Playground) because "It was the only way I could reach the hoop when I was a little kid." According to Dick Friendlich, a San Francisco basketball writer for many years, others before Luisetti at Galileo had done the same thing. Hank just perfected the method. Still, he scored only 54 points his whole senior year and was sought by the local colleges more for his tough defense and clever dribbling and passing than for his scoring potential.

Stanford got him and, of course, most of his heroic deeds were performed on the West Coast. With eleven minutes left against Southern California (during his sophomore year) he had only six points. In the last minutes of the game he hit 24 points to lead the Indians to a 51–47 victory. He scored 20 points against Oregon one night, mostly from inside. The next night the Ducks wouldn't allow him anywhere near the hoop, so he lofted in 26 points from outside. In March of 1938, his senior season, Stanford battled California in Berkeley for first place in the Pacific Coast Conference's Southern Division. Luisetti ended the first half with a 50-foot field goal, was knocked cold in the second half, returned to the game and ended up with 22 points. Stanford won 63–42 and took the division title for the third straight season.

Charles Hyatt, a Hall of Fame player from Pitt, thought that Luisetti was the greatest player up to World War II.

"I've seen most of them—Beckman, Holman, Dehnert, Banks and the others," he said, "but this boy is the last word."

Recollections of Luisetti might be even more vivid today if he had ever played pro ball. He never did, although the Amateur Athletic Union had him labeled as a professional for a year. That happened because Hank and several of his teammates appeared with Betty Grable in a college basketball movie *Campus Confessions.* Hank received ten thousand dollars and the AAU figured he was naughtily trading on his basketball fame. He was reinstated in 1940 and played parts of two seasons with the San Francisco Olympic Club and the Phillips 66ers before joining the Navy.

Playing for the Navy's St. Mary's Pre-Flight team, Luisetti probably was at the top of his game. People who followed Bay Area basketball at that time say he invariably outplayed another ex-Stanford star, Jim Pollard (later to be a pro all-star), whenever they met. Twice he scored 32 points in a game. In 1944 he was assigned to the aircraft carrier *Bonhomme Richard* as athletic officer. He traveled to the East Coast, but before he shipped out he contracted spinal meningitis and was in a coma for a week. Although he recovered (thanks to the miracle sulfa drugs, he says), doctors warned him to stay away from competitive basketball. Thus, when major-league professional basketball was in its infancy in the late 1940s and early 1950s, perhaps the greatest player who ever lived was home in San Francisco coaching an AAU team, the Stewart Chevrolets.

The NCAA Tournament started in 1939, one year after the NIT. The first championship game was in Northwestern's Patten Gym, where Oregon defeated Ohio State 46–33. To get there, the Ducks from Eugene, Oregon, had won a playoff for the Pacific Coast Conference title, then defeated Texas and Oklahoma. Because of their front line, 6 foot-8 inch Urgel (Slim) Wintermute, 6 foot-4 inch John

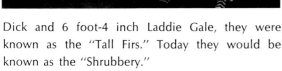

LEFT: Young George Mikan of Joliet, Illinois, gets instructions from DePaul coach Ray Meyer. BELOW: Oklahoma A&M's giant Bob Kurland gets NCAA most valuable player medal, 1946.

Dick and 6 foot-4 inch Laddie Gale, they were known as the "Tall Firs." Today they would be known as the "Shrubbery."

Their victory might not have meant much to most of the country (only slightly more than 15,000 fans attended tournament games), but in Oregon it was big news. The team came home by train and thousands of people crowded the depots at Pendleton and The Dalles to catch glimpses of their heroes. A crowd of about 10,000 met them at Portland and paraded them through the downtown streets, and the next day in Eugene they basked in still more adulation.

In 1942 two awkward midwestern giants entered college, fortunately came under the influence of intelligent, patient coaches and later exercised tremendous influence on the NCAA, the NIT and even the history and rules of the sport. They were George Mikan, 6 foot-9 inch center at DePaul (later in the pros he was listed at 6 feet 10 inches), and Bob (Foothills) Kurland, 7-foot center for Oklahoma A&M (later renamed Oklahoma State). Both were born in 1924, Mikan six months before Kurland.

Mikan, of Croatian and Lithuanian descent, grew up in Joliet, Illinois, southwest of Chicago. When he was twelve years old, his brother—while whittling—accidentally cut him in the right eye with the knife, and he had to wear strong glasses after that. George dropped out of Joliet Catholic High School and enrolled at Quigley Preparatory Seminary in Chicago with the intention of becoming a priest. His basketball training took place in his own yard and in Catholic Youth Organization leagues. In a 1939 CYO game in Waukegan he suffered compound fractures of his right leg. He was carried home in a pickup truck, and was in bed, on crutches and walking with a cane for eighteen months.

George gave up the idea of entering the priesthood (a deficiency in Greek and an efficiency in basketball had something to do with it). Notre Dame coach George Keogan saw him in a 1941 workout and turned him down for a grant-in-aid but, not long after, an ex-Notre Dame assistant, Ray Meyer, recruited Mikan for DePaul, a Catholic school in Chicago.

"I had some speed, but I was not agile," said George later. "I could shoot only with my right hand. Meyer went to work on me. He gave me the correct outlook. I remember how he stressed work as the prime factor in success. Every night he kept feeding me the ball on my left side. It took me two years to master the shot, but now it is more accurate and natural than my right."

Kurland was even less an obvious prize than Mikan. He was 6 feet 6 inches tall at age 13 and 6 feet 10 inches as a senior at Jennings High School near St. Louis. His high school coach knew A&M coach Henry Iba, and Iba worked with the youngster in the summers.

"One afternoon that I recall, Bob must have tried 600 hooks with his left hand," said Iba. "The first 100 didn't hit either the rim or the backboard. The next 100 didn't go in. After that, he started to connect."

"Neither St. Louis U. nor Washington U. (in St. Louis) was playing top-rung teams in basketball at that time," said Kurland. "I wanted to go to the University of Missouri, but football was the big sport there at that time and I wasn't offered a scholarship. I at least had to have my board and room furnished. Hank [Iba] told me that if I kept up my grades and did the outside jobs that I was assigned to, he'd see that I graduated, regardless of how I played."

Iba was the master of discipline, organization and defense. He would not tolerate sloppy play. ("I've seen Mr. Iba cringe when the *other* team makes a mistake," said his longtime assistant and recent successor, Sam Aubrey.) A&M once lost a game to George Washington University by four points and the GW fans went wild and their band played "Happy Days Are Here Again" eighteen times. On the train out of Washington, D.C., Iba sat slumped in his seat. Suddenly he straightened up.

"Those people sure were happy," he said. "I don't believe I've ever seen a happier group of people. Hell, we can't go around the country making people happy!"

Kurland was a varsity substitute as a freshman in 1942–43 and averaged only 2.5 points a game. He improved to 13.5 as a sophomore and developed into a fine shot blocker. (He, Mikan and 6 foot-11½ inch Don Otten of Bowling Green were primarily responsible for the NCAA's rule against goal tending, i.e., interfering with a shot on its downward flight to the basket.) In 1944–45 everything fitted together and the Cowboys went to the NCAA Tournament with a 23–4 record. One of their losses was to DePaul 48–46 early in the season.

A&M's excellent starting five—Kurland, Cecil Hankins (also a good football player), Weldon Kern, Doyle Parrack and Blake Williams—were well-schooled in Iba's disciplined offense and tough defense. They made it into the final at Madison Square Garden versus New York U. and won a close battle 49–45. Kurland scored 65 points in the three games and was voted the most valuable player.

But in those days the NCAA playoffs were matched in importance by the NIT, and in that tourney, held at the Garden earlier, Mikan was the hero. Big George's game apparently was not affected by spending nights away from the 8-foot-long, 6-foot-wide bed made for him by inmates —and fans—at Joliet State Penitentiary. He scored

33 against West Virginia, 53 against Rhode Island State and led DePaul's Blue Demons to an easy 72–54 victory over Bowling Green in the final.

Bowling Green had tall Don Otten, but Mikan outscored him 34–7, upping his point total for three games to 120. He was the MVP, of course.

"Mikan was the head man," said The New York Times, "an inspiration to his mates and a hero to the crowd that boosted the four-night total . . . to 72,622, a tournament record."

Then came the fans' strawberry shortcake, a special match in the Garden to benefit the American Red Cross: NIT versus NCAA, DePaul versus Oklahoma A&M, Mikan versus Kurland.

(This was the third NCAA-NIT game played in the Garden for charity. In 1943 the Whiz Kids of Illinois, starring Andy Phillip, didn't enter any tournament because some of them were taken into the service. Wyoming, with Milo Komenich and Kenny Sailors, won the NCAA. St. John's, led by Hy Gotkin and Harry Boykoff, won the NIT. Wyoming took the Red Cross game in overtime 52–47.

(In 1944 Utah was eliminated in the NIT's first round and sadly went home to Salt Lake City. However, at the last minute the Redskins received an invitation from the NCAA to substitute for Arkansas. They surprised everyone by winning, beating Dartmouth in the overtime championship game. St. John's again won the NIT—over Mikan and DePaul —and again lost to the NCAA champ in the Red Cross game.)

DePaul was a seven-point betting favorite against A&M, but the Demons' chances and most of the game's excitement disappeared when Mikan fouled out less than fourteen minutes after the opening tipoff. The crowd of 18,158 saw the Cowboys win 52–44. (The Red Cross raked in close to fifty thousand dollars.) Kurland scored a modest fourteen points; Mikan had nine when he left the game. Still, George was the national scoring cham-

pion (23.3 points a game, compared to Kurland's 17.1) and the New York sportswriters named him the outstanding visiting player of the season.

Mikan led again in 1945–46 with a 23.1 average, but DePaul didn't enter either of the tourneys. Oklahoma A&M, after splitting with the Blue Demons in the regular season, won a second-straight NCAA title, beating North Carolina 43–40 in the final. Kurland ended his college career by being named MVP again (he also was an A-student in chemistry, president of the A&M student association)

"He thought he did very well and I thought I did very well," said Bob of his battles with Mikan. "Individually, I think he made more total points."

Of course, Kurland could score plenty of points when Iba unleashed him. He was ordered to shoot on February 22, 1946, against St. Louis and its freshman center, Ed Macauley. He scored 58, breaking Mikan's record of 53. The two of them could have gone on smashing each other and each other's records for many years, but they chose different postgraduate paths, Mikan the pros and Kurland the Amateur Athletic Union, the Olympic Games and a job at the Phillips Oil Company.

The state of Kentucky's two most venerable heroes are Colonel Harlan Sanders, the fried-chicken king, and Adolph Frederick Rupp, the cantankerous basketball coach of the University of Kentucky Wildcats. The fact that neither one of them is originally from the state (Sanders is from Indiana, Rupp from Kansas) doesn't seem to bother the good folks in places like Carr Creek, Ashland and Horse Cave. Rupp, a tobacco farmer and raiser of Hereford cattle, is known as The Baron of the Bluegrass.

He is also known as The Man in the Brown Suit and, to some of his opponents and even some of his own players, as something much less complimentary. A no-nonsense, Germanic tyrant, his hard work and coaching genius have made basketball an

ingrained part of Kentucky culture, as prevalent as bourbon whiskey, horse racing, and finger-lickin' good drumsticks.

In a sense, he is a direct descendant of James Naismith, inventor of the game. Rupp left his family's farm in Halstead, Kansas, to play (but not much) at the University of Kansas for Phog Allen, who in turn had been taught by Naismith. After coaching wrestling and basketball at high schools in Iowa and Illinois, Rupp beat out 69 other applicants for the Kentucky job in 1930. The Wildcats had a 15–3 record his first season and they've been big winners almost every year since. In the late 1960s Rupp passed Allen as the winningest coach in college basketball history. He had accumulated 831 victories at the end of the 1969–70 season.

In the hollows and hills from Appalachia west to Paducah, mothers would just as soon have their sons be starters at Kentucky than be in the President's cabinet. When the Wildcats play their annual game in Louisville's Freedom Hall against Notre Dame, people jam the place the previous day just to

see them warm up. In December of 1967, for instance, 5,000 fans came to the open practice. When Rupp stood up to instruct the team about something, the crowd gave him a big hand. Last fall 13,500 filled Kentucky's Memorial Coliseum to see an intrasquad scrimmage. An estimated 2,000 were turned away.

Rupp developed his first strong national contenders in the 1940s. In 1946, Kentucky met Rhode Island State for the NIT championship. The game was tied twelve times before a gum-chewing sophomore guard named Ralph Beard made a free throw in the last seconds to give UK a 46–45 win. Beard also held Rhode Island's Ernie Calverley to eight points. Kentucky finished with a 28–2 record and was generally considered the second-best team in the nation, behind Oklahoma A&M.

In the next two seasons the Wildcats were improved, so much improved that their leading scorer and All-America from the NIT-championship team, Jack Parkinson, couldn't crack the starting lineup! Playing before more than 250,000 people in

1946–47, they won 34 and lost only three. One of the three losses came to Utah in the NIT. The team gave Rupp his first NCAA title in 1947–48 and earned a flattering nickname, "The Fabulous Five." One of their three losses in 39 games was to the Phillips 66 Oilers in the Olympic trials 54–49; all five Kentucky starters were chosen for the Olympic team and won gold medals; Rupp was assistant coach.

The Fabulous Five was made up of Beard, the youngest and smallest at 19 and 5 feet 10 inches (his brother Frank is now a big money winner on the professional golf tour); 6 foot-7 inch center Alex Groza from Martin's Ferry, Ohio, leading rebounder and scorer (he has a famous brother, too: ex-pro football star Lou Groza); 6-foot guard Kenny Rollins, a World War II veteran who usually guarded the opponent's toughest man; 6 foot-4 inch Wallace (Wah Wah) Jones, also an All-Southeast Conference end in football, and 6 foot-2 inch forward Cliff Barker, another veteran.

Barker was an unusually good ballhandler. He had been a sergeant in the Air Force and was shot

down over Germany in 1944, captured and put behind barbed wire. He would have gone stir crazy were it not for the Red Cross, which gave him a ball. He spent long hours playing with it.

"We had great material," said Rupp. "We had some kids who were 26 years old coming back from the war and some who were nineteen, fresh out of high school. My big problem there was to play enough boys to keep them all happy. There's never been any question about that being a great crowd. Those boys were cruel and cold-blooded. They destroyed an opponent as quickly as possible. Within five minutes some games they'd be sitting on the bench, having given the second team a 22–5 lead."

This must have frustrated Adolph, who has a reputation as a half-time hell-raiser. Once The Fabulous Five had a 38–4 lead at half time in Kentucky's old Alumni Gymnasium. All four of the opponent's points were by one man.

"Somebody guard that man," bellowed the Baron. "Why, he's running wild!"

Rollins was graduated, but Jim Line stepped into his spot and the Wildcats rolled to a second-straight NCAA title in 1948–49. In the NCAA final in Seattle, they beat Oklahoma A&M 46–36. The Aggies that year led the nation in fewest points allowed, but Kentucky gave them a lesson in how to play defense. A&M had only two field goals in the second half.

The reputation of that team became considerably less savory a few years later when Beard, Groza and Dale Barnstable, caught up in the first big scandal to shock college basketball, confessed to accepting bribes from gamblers to manipulate point spreads—"shaving points." (For instance, if Kentucky was favored by ten points, the gamblers might pay the players to win by nine or less.) The manipulating got out of hand and caused Kentucky's upset loss to Loyola of Chicago in the 1949 NIT.

Before the scandal broke, Kentucky, led by 7-foot Bill Spivey, won another NCAA championship in 1950–51. Spivey had 22 points and 21 rebounds in the 68–58 final-game victory over Kansas State. He was later indicted in the fixing mess but never convicted. Although he denied any guilt, he was never allowed to play major-league pro basketball.

Following revelations of illegal, under-the-table payments to athletes at Kentucky (Beard, Groza and Barnstable spilled the beans), the NCAA forced the school to cancel its 1952–53 schedule. The great team of Cliff Hagan, Frank Ramsey and Lou Tsioropoulos had nothing to do but stay on campus, practice and seethe. When 1953–54 rolled around they were ready.

"There's not going to be any of this point-shaving business by Kentucky this year," said Adolph. "When we run up one of those 95- or 97-point totals against a team—we used to do it often—and there's still a couple of minutes left to play, I'm not going to pull my boys up and have them

LEFT: Soaring high to score against the California Bears, UCLA's Lew Alcindor shows form that made him outstanding college player three years running. BELOW LEFT: Purdue's Rick Mount takes a breather to rest his shooting arm; he never was bashful about field-goal attempts. BELOW: Gary Bradds of Ohio State, one of many excellent players developed in Columbus, yanks down a rebound versus West Virginia.

stand around at midcourt and try to hold the score down so we don't humiliate anybody. We'll just keep playing our game right to the last second."

Forewarned, the teams on Kentucky's schedule couldn't do anything about it. The Wildcats raced to a perfect 25 and 0 record and were seldom extended. They chose not to participate in the NCAA Tournament because the fifth-year players were ineligible for post-season games. That is, Rupp chose not to go. The squad voted 9–3 to enter (the three against were the three ineligibles), but Rupp exercised his veto power, saying he wasn't going to let a bunch of substitutes ruin an unbeaten season.

Rupp's fourth NCAA championship came in 1957–58, when his "Fiddling Five"—so nicknamed because they fiddled around before they got rolling —upset Seattle and Elgin Baylor in the final 84–72. They were the first NCAA champions who had lost as many as six games, but Adolph didn't mind. He had vowed he "wasn't going to rest until the man who said Kentucky couldn't play in the NCAA hands me the national championship trophy."

Until UCLA came into national prominence in the 1960s, the four NCAA titles were a record. Crusty old Adolph credited his stress on discipline and fundamentals for the success. And he's stressing the same things today.

Practices at Kentucky are as austere as prison-camp lineups. At the precise minute a session is to start, the student managers close off access routes to the floor with iron gates and heavy curtains. Rupp and his assistants wear starched khaki shirts and pants. Adolph sits there with a perpetual scowl on a face etched by crags and seams developed in 40 seasons as boss of the Wildcats. His forehead has more furrows than any Fayette County farm and his upside-down U of a mouth is accentuated by two deep creases that run from the corners down to under his chin. The players zip through their basic 10 plays over and over again. Minutes go by without a dropped pass or a missed basket. Except for the squeak of sneakers and the thump of bouncing balls, there is strict silence from the athletes.

"Why should boys constantly chatter in a class in basketball any more than they do in a class in English?" says Rupp. "Why should they whistle and sing? If you let 'em talk and wisecrack around, they don't concentrate. I tell the boys if they want to talk, we've got a student union for visiting purposes. And if they want to whistle, well, there's a music academy, too."

But Rupp himself doesn't keep quiet. When something or someone isn't going right, he dips into his vast reservoir of sarcasm:

"Go back up in the stands and read your press clippings!"

"Boy, will you pass that ball to someone who knows what to do with it!"

"Some day I'm going to write a book on how not to play basketball, and I'm going to devote the first 200 pages to you!"

Adolph was once asked to cut short a workout because a well-known pianist needed the arena to practice for his concert that night. The ensuing growls and screams were predictable.

"That guy could miss a note tonight and nobody would know the difference," said the Baron, "but let one of my boys miss a free throw and it's all over the state."

After the Wildcats upset Seattle to win the 1957–58 NCAA championship, Rupp was accused of running a joyless program. His players didn't have any fun.

"Comes March 24 and who has the fun?" he snorted. "Where was Wilt Chamberlain when we were winning the championship? Where was Oscar Robertson? I'll tell you where. Home listening to the game on the radio. Who was having the fun then?

My kids. What do you start a season for if not to be the national champions? Who has won more championships than my teams?"

Irascible as he normally is, Baron Rupp can be charming and funny when the mood strikes him. He is notorious for getting large fees for speaking at coaching clinics and then giving forth with more humorous stories than techniques.

On married players: "I won't have a married man on my squad. First, they must think of their family. Then they think about how they are going to put food on the table. Next, they think of their studies—and finally they think of Adolph. That puts me too far down on the list."

On his own meanness: "Those newspaper guys up east are always throwing darts at me. They try to get people to believe the only reason I win is because I'm an SOB. But I know a lot of losers who are SOBs, so that's not the answer."

On Kentucky fox hunting: "It's the best sport for a man my age. You turn the dogs loose and sit down and listen to them with some sandwiches and a fifth of bourbon. The fox holes up and doesn't get caught. The dogs have a happy time running about. Nobody wins and nobody loses—and the alumni don't write letters."

A favorite biblical quotation on the country-boy basketball talent in Kentucky: "I will lift up mine eyes unto the hills, from whence cometh my help."

On whippersnappers: "I see these young coaches come along with theories opposite to mine. So I go to the farm and think things over. Then I figure out that if these coaches begin at the age of 25 and win at least 20 games a year—then it's still going to be 45 years before they'll be able to match me in wins."

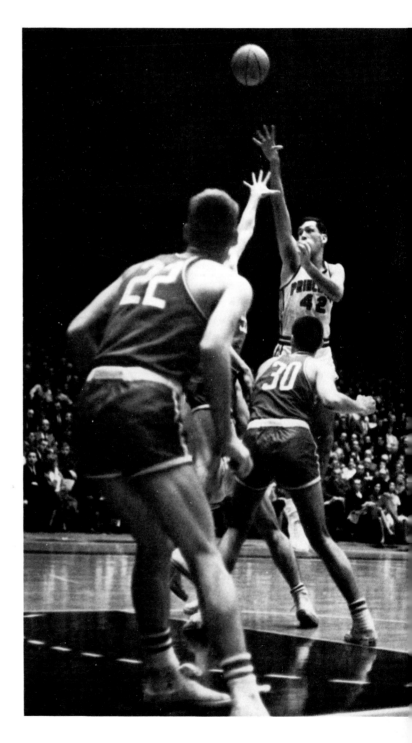

Firing his jump shot against Wisconsin, Bill Bradley of Princeton is on his way to scoring 48 points. A banker's son from Crystal City, Missouri, he became a Rhodes scholar.

By the time the Baron neared the mandatory retirement age of 70, old-timers in Lexington insisted he had mellowed, although he was often as mean and egotistical as ever. Why, there were even some married men allowed on his team, including All-America center Dan Issel. And, wonder of wonders, in 1970–71 Kentucky had its first black basketball player, Tom Payne, which—temporarily, at least—quieted the tiny corps of UK campus liberals who referred to Rupp as The Bigot of the Bluegrass.

Adolph's best chance for a fifth NCAA title seemed to be in 1965–66. UCLA was somewhat depleted in talent after two straight championships, but giant Lew Alcindor was on the Bruin freshman team and most people thought UCLA would win three straight with him on the varsity. This interval year was the time to grab another trophy.

It turned out to be one of Adolph's greatest coaching jobs. The Wildcats had been 15 and 10 the season before, their worst record in the Rupp era, and his starters were so small they came to be known as "Rupp's Runts." There was 6 foot-3 inch forward Pat Riley, who had been a high-school football and basketball star in Schenectady, New York; 6 foot-5 inch center Thad Jaracz, a Lexington boy nicknamed "The Bear"; 6 foot-5 inch guard Tommy Kron, tough on defense; and 6 foot-3 inch forward Larry Conley, a superb passer who was the team catalyst. The best shooter was 6-foot Louie Dampier from Indiana. ("God taught Louis how to shoot," said Rupp, "and I took credit for it.")

The Runts, pretty much the same men who had been split by dissension the season before, grew very close and played beautifully. They whipped through the season with just one loss, won the Mideast Regional and defeated Duke in the semifinals at the University of Maryland. That put them in the final against an obscure newcomer, Texas Western (the University of Texas' El Paso branch), which had not placed one man on its all-district team.

Coach of the Texas Western Miners was Don Haskins, who had learned all about stingy defense while playing for Hank Iba at Oklahoma State. He had recruited talented but undisciplined players from sooty playgrounds in Detroit, Gary, Indiana, and the Bronx and welded them into a team. In his pestering man-to-man defense, the players considered any undeflected pass or unobstructed dribble a personal affront. And in Orsten Artis, Haskins had a Hoosier deadeye to match Kentucky's Dampier. When Artis first went down from Gary to visit El Paso, he was kiddingly told that baskets in the Southwest were smaller than up north. He just shrugged.

"Don't matter none," he said. "I don't use the rim much anyway."

When the Miners and Wildcats met an extra undercurrent of interest was buzzing around Maryland's field house because Texas Western's starting lineup was all black, Kentucky's all white—the first time that had ever happened in an NCAA championship game. "Outlaw-school" jokes about Texas Western were big favorites around the coaches' convention, which always coincides with the tournament. Smirking detractors even dragged out the ancient line, "They can do anything with a basketball but autograph it."

The score was tied at 9–9 in the first half when Texas Western made a free throw and Kentucky's Tommy Kron dribbled over the center line. Miner guard Bobby Joe Hill (full name: *Tyrone* Bobby Joe Hill), probably the quickest player in the country, stole the ball from Kron and scooted in for an easy lay-up. Dampier then brought the ball upcourt. Bobby Joe cleanly swiped it again and made another cinch lay-up. The Wildcats did not fold after that, but Texas Western led the rest of the way and won 72–65. There was a riotous celebration that night down by the Rio Grande.

"I'm just a young punk," said Haskins afterward. "It was a thrill playing against Mr. Rupp, let alone beating him."

"This is the grandest bunch of boys a man ever had," said the Baron sadly.

He said later the Wildcats would have won if Larry Conley had not had the flu. He conveniently forgot that Duke star Bob Verga had been ill when he played against Kentucky in the semifinals. There was some solace, however. The U.S. Basketball Writers Association, before the final game, had named Adolph coach of the year. And a furrier in Kentucky made the team a basketball out of autumn-haze mink.

Adolph's own coach, Phog Allen of Kansas, won his first and only NCAA championship in 1952. (However, the Jayhawks had many fine teams before the tournament started in 1939, most notably in 1922–23 with Paul Endacott—and a bench-warmer named Rupp.) Kansas beat St. John's 80–63 in the final and 6 foot-9 inch center Clyde Lovellette was named the most valuable player. A pale, slope-shouldered import from Terre Haute, Indiana, Clyde loved to clown but still averaged 28.6 points a game in the regular season and scored a record 141 points in the NCAA Tournament. He gave most of the credit for his success to his one-quarter-Cherokee mother, Myrtle.

"I'll bet I set some sort of a rope-skipping record," said Clyde. "Mother had me skipping rope as soon as I got up in the morning. I was ashamed to have the other boys see me. And when other kids my age were going to picture shows at night, I was out back of the house skipping rope. But I soon lost my awkwardness. Mother had other exercises. She even boxed with me to develop my footwork. I took dancing lessons. By the time I entered high school, I could dance and wasn't embarrassed about my height. I feel that my mother is one of the best physical trainers in the country."

Myrtle stayed home when Clyde went off to college, but after a while she just couldn't resist going to see Kansas play. She was every bit as enthusiastic a rooter as she had been a trainer.

"I'm terribly happy when they say that I am worth ten to twenty points to the Kansas team," she said. "I love basketball and I get more fun out of the games than perhaps the players."

Allen didn't need people like Myrtle and Clyde around to liven up things. He was enough of a character himself for any one school or conference.

His nickname originally was Foghorn, stemming from the days when he umpired baseball games and bellowed his decisions for the whole county to hear. A sportswriter shortened and fancified it to Phog. Actually, most people around the KU campus called him Doc. (He was a doctor of osteopathy, as well as a Sunday-school teacher and a member of the local draft board.) He always had a cause, be it getting basketball into the Olympics, saving the dribble, raising the basket, bringing in fan-shaped backboards or getting a commissioner for college athletics. He drank huge quantities of water during games. Sometimes he would use a zone defense but insisted on calling it a "stratified, transitional man-for-man with a zone principle."

He had unique theories on getting his players ready to win. He showed them a movie, *Killing the Killer*, about a mongoose fighting a cobra. Before home games, he made them take naps in a dormitory, then take long walks. He was afraid of cold feet, so he insisted his men warm their bare toes in front of a fire.

No matter how nutty his theories may have appeared, they seemed to work—or at least they didn't hurt. The Jayhawks were right back in the national final in 1953 against Indiana, which was coached by another old-timer, Branch McCracken. The Hurryin' Hoosiers won 69–68 when guard Bob Leonard made a free throw with 27 seconds left.

His teammate, center Don Schlundt, scored 30 points.

Phog was forced to retire after the 1955–56 season because, he said with some bitterness, he had reached age 70 and the state of "statutory senility." His 43-year head-coaching record was 771 and 233. It could have been even better if the State Board of Regents had let him stay on because, while Doc was practicing osteopathy in downtown Lawrence, 7-foot Wilt Chamberlain became eligible for the Kansas varsity. Phog's assistant, Dick Harp, was in command.

In Wilt's first varsity game, against Northwestern, he scored 52 points and took 31 rebounds. At one point he dunked the ball and it went through and hit a Northwestern player on the head. Behind Wilt and his startling feats, Kansas moved to the NCAA final in Kansas City.

There the Jayhawks met undefeated North Carolina, coached by Frank McGuire, whose St. John's team had lost to Kansas back in the '52 final. Looking at his Carolina roster made you think he might as well still have been at St. John's—nearly 100 percent of the players, including star Lennie Rosenbluth, were from New York and New Jersey. The Tar Heels barely made it into the final. It took them three overtimes to beat Michigan State the night before.

Carolina double- and triple-teamed Wilt and held him to 23 points, and the game was another heart strainer—in fact another triple overtime. With six seconds to go in the third extra period, Joe Quigg made two free throws to beat Kansas 54–53 and make Carolina's final season record a perfect 32–0.

"We made it a personal challenge," said McGuire. "It was North Carolina against Chamberlain. We had three men around him on every play —a man in front, one behind and a third dropped off as soon as the ball was thrown in.

"We gambled. We played Chamberlain and hoped the rest of his team would tighten up. That's exactly what happened. His teammates were so wound up trying to force the ball in to Wilt that they didn't take their own shots. We left a lot of openings for them, but they just didn't take advantage of them. On another night, they could have hit from the outside and beaten us by 20 points."

In Wilt's junior year, Kansas lost five games and again failed to win the national championship. The Jayhawks didn't even finish in the top four and, what was worse, arch rival Kansas State did. There were strong rumors that Chamberlain would quit school and turn professional, but he kept denying it—right up until *Look* hit the stands with his exclusive story, "Why I Am Quitting College." One reason he gave for dropping out of school: "It wasn't basketball at KU. I always had three or four guys hanging on me."

Some people believe the University of San Francisco Dons of 1954–55 and 1955–56 were the greatest college teams of all time. Two players, Bill Russell and K. C. Jones, were the key men both years. The Dons won the NCAA championship both seasons, losing only one game, to UCLA late in 1954.

"I can't imagine a better college team," coach Phil Woolpert said later. "We had fine balance, excellent shooting and tremendous defense. The thing that impressed me most about these boys was their ability to come off the bench and stop every rally. This was because they had mastered the art of defensive play."

An outsider, and perhaps an insider, too, would have thought there was only mild reason for optimism at USF at the beginning of the 1954–55 season. The Dons, who had a mediocre 14 and 7 record the previous year, played their home games in Kezar

Pavilion (5,500 capacity), the Cow Palace and a court in nearby San Jose, and had to practice at St. Ignatius High School. They had no gym of their own. Woolpert's record since taking over the job in 1950 was 45 and 49. Guard K. C. Jones had been sidelined by appendicitis the previous season, and Jerry Mullen from Berkeley had been injured. Hal Perry, who had no grant-in-aid, had been only so-so as a sophomore. And there was Russell.

Bill was born February 12, 1934 in Monroe, Louisiana. His parents named him after William Felton, president of Southeastern Louisiana College in Hammond. He was naturally right-handed, but his Uncle Bob had been unsuccessful in becoming a first baseman in the Negro baseball leagues and blamed the failure on not being left-handed. He was therefore determined to make his nephew a southpaw.

"One time we bought a 22-pound turkey and Bill started in on the leg," recalled Russell's dad. "Before he got through he fell asleep with the unfinished turkey leg in his right hand. Uncle Robert went over and switched it to his left. Billy's been a left-hander ever since."

When Bill was nine the family moved to Detroit and then Oakland, where his father went to work in the shipyards. His mother died when he was twelve. Older brother Charles Jr., who had always been a good natural athlete, went to Oakland Tech, so spindly, unagile Bill decided to avoid embarrassing comparisons and enroll at McClymonds High—later to become well known as the alma mater of baseball stars Frank Robinson, Vada Pinson and Curt Flood, and basketball stars Joe Ellis of USF and Paul Silas of Creighton. He entered high school in the fall of 1949, an emaciated 6 feet 2 inches and 128 pounds. As a sophomore he was understandably cut from the junior varsity football team. Out of the kindness of coach George Powles' heart, he made the JV basketball squad. Since there were fifteen

boys and fourteen uniforms, he had to share the last uniform with another fellow.

He was third-team varsity center as a junior. By the end of the season he had grown to 6 feet 5 inches and actually showed a little promise. Powles got him a membership in a local athletic club, so he could practice all spring and summer. He worked as a typist before and after classes, made his father's dinner most nights and worked out at the club until the director chased him home. Bill's determination to succeed paid off because as a senior he was the 6 foot-6 inch starting center and scoring well when his class was graduated at mid-term. He was grateful for Powles' patience.

"He may not have known too much basketball," said Bill, "but he taught me a lot of other things, how important heart and attitude are."

No colleges were beating on Russell's door; there were no charges of illegal recruiting procedures hurled about, no jobs promised to his father. USF, a relatively poor Jesuit school, took a chance on him because a scout had seen him play a good game. The scout wasn't wowed but did recommend him to Woolpert.

"Woolpert didn't think much of my ability either," says Russell. "No one had ever played basketball the way I played it, or as well. They had never seen anyone block shots before. Now I'll be conceited. I like to think I originated a whole new style of play. It wasn't anything I thought about, though. I had always played that way, and it was always purely automatic."

Bill, growing steadily and getting a little heavier too, got up to 6 feet 8 inches in his freshman year and worked on his hook shot under frosh coach Ross Giudice. He averaged 20 points a game. When he made his varsity debut against California he had grown to 6 feet 9 inches and 200 pounds. The Bears had a husky All-Coast center, Bob McKeen, and Russ outscored him 23 to 14 and blocked eight of his shots. But K.C. suffered an appendicitis attack early in the season and the team was just so-so.

USF started off 1954–55 with two easy victories, then lost to UCLA 47–40. It was the last loss of Russell's college career. In a return match the Dons won 56–44, thanks to Russell's 28 points, 21 rebounds and 15 blocked shots. Local rival Santa Clara had a 14-point lead at half time, but Russ made fourteen points in four minutes, allowing USF to take the lead and win going away. Against Stanford he scored 23 points in less than 30 minutes and was even more impressive on defense, leading Stanford coach Howie Dallmar to rave:

"He can jump higher than any man in basketball. Mikan would get four field goals a game off Bill. He might get the ball, but he just wouldn't get the shots."

USF went into the NCAA West Regional with a 23 and 1 record and bashed West Texas State by 23 points and Utah by 12. In the latter game Russell held Ute star Art Bunte to four baskets. In the regional final, Bill was up against Oregon State's Wade (Swede) Halbrook, who was four inches taller and 40 pounds heavier, and outscored him 29 to 18 on OSU's own court in Corvallis. The Dons were off to Kansas City for the semifinals.

They took Colorado with little trouble and found themselves in the national championship game against LaSalle. The Explorers were led by 6 foot-6 inch Tom Gola, a handsome Pole from Philadelphia considered by some to be the best college basketball player up to that time. *Sport* had had a photo layout on him the year before entitled, "Tom Gola, Basketball's Best."

"I'm not worrying about Gola," said Russell, "I'm just trying to help my team win. But, man, that Gola could really give the coach an ulcer."

Woolpert made a surprise move and put Jones on Gola, figuring K.C.'s quickness would make up for the five-inch difference in height. Besides, Russell would always be there as a backup. It worked nicely. Jones held Gola to 16 points and made 24 himself. Russell amazed the 10,500 fans in Kansas City Municipal Auditorium with 23 points, 22 rebounds (to Gola's commendable 14) and 11 blocked shots. USF won 77–63 for its twenty-sixth victory in a row, and Bill was the unanimous choice for MVP.

The former fifteenth man on the McClymonds junior varsity was so excited that he pounded Woolpert on the back like a madman and shook hands twice with the dejected Gola. Kansas coach Phog Allen, stunned like everyone else at Bill's leaping ability and timing, said, "I'm for the 20-foot basket!"

Russell had made such an impact on the game that the NCAA doubled the width of the foul lane from six feet to twelve. It was dubbed the "Russell Rule."

"They certainly aren't hurting Russell," said Woolpert. "As a matter of fact, this rule was made for him because he's as fast as he is big. He's so much the fastest of the big men that now he'll just leave them further behind."

"I think it's a good rule," said Bill. "It doesn't bother the tall players, but as for the fat ones and the slow ones, it kills them."

In the off-season Russ visited President Eisenhower in the White House, worked as a shoe salesman and dabbled in high jumping. He originally went out for track and field because the track team gave lettermen a cardigan sweater and at the time Bill had only a tight pullover that he didn't like. In his first meet he leaped 6 feet 7 inches and his best competitive jump in college was 6 feet 9½ inches.

In his last season he had grown to a fraction under 6 feet 10 inches and had a group of talented teammates with him: K.C., Mike Farmer, Carl Boldt, Hal Perry and Gene Brown. They stormed through the regular season undefeated, winning a four-team tourney in Chicago Stadium and the Holiday Festival in Madison Square Garden. Against Holy Cross in the Garden, Russell held Tom Heinsohn, later to be his teammate on the Boston Celtics, to 12 points, all on long shots. In the West Regional USF beat UCLA, which had won 17 straight since losing to the Dons in the Holiday Festival final, and Utah. SMU fell in the semifinals 86–68.

The final, before 10,653 fans in Northwestern University's McGaw Memorial Hall, was close at first. In fact it was one-sided in favor of Iowa, which jumped off to a 15–4 lead. USF was missing K.C., ineligible for the tournament because it was his fifth year of college competition. Russell pulled the Dons to a five-point lead at half time. They ran off to a 13-point lead before the second half was five minutes old and won 83–71. It was their 55th straight victory.

The foggy shores of San Francisco Bay seemed to be conducive to coaches preaching deliberate offense and stingy defense. The next such team to win an NCAA championship was the University of California at Berkeley coached by Pete Newell. The Golden Bears won in 1959 and were beaten in the final in 1960.

Newell was a close friend of Woolpert's. He played with Phil at Loyola of Los Angeles and preceded him as coach at USF. Pete's 1949 USF team won the NIT; the following four years he spent refurbishing Michigan State's program before taking the job at Cal. He was infamous as a practical joker and one of his victims in the USF days was the school's young sports information director, Pete Rozelle (now commissioner of the National Football League).

At that time USF had a player named Willie (Woo Woo) Wong. Newell phoned Rozelle and, using a phony Chinese accent, represented himself as Charlie Lee from the Chinese Press. He asked about Woo Woo's chances of making the trip to the NIT.

"He filst team, he make tlip?" asked Newell/Lee.

"No, he hasn't quite made the first team," answered Rozelle diplomatically.

"What's the matter you?" screamed Newell. "You against Chinee boy?"

"Oh, no, Mr. Lee," sputtered Rozelle, "I'm sure Willie will make the trip to New York."

Newell paused for a moment. Then he resumed his own voice.

"Rozelle, I told you you were the leak [to the press]. Now you're trying to name my traveling squad for me!"

Newell also was one of the most nervous coaches who ever suffered through a close game. He lived off coffee and cigarettes, and during the six days with USF at the NIT he lost 14 pounds. He risked a bellyful of lint in every game he coached because he chewed a towel throughout.

"It's a funny thing about that towel business," he said. "When I first started coaching at USF, my hands got moist. I started with a dry towel. Then my mouth got dry. I got tired of getting up for water, so I started wetting the towel to keep my mouth moist."

In a game at Reno, Nevada, Pete got so sore at a referee that he threw the towel at him. It wrapped itself around the official's head like a turban and covered his eyes.

"Pete, you shouldn't have done that," screamed the ref.

"You should have made the call when you were running in blinkers," Newell yelled back. "You'd have made the best call of your life."

The ref stopped short and laughed.

"Hey, Pete," he said, "that's a pretty good one."

Newell's unflappable Cal team of 1958–59 had two strong rebounders, 6 foot-10 inch center Darrall Imhoff and forward Bill McClintock, but its forte was persistent, intelligent defense. The Bears allowed an average of only 51 points a game by their opponents. And even when they were behind, they would take their time on offense and never get panicky. If they were down 10 points, they behaved as if they were comfortably ahead, and somehow they usually ended up winning. The style worked nicely and Cal had won 14 in a row when it met Cincinnati and the great Oscar Robertson in the NCAA semifinals at Louisville.

Cincy was averaging 20 points a game more

than Cal, and Oscar, who could have made it as a pro right out of his Indianapolis high school, was averaging 33 points all by himself. In his debut in Madison Square Garden the previous year he had scored 56 points. The stubborn Bears held him to one field goal in the second half—19 points altogether—and won 64–58.

The final was against West Virginia, which had still another all-time college great, Jerry West. Cal didn't clamp down on him quite so well (he scored 28, better than his average), but the Bears won 71–70 when Imhoff tipped in a basket with 17 seconds left. Their rowdy and raucous straw-hat band was ecstatic.

The Bears seemed even stingier in 1959–60. They got another chance at stopping West in the Los Angeles Classic holiday tournament and restricted him to one field goal in a 65–45 romp. They made it again to the NCAA semifinals and had a rematch with Oscar, who was to become the first man ever to lead the nation's major colleges in scoring for three straight years. Robertson managed only 18 points and Cal won 77–69. The tournament was being held at the Cow Palace, in a suburb south of San Francisco. (Perhaps Cal arranged that so they wouldn't have to lug the championship hardware so far.) But Ohio State spoiled it all.

It was the fine Ohio State team of John Havlicek, Larry Siegfried, Mel Nowell, Joe Roberts and 6 foot-8 inch sophomore Jerry Lucas. It is doubtful if the National Guard could have stopped the Buckeyes that night—they made an amazing 68.4 percent of their shots. OSU's Fred Taylor knew something about defense, too. Lucas held Imhoff to eight points. The 75–55 loss was Cal's first in 20 games.

The era of tough defense continued for three more years, but the scene shifted from California to Ohio. Specifically, Cincinnati. Oscar had gone on to the pros, but Ed Jucker, assistant of seven years, took over as head man and worked wonders. Sud-

denly the Bearcats downshifted their offense from fast break to deliberate.

"We never hold the ball to keep the score down," he said. "We handle it to get the best percentage shots. There are two ends to a basketball court and our players have to know what to do at either end."

For two straight seasons the NCAA final was an all-Ohio party. Cincinnati, champion of the Missouri Valley, versus Ohio State, champion of the Big Ten. In 1961 Lucas had an injured knee and was held to 11 points by Cincy's Paul Hogue, a transplanted Tennessean. The Bearcats won 70–65 in overtime. In 1962 Hogue and Tom Thacker starred as Cincy beat OSU more easily, 71–59. Hogue scored 22 points over Lucas and was named the tourney MVP.

Oklahoma A&M, Kentucky and USF all had won two NCAA championships in a row, but no team had won three. Cincinnati should have done it in 1963. Its opponent in the final was Loyola of Chicago, coached by George Ireland. The game pitted the irresistible force against the immovable object because Loyola, an exceptional sprint-and-shoot team, was leading the nation with an average of 91.8 points. Cincy was allowing an average of only 52.9.

Cincinnati led by 15 points, 45–30, with 11:45 left in the game at Louisville's Freedom Hall, but coach Jucker ordered the Bearcats into a stall with too much time left and they lost their momentum. Loyola caught up and tied the game on Jerry Harkness' jump shot with five seconds left. With one second remaining in the overtime, Loyola's Vic Rouse tapped in a rebound for a 60–58 victory.

Despite the upset, Cincinnati could be proud of its record: five times in five years it had climbed as high as the semifinals, three times it had reached the final and twice it had won the championship. Yet, impressive as Cincinnati's record was, it was

ABOVE: *Bobby Joe Hill of Texas Western drives
in NCAA semifinal game. RIGHT: Driving into
the key, Notre Dame's prolific scorer Austin Carr
gets set to give one last fake before shooting.*

quickly forgotten because just a few months later UCLA began the most incredible domination of a team sport in the history of collegiate athletics.

From 1963–64 through 1969–70, the Bruins won six out of seven NCAA championships. They were the first to win three in a row, the first to win four in a row and eventually they might become the first to win 10 in a row. Those titles were won in actual competition, not in polls taken by United Press International or the Associated Press. The man most responsible is not 7 foot-2 inch Lew Alcindor—although he certainly was no hindrance—but a meticulous, hard-driving coach named John Robert Wooden. He already has a niche in the Basketball Hall of Fame, but he deserves an entire wing.

Wooden was an outstanding professional player for six years. Before that he was a consensus All-America guard at Purdue for three straight seasons. In his high-school years he starred on one of the finest teams ever to play in Indiana. As a coach, he has had only one losing season, his first. His UCLA teams won two national titles before Alcindor and one after. They were the favorites again in 1970–71, while waiting for one of the best freshman crops in the nation to move up in 1971–72.

Away from games, Wooden is a soft-spoken gentleman with a trace of homespun Hoosier in his voice, a human *Poor Richard's Almanack* who has inspirational sayings filed in a loose-leaf notebook, taped to his pencil box, framed on his walls, tucked away in his wallet: "Make each day your masterpiece." "Build a shelter for a rainy day." "It's better to go too far with a boy than not far enough."

Somewhere between "Be true to yourself" and "It's the little things that count," a visitor begins to think it is all just a giant put-on. Nobody could be that square. But Wooden is real all right, sitting there in his office overlooking UCLA's basketball palace, Pauley Pavilion. He can thumb quickly through a notebook and find his drill-by-drill plan

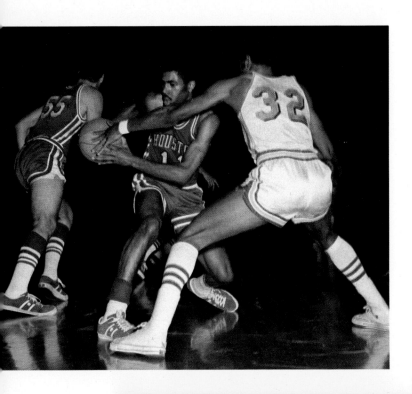

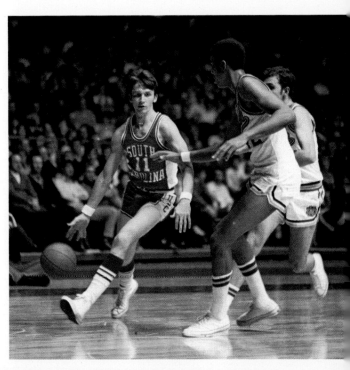

CLOCKWISE FROM BOTTOM LEFT: Astrodome game in 1968
between Houston and UCLA attracted a record number of
fans, many of whom needed telescopes; Houston's Bonney
controls rebound against Southern Cal's Nash; South Carolina's
John Roche, a slick passer, careens toward hoop; Curtis Rowe
of UCLA outleaps Austin Carr in game at South Bend.

ABOVE: One of the greatest shooters in the history of college basketball, Rick Mount of Purdue rockets past his opponent, freeing himself for one of his jump shots that seldom miss. Mount was a legend while still in high school in Lebanon, Indiana, and he was the state's "Mr. Basketball." He was just as much a scoring threat in college, but not very strong on defense. RIGHT: Performing a pas de deux with a rival, LSU's "Pistol Pete" Maravich prepares to show off one of his dipsy-doodle passes. UCLA coach John Wooden called him the greatest ballhandler in the game's history. FAR RIGHT: Menacing Bruin Sidney Wicks, infamous for his glare, drives past New Mexico State player in 1970 NCAA semifinal game at College Park, Maryland. Wicks, 6 feet 8 inches and quick, was considered a first-class prospect to play forward in the pros—and excel.

CLOCKWISE FROM FAR LEFT: Michigan's Henry Wilmore dribbles through his Big Ten opposition, establishing himself as a worthy successor to ex-Wolverine aces Cazzie Russell and Rudy Tomjanovich; UCLA All-America Sidney Wicks listens to coach's instructions; Pennsylvania's teeny guard Steve Bilsky helps Quakers rule Ivy League for a second consecutive season; UCLA coach John Wooden is a tough, give-no-quarter competitor who drives himself and his players to victory after victory; St. Bonaventure, shown here in action against Toledo, has been the traditional power in upstate New York despite its campus being in the boondocks.

for a practice 17 years ago or he can flip through another one and find a short essay on how the world today maybe could use a few more squares. His *Pyramid of Success* chart ("industriousness," "loyalty," "self-control" are some of its building blocks) hangs on the wall near his desk; he once talked about it on his Los Angeles TV show and was buried under 7,000 requests for copies.

When Wooden gets off a small joke or receives a compliment, he does not flash a white-neon smile, he ducks his head and grins sheepishly. It is easy to imagine him as a deacon of his church or a kindly grandfather, both of which he is. Not so easy to imagine, but real nevertheless, is the intensely competitive John Wooden of the Bruin bench whose angry, sometimes scathing comments can melt a referee's whistle in mid-tweet. He sits there wielding a rolled-up program and, like most members of his ulcerated profession, suffers while an entire year's work, or maybe more, is compressed into an hour-and-a-half game.

"I've seen him so mad that I've been afraid he'd pop that big blood vessel in his forehead," said a Pacific Coast official, "but I've never heard him curse."

"Dadburn it, you saw him double dribble down there!" hollers Wooden, now about as soft-spoken as an electric guitar. "Goodness gracious sakes alive! Everybody in the place saw that."

He admits he has yelled at opposing players and isn't proud of it.

"Not calling them names," he said, "but saying something like 'Keep your *hands* off of him' or 'Don't be a butcher' or something of that type."

Walt Hazzard, the high scorer and imaginative passer who sparked Wooden's first NCAA title team in 1963–64, is a great admirer of the coach's needling. "He is one of the best bench jockeys in the world. He has an 'antiseptic needle'—clean but biting. I've seen opposing players left shaking their

LEFT: Jacksonville's 7 foot-2 inch Artis Gilmore (leaping, right) helps nation's tallest team dominate St. Bonaventure. ABOVE: Western Kentucky's Jim McDaniels, rebounding, caused furor in ABA draft.

heads, but there was nothing they could say."

Wooden is not exactly the most popular figure within the coaching fraternity. What man with his winning record would be, asks Ted Owens of Kansas. "I know that after finishing second in the Big Eight one season I was a lot more popular than I was the previous two years when I won the title. But Wooden is highly respected by his fellow coaches."

At the coaches' national convention Wooden is not the hotel-lobby raconteur regaling a circle of admirers with funny stories. One reason for that is he's usually busy preparing his team for the next game in the NCAA tourney, which coincides with the convention. He does not socialize much because he does not drink and he is shy. Says a West Coast rival: "He's the sort of guy who goes to the conventions with his wife and they sit in the lobby and watch *you* come in drunk."

When he says he does not much believe in scouting opponents, some other coaches feel he is trying to show them up. They observe his gentlemanly manner and hear his fund of homilies, then react angrily when their players get zapped by his needle. A few believe he is a sanctimonious hypocrite and privately call him "Saint John."

There are those among his ex-players who think sainthood—or at least knighthood—would be perfectly suitable. Eddie Sheldrake, a fine little backcourt man on Wooden's first teams at Westwood, married and had children while he was still in school. Shortly after graduation, his father died. Not long after that his wife became critically ill with cancer and finally died. Wooden and his wife, Nell, stayed at Sheldrake's side and helped raise four thousand dollars to pay the medical bills.

"He was as good as a dad could be," said Sheldrake, who had to fight back tears as he told the story.

"The finest man I've ever met," says another ex-player, Ron Pearson.

"The true man comes out on the bench," says a Midwest coach. "He's a vicious ——."

"No regrets if you can answer to yourself," Wooden likes to say.

John Robert Wooden grew up on a farm eight miles from Martinsville, Indiana. His father, Joshua, who never had much money or good fortune, was a pretty good pitcher and built a diamond among the wheat, corn and alfalfa. To this day baseball, not basketball, is Wooden's favorite sport. But there also was a hoop nailed up in the hayloft, and he and his older brother, Maurice, played there with any kind of ball they could find.

John attended the four-room Centerton grade school, where he was the star athlete. Centerton's principal, Earl Warriner, was one of the important influences in his life. Once, when John was being recalcitrant, Earl Warriner, who also coached basketball, made his high scorer sit out an entire losing game. "After it was over," said Wooden, "he put an arm on my shoulder and said, 'Johnny, we could have won with you in there, but winning just isn't that important.'"

Years later Warriner retired to a farm in Indiana. UCLA was to play in a doubleheader at Chicago Stadium not long ago, and he wrote John for tickets, sending along a blank check. Back with the tickets came the check and in the space for the amount was written, "Friendship far too valuable to be measured in dollars."

Wooden's dad lost the farm because of some bad investments and the Woodens moved into Martinsville in 1924, at about the same time the red brick high school gym was built on South Main Street. The population of the town was 5,200 and the gym held, as noted at the time in Ripley's *Believe It or Not*, 5,520. John Bob soon made the transition from hayseed to sharp dude, Central Indiana version. Hanging around with his buddies at Wick's Candy Kitchen, he wore his letterman's sweater and a green hat Maurice had brought home from Franklin College. He usually had a toothpick in his mouth.

John Bob always worked hard—digging sewers one summer—and he was a good student, but, as longtime friend Floyd Burns remembered, "He always had time for basketball, baseball and Nellie Riley." Nell played the trumpet in the school band and John, as a sophomore starter in 1926, got in the habit of winking at her before each game. He's still doing it more than 40 years later.

It was not easy making the Martinsville High team, which had won a state title not long before Wooden arrived. The team, in fact, went all the way to the state finals before losing to Marion 30–23 in his sophomore year. Wooden did not score, but he was second leading scorer in the 16-team finals the next year. Playing on the final day, Martinsville won the championship by beating Muncie 26–23, and Wooden hit 10 points. In 1928 the same two teams reached the finals again, and Martinsville led 12–11 with 30 seconds to go before it was defeated by the most amazing shot Wooden has ever seen.

"On a center jump their center tipped the ball back to himself," he said. "In those days it was legal. He pivoted and let loose an underhand scoop shot that had the highest arch I have ever seen. The ball seemed to disappear in the rafters. It came straight down through the hoop, not even swishing the net."

Wooden made the All-State team for the third straight year. Six boys from that 1928 team went to six different colleges and were starters as sophomores. Little has changed in Martinsville since those days. Farmers come to town in summer and sell tomatoes, corn and peaches from their ancient pickup trucks parked around the square. A Chamber of Commerce sign on the edge of town says, "Home of John Wooden." The Town House Cafeteria has pictures on the walls of Wooden and the famous Artesian basketball teams. For a long time a crew cut in Martinsville was known as a "Johnny Wooden."

"About three or four years ago," said Town House proprietor Bill Poe, "he gave the commencement address at the high school, and before he talked, he walked in here to eat. It was early and he asked me how Aunt Edna Hyah was–she was a friend of John's mother.

"I said she had just come back from the hospital that day. He said, 'I think I'll drop by and say hello.' So instead of going down to the Elks Club to renew old acquaintances, John went by and talked to an old lady who was a friend of his mother's. Then he went to the gym and gave his talk. John Wooden is a yard wide."

Kansas and most of the Big Ten schools invaded Martinsville to try to recruit Wooden, but Purdue got him because of its engineering school and its fine coach, Ward (Piggy) Lambert, an early advocate of the fast break. Wooden soon switched to a liberal arts major. He not only made All-America three times, he led the Boilermakers to two conference championships and won the Big Ten medal for excellence in scholarship and athletics. A "floor guard," as opposed to the "back guard" who rarely got to shoot, he played at 5 feet 10½ inches and 183 pounds and was so slashing and daring that sometimes school officials stationed two men behind the basket to catch him after his wild drives. In a game against Indiana he was knocked to the floor near the free-throw line. Before he could get up a rebound came to him and still sitting down he made the shot that won the game.

He could take off near the foul line and sail up to the basket "as smooth and pretty as a bird." Or he would drive in for a lay-up with such determination that his momentum would carry him into the fifth row of the school band at the end of the court. He'd have to pull his head out of the tuba and race back on defense. He bounced off the floor so often that people called him the India Rubber Man.

"He had a way of stalling the game by fantastic dribbling," said teammate Dutch Fehring, later intramural sports director at Stanford. "He would dribble from backcourt to forecourt, all around, and nobody could get that ball away."

Sportscaster Tom Harmon, who won the Heisman Trophy as a Michigan halfback, was a schoolboy in Gary, Indiana, in the early 1930s and used to go down to Lafayette to watch Purdue. "Wooden was to the kids of my era what Bill Russell, Wilt Chamberlain or Lew Alcindor is today," he said. "He was king, the idol of any kid who had a basketball. In Indiana that was *every* kid."

It all sounds glorious, yet college was no lark for Wooden. To pay for his meals he waited on tables at his fraternity house. He produced the Purdue basketball programs and split the proceeds with the high school boys who sold them for him (he kept the advertising income). On the annual train ride to Chicago for the Purdue-Chicago football game he raced up and down the aisles selling sandwiches. He called it "my annual walk to Chicago."

Wooden played some semipro and pro ball right after being graduated in the depths of the Depression and managed to save 909 dollars and a nickel—he remembers the exact figure. Two days before he was to marry Nellie Riley, the bank where he had his savings failed to open (the directors later went to prison). He had to scurry around and borrow two hundred dollars to pay for the wedding and a one-day honeymoon in romantic downtown Indianapolis. Buying a car was impossible, so some relatives drove them to Dayton, Kentucky, where Wooden's first coaching job was waiting.

While coaching at high schools in Dayton and South Bend, Indiana, he continued his part-time pro career, most of the time earning 50 dollars a game playing floor guard for Kautsky of Indianapolis.

Once he made 138 consecutive free throws in competition. Those were the disorganized pre-NBA days —with games in places like Kokomo, Oshkosh and Sheboygan—when anything could and did happen. There was the time in Detroit when the Kautskys had a 10- or 12-point lead with two minutes to go. They played at least three or four minutes more, but the timer insisted that there were still two minutes left to play.

"We finally got the idea," said Wooden, "so we went back to the center jump and each time they'd throw the ball up we'd stand there and not move. They would take the tipoff and go down and score and bring it back to the center jump. When they made the basket that put 'em ahead, why the game was over."

The center jump after each basket finally went out before his last pro season in 1938 and Wooden, described by a fellow pro as "fast as the wind, quicker than a cat and the best ballhandler and dribbler I have ever seen," enjoyed his highest-scoring season. But an old leg injury forced him to quit the game.

Wooden's 11 years as a high school coach—nine at South Bend Central—were very successful (218 wins, 42 losses). Even more impressive if you know that he also had to coach baseball and tennis, teach English and serve as comptroller and athletic director. Then, as now, his practices were organized down to the last dribble and he was a fanatic on fitness. ("They may beat me on ability," he had said at Purdue, "but they'll never beat me on condition.") World War II ended Wooden's high school coaching career.

He was a Navy officer, helping to get pilots in shape for combat flying. When he got out in 1946 there was no house to go back to. Wooden had been unable to keep up the payments and lost it. He immediately got all his jobs back at South Bend Central, but some of his friends were not so fairly treated and he became disenchanted with the school system. When a job opened at Indiana State Teachers College in Terre Haute, he took it, bringing along a load of former Central High players just getting out of the service themselves. With 14 freshmen and one sophomore that first year, Indiana State had an 18 and 7 record. The same cast improved that to 29 and 7 the next year.

As long as he had taken the reluctant step from high school to college coaching, Wooden figured he might as well go on to a major university; both Minnesota and UCLA were after him. Minnesota offered more money, but the Gopher officials were delayed somewhere by a snowstorm on decision day and did not call when they said they would. Wooden accepted the UCLA job and an hour later Minnesota got him on the phone—too late.

Wooden was not a big hit at southern California cocktail parties. Most of the time he stood ill at ease in a corner holding a glass of something like sarsaparilla while assistant Eddie Powell rounded up people to come meet him. It was not that Wooden lacked confidence. On a spring evening in 1948 he told a UCLA banquet audience: "The fast break is my system and we'll win fifty percent of our games by outrunning the other team in the last five minutes."

It was no exaggeration. Most West Coast teams played slowly and deliberately and several times against league opponents, Powell swears, UCLA actually had *five-on-zero* fast breaks.

"Wooden's success is based on upsetting the tempo and style of his opponent," said a rival coach. "He does it by running, running and running some more. He mixes that up by hawking, by grabbing, by slapping and by hand-waving defense. His clubs dote on harassing the man with the ball."

Foes hated to visit the old UCLA gymnasium, a small place that steamed when packed with people, and was known, not without reason, as the B.O.

Losing the ball and getting hit in the mouth with his own medallion, LaSalle's Larry Cannon gets an A for effort anyway. He was coached by ex-Explorer high-scorer Tom Gola.

Barn. Wooden insisted that if he was turning up the heat, as some people claimed, he would be doing more damage to his running clubs. "I wanted a better place to play," he says, "but it didn't displease me that the other teams dreaded to come in there."

Despite numerous division and league championships, UCLA really was not a national power during Wooden's first 13 years there. He had a fine center, Willie Naulls, in the mid-'50s, but that era was dominated by USF and Bill Russell. Then Cal, coached by Pete Newell, came up to frustrate the Bruins. Newell's teams beat Wooden's the last eight times they met.

The thrust into the national spotlight came in the early '60s with the arrival of some gifted athletes, notably Walt Hazzard and Gail Goodrich, and the introduction of the full court zone press, known as the "Glue Factory"—the first major change in college basketball in a number of years.

The Glue Factory, devised by Wooden and his assistant coach/recruiter Jerry Norman, opened for business in the 1963-64 season, and the Bruins had just the right manpower—five fast, cocky players: Hazzard, Goodrich, Fred Slaughter, Jack Hirsch and Keith Erickson. Not one of them was taller than 6 feet 5 inches but they full court-pressed and fast-broke their way to a 30 and 0 season and the NCAA championship.

A sixth player also had an important role. He was Kenny Washington, a sophomore from Beaufort, South Carolina, who went in as a sub in the final against Duke and scored 26 points. UCLA beat the Blue Devils 98–93.

Hazzard was gone in 1964-65, but Goodrich and Erickson were back and the Bruins again battled their way into the NCAA final, where they met the tough Michigan team led by Cazzie Russell, Bill Buntin and Oliver Darden. Michigan jumped off to a seven-point lead, 20–13, but only temporarily.

UCLA outscored the Wolverines 10–1 in the last three minutes of the first half and went on to win its second-straight championship 91–80. UCLA had much more speed, the sticky zone press and scrawny Goodrich, who scooted in and around Michigan's muscle men as if they were trees rooted in the floor of Portland's Memorial Coliseum. (Wooden had recognized his potential early and offered him a scholarship at the end of his junior year in high school, when he was only 5 feet 8 inches and 120 pounds.) Kenny Washington had another good game going in off the bench: seven baskets in nine tries.

Washington was just one of many black athletes who had been attracted to UCLA's basketball program from around the country. The list included Johnny Moore from Gary, Indiana, Ron Lawson from Nashville, Fred Slaughter from Topeka, Kansas, Hazzard from Philadelphia and others. In 1965-66 the biggest recruiting plum of all arrived. At 7 feet 1 inch (or thereabouts), Lew Alcindor was also *literally* the biggest.

Even though he was shielded from reporters by his high school coach, Jack Donohue (now the coach at Holy Cross College), Alcindor was a highly publicized prospect at Power Memorial High in Manhattan. Not only was he the most agile 7-footer ever to come along, but he was a good student, too. Some sportswriters and coaches felt that the school that landed Lew was assured of winning three consecutive NCAA championships. When that school turned out to be UCLA, the rest of the country shuddered.

UCLA's handsome, 13,000-seat Pauley Pavilion opened that year and was quite a contrast to the old B.O. Barn. The new arena's first basketball program was "A Salute to John R. Wooden" and a varsity-freshman game. Wooden received three standing ovations, but the real hero of the night was Lew. Playing on a frosh team with three other ex-high school All-Americas, he scored 31 points, took

31 rebounds and blocked seven shots. The freshmen beat the defending national champions by 15 points and led at one time by 18!

The varsity did not win the NCAA championship—and the frosh were not eligible to try for it—so the record for consecutive titles remained at two.

Lew's varsity debut was against USC, which bravely and foolishly tried to stop him with a straight man-to-man defense. He scored 56 points. Duke arrived next for a two-game series and tried a zone defense, draping three or four men on Lew. He scored 57 points for the two nights. Nobody stopped him or UCLA in 1966–67 and the Bruins romped to their third title in four years, beating Houston and Elvin Hayes 73–58 in the NCAA semifinals and Dayton 79–64 in the final.

UCLA Athletic Director J. D. Morgan, a sound businessman, made good use of Alcindor. In Lew's three years, the Bruins appeared in Madison Square Garden, Chicago Stadium and other big arenas and raked in a lot of money. The best payday of all was in January of 1968 in Houston's Harris County Domed Stadium, better known as the Astrodome, where UCLA again met Houston.

It was the first basketball game played in the Astrodome (except for the preceding freshman game that night). Houston, with senior Elvin Hayes, had won 48 straight home games. UCLA had never been beaten with Alcindor. The match drew 52,693 fans, the largest crowd ever to see a basketball game in the U.S. It had the biggest television audience in the history of the sport (150 stations in 49 states), and the U.S. Information Agency was there to make a five-minute TV show to be shown in 33 countries.

Only a couple of things were not just right. Except those for the reporters and the bands, the nearest seat to the floor was about 100 feet away. People in the worst seats needed binoculars to follow the action, and basketball is not a sport that should be watched through binoculars. Secondly,

Alcindor had suffered a scratched left eyeball in a game against Cal and had missed two games. There was some question as to how well the eye had healed and what kind of shape he was in. Everything else under the dome was ready, including the 225-panel, 18-ton portable floor which had been brought in all the way from the Los Angeles Sports Arena.

To the delight of the Texas crowd, Elvin completely outplayed Lew. The Big E from Rayville, Louisiana, scored 39 points, took 15 rebounds and made the free throws that decided the game in the Cougars' favor, 71–69. Alcindor, no doubt bothered by the layoff, made only four of 18 shots. To rub it in, every time Elvin scored, the Astrodome's giant message board flashed an E two stories high. The crowd chanted E, E, E, E until it sounded like one long EEEEEEEE.

Gone was UCLA's chance to play three straight seasons without a defeat, but it could still win three straight championships. The Bruins pointed for a rematch with Houston in the semifinals of the NCAA Tournament, held that year in L.A.'s Sports Arena, which had reclaimed its floor from the Astrodome. No matter which team won in the other bracket, North Carolina or Ohio State, everyone was certain that UCLA versus Houston was really the championship game.

The Cougars had been enjoying their California holiday, staying at the Beverly Hilton Hotel, touring the movie studios and eating sweet-and-sour ribs at the Luau. Their evening out at the Sports Arena began inauspiciously, however. Student manager Howie Lorch was arrested outside for scalping tickets.

UCLA got off to a good lead at the beginning of the game, but Houston closed it to 20–19 and the fans settled back in their seats to watch a dogfight that might go into five or six overtimes. Maybe Howie would get bailed out in time to see the finish. But Howie was out of luck because in the next four minutes and 17 seconds, UCLA outscored Houston 17–5 and the rout was on. The Bruins had a 22-point lead at half time and at one point in the second half stretched it to 44. They won 101–69. Hayes played like a sleepwalker and Houston made only 28.2 percent of its shots. Lew was the most valuable player.

"That's the greatest exhibition of basketball I've ever seen," said Houston coach Guy V. Lewis.

UCLA's 78–55 victory over North Carolina in the final was an anticlimax. So was most of Alcindor's senior year, although USC did defeat the Bruins with a well-executed stall just before the NCAA Tournament, and Drake played a good but losing game against them in the semifinals. In the final at Louisville's Freedom Hall, UCLA beat Purdue 92–72 as Lew's dad, a New York City transit cop, sat in with the Bruin band and played trombone.

Three consecutive national championships!

"It was not as easy an era as it might have seemed to outsiders," said Wooden. "But it's been a tremendous era, I think. I've heard it said that any coach would have won championships with Lewis. That might be true, it really might. But they'll never know. I do."

Although Wooden did not say so publicly, it was known that he did not particularly enjoy the Alcindor years and would be pleased to get back to the racehorse basketball he loves to teach. Lew and some of his teammates were difficult to handle off the court, and there was always the peculiar pressure of trying to avoid defeat rather than trying to win.

In 1969–70 he had an excellent front line: 6 foot-8 inch Sidney Wicks, 6 foot-9 inch Steve Patterson and 6 foot-6 inch Curtis Rowe, all from California, plus two guards who were accurate outside shooters, John Vallely and Henry Bibby. The Bruins were beaten twice in their tough conference

but made it again to the NCAA semifinals, held that year in College Park, Maryland.

"My wife Nell was saying before the season started that maybe this year we could go back to the coaches' convention and the Nationals and just relax," said Wooden. "Without any pressure at all. It didn't turn out that way, but of course I didn't really want it to."

UCLA beat New Mexico State in the semifinals. Its opponent in the final was a new basketball power, Jacksonville, which had built a 24 and 1 record with 7 foot-2 inch Artis Gilmore. It was UCLA's turn to try to cope with an outsized pivot man. JU got off to a 14–6 lead, but Wooden made a quick, simple adjustment, moving Wicks around behind Gilmore and having Patterson and others sag in on him. Wicks, giving away six inches in height, blocked four of Gilmore's shots and out-rebounded him 18–16.

"We knew the first couple of minutes of the second half would determine the outcome," said Patterson. "They were down by five and could catch us, or we could move out by 10. We moved out. They weren't used to playing *behind* teams—they don't play the kind of rough schedule we do."

The Bruins won 80–69 for their fourth title in a row. A sixth NCAA championship banner to hang in Pauley Pavilion, a banner won without the aid of Lew Alcindor.

Recently, some old friends from Indiana, Floyd Burns and his wife, were passing through L.A. and gave the Woodens a surprise call. After dinner and a campus tour, they were shown UCLA's modern arena, silent and empty except for John, Nell and the other couple. They all sat down in the plush theater seats and gazed at the gleaming floor and the banners hanging far above.

"John," said Burns, "it sure is a long way from Martinsville to all this."

"Yes, Floyd, it is," said the India Rubber Man.

The shot has missed, but basketball players are taught to try, try again, and Skip Thoren of Illinois (35) has obviously learned his lessons well. Here, he tries to nudge the ball back in.

The essential big man

It was christened the Basketball Association of America, which certainly *sounded* grand enough. In truth, however, it was merely ice hockey's foster brother, adopted in 1946 by the Arena Managers Association as a means of filling empty seats on those winter nights when pucks weren't flying about. BAA players traveled by train, bus and their own cars. There was no all-star game, most valuable player, rookie of the year or 24-second clock. The commissioner was a roly-poly minor-league hockey executive who didn't know a backboard from a backcourt.

Today, 25 years, 32 cities and 32 franchises later, the league is called the National Basketball Association, and more than five million people have watched its teams in a single season. Any individual or group wanting to join will have to cough up at least 3.7 million dollars.

The struggle for survival and then success was not easy. Cities, teams and owners came and went like truck drivers at a highway cafe. The original eleven teams were the Chicago Stags, Cleveland Rebels, Detroit Falcons, Pittsburgh Ironmen and St. Louis Bombers in the Western Division, the Boston Celtics, New York Knickerbockers, Philadelphia Warriors, Providence Steamrollers, Toronto Huskies and Washington Capitols in the Eastern Division. Only two of them operate today in the same cities. Only three operate at all.

The impetus behind the formation of the BAA came mainly from Max Kase, sports editor of Hearst's afternoon *New York Journal-American*. World War II was over and Kase felt the time was ripe for professional basketball. He expected that he would get the New York franchise and be able to rent Madison Square Garden for his home games. But he got nowhere with his idea until he decided to talk to some arena owners. Walter Brown of Boston and Al Sutphin of Cleveland were interested and helped recruit others.

Ned Irish was doing nicely indeed with college-basketball promotions at the Garden and was not enthusiastic about a new pro league, but when he saw the interest of some of his fellow arena managers, he joined up. Kase, who couldn't very well have a team play in the city room of the *Journal-American*, was out of the picture.

The organizational meeting was held in New York City on June 6, 1946 (Oscar Robertson was seven years old at the time, Walt Frazier was one and Lew Alcindor wasn't born yet). Among those present were Walter Brown, president of the Boston Garden; lawyer Arthur Morse, representing the Chicago Stadium interests; John Harris of Pittsburgh, well known for his ice shows; Al Sutphin of Cleveland, and Ned Irish. The BAA adopted a hockey-style playoff system and a hockey-style financial arrangement whereby home teams would keep gate receipts and visiting teams would get paid off in boos. The influence of hockey was so pervasive in the room that the new basketball magnates could almost feel the chill from the ice.

Perhaps overdoing the theme, the owners picked a hockey man for commissioner. He was Russian-born Maurice Podoloff, a Yale Law School graduate, commissioner of the American Hockey League and co-owner of the New Haven Arena (he kept his job as head of the AHL until 1952). A good compromiser and tireless worker, he knew very little about basketball and didn't particularly care to learn more. He scoffed at public relations, saying that a behind-the-back pass from Boston's Bob Cousy was all the PR he needed.

Out-and-out publicity Podoloff could understand. To help get some, the BAA hired Walter Kennedy, who had been sports information director at Notre Dame for three years. He had left Notre Dame to run a high school sports program—the Scholastic Sports Institute—for Coca-Cola. This Coke subsidiary folded, however, because a scar-

A giant among giants, Wilton Chamberlain of Los Angeles rebounds (and grimaces) in a game against Cincinnati. Wilt holds NBA records in almost every category but championships.

RIGHT: Muscleman of the Minneapolis Lakers was center George Mikan, who helped his team dominate the NBA. FAR RIGHT: Boston's Bob Cousy tries to free himself for a shot under the hoop.

city of sugar was making things difficult for the parent company.

Kennedy was responsible for finding the league's first digs. Podoloff was looking for office space, not plentiful at that time, so Kennedy told him about the vacated headquarters of the defunct institute on the 33rd floor of a building at 53rd Street and Madison Avenue. The league moved in and stayed there until switching to the Empire State Building in 1951. Today the offices are in Suite 2360 of the Penn Plaza building, conveniently adjacent to Madison Square Garden and Penn Station. And the man in the commissioner's chair is Walter Kennedy, who took over from Podoloff in 1963.

The first game was played November 1, 1946, at Maple Leaf Gardens in Toronto. A crowd of 8,000 fans paid from seventy-five cents to two and a half dollars and saw the New York Knicks beat the Toronto Huskies 68–66. Any fan taller than Toronto's 6 foot-8 inch George Nostrand got in free. New York did much better at the gate for its first home game, drawing 17,205.

Eddie Gottlieb, connected for so many years with the Philadelphia Sphas, was the first coach of the Philadelphia Warriors and later bought the club for 25,000 dollars. He remembers that the BAA initially stocked its teams with weekend American League players willing to play every day (the A.L. died in 1952), college stars and veterans back from the war.

The league's first hero was ex-Marine Joe Fulks, who had seen action on Iwo Jima and Guam. Before that he had played at Murray State in Kentucky, but Gottlieb heard of him as a service player from ex-Spha Petey Rosenberg. Joe was a broad-shouldered, long-armed, poker-faced country boy who had been reared by the banks of the Tennessee River in Marshall County, Kentucky, but he knew how to drive a hard bargain. He demanded 8,000 dollars to play for the Warriors. The BAA had a 50,000-dollar pay-

roll limit on each club at that time, Gottlieb says—and besides that, he had never seen Fulks play. He argued, pleaded and cried, but Fulks wouldn't give in and finally got his eight thousand.

Joe was 26 when he joined the team and he brought his philosophy with him: "To win, you've got to have points, so I fire away at every opportunity." His firing was effective—he scored 1,389 points and led the league with a 23.2 average—but the Warriors finished second in the Eastern Division. They made up for it by beating St. Louis, New York and Chicago in the playoffs to win the first cham-

pionship. The first all-league team consisted of Fulks, Bob Feerick and Horace (Bones) McKinney of Washington, Stan Miasek of Detroit and Max Zaslofsky of Chicago.

Cleveland, Detroit, Pittsburgh and Toronto dropped out after one year, and the Baltimore Bullets came in from a minor league. Once again in 1947–48 a division second-place team won the overall championship. This time it was newcomer Baltimore, led by player-coach Buddy Jeannette, beating New York, Chicago and Philly in the playoffs.

People flipping through their *NBA Guides* today tend to think of 1946 as the start of real big-league basketball. The BAA had the large cities, bright lights and big arenas, but the truth is that the league was second-rate in talent its first two seasons. The best players were performing out in Oshkosh and Moline in the National Basketball *League*, which had been operating since 1937. The NBL also had some sizable cities—Chicago, Detroit and Indianapolis—but there were too many towns like Anderson, Indiana and Sheboygan, Wisconsin. Here was George

Mikan, the great star from DePaul, playing for the Chicago American Gears and having to trade elbows with the Anderson Duffey Packers. It was embarrassing. However, it was equally embarrassing to the BAA that it didn't have Big George appearing in Madison Square Garden.

Mikan signed with the Gears in March of 1946. Maurice A. White, president of the American Gear Co., bragged that the five-year, 60,000-dollar contract (including a juicy 25,000-dollar bonus for signing) made George the highest-paid pro basketball player of all time. Apparently George didn't think it was all that glorious, because in December he sued to have the contract broken so he could become a free agent. He claimed he had not seen any of the bonus money and that the contract was "one-sided" because he could be fired at any time. There was a compromise and he returned to the club in January and helped the Gears mesh again.

Then came one of those complicated sequences entwined through the history of pro basketball. For the 1947–48 season, White set up his own circuit,

the Professional Basketball League, which folded after a few weeks. Rights to the PBL players were distributed among the NBL clubs and the new Minneapolis Lakers (formerly the NBL Detroit franchise) drew Mikan's name. The Lakers already had coach John Kundla, Herman Schaefer from Indiana and 6 foot-5 inch Jim Pollard, the Kangaroo Kid who had been a star with Stanford, a Coast Guard team and two AAU clubs. Mikan's arrival in Minnesota was the beginning of the first dynasty in modern pro basketball history.

It doesn't show up in the *NBA Guide,* but the Lakers won the NBL title in 1947–48 and Mikan, joining the team for its fifth game (and scoring just one basket that day) led the league in scoring with 1,195 points in 56 games and a 21.3 average. He got all 240 votes for most valuable player.

BAA Commissioner Podoloff wanted Mikan and the Lakers to defect, but the Minneapolis owners said no. The second-best team, the Rochester Royals, was skipped over and Podoloff went to work on Indianapolis and Fort Wayne. When he succeeded in luring those two franchises into the BAA, Minneapolis gave in and followed. Rochester asked in too and was accepted. Thus the 1948–49 season was the real start of major-league basketball.

Mikan went right on scoring in bunches in the

BAA, especially since the games were eight minutes longer than in the NBL. He scored 1,698 points in 60 games, averaged 28.3 points and was second in field-goal percentage and seventh in assists. He hit 53 points against Baltimore and seven times scored 40 or more points. The Lakers were a stronger team, mainly through the addition of a 6 foot-8 inch Dane named Arild Verner Agerskov Mikkelsen—Vern for short. He had been a hook-shooting center at Hamline University in St. Paul, but since nobody short of Paul Bunyan was going to beat out Mikan, he adjusted quickly to playing forward. Mikan, Pollard and Mikkelsen dominated the backboards against every other team in the league.

The Lakers were second in the Western Division to Rochester that first season after the "merger," but in the playoffs they beat both Chicago and Rochester 2 to 0 to reach the best-of-seven finals against the Washington Capitols, coached by Red Auerbach and starring Bones McKinney and Fred Scolari (Bob Feerick missed the playoffs because of a knee injury). Near the start of the fourth game George crashed into the Caps' Klegie Hermsen and hurt his right wrist. He stayed in the game and scored 27 points. X rays afterward showed that the wrist was broken. Mikan played the last two games with a cast on the wrist and still averaged 30.3 in the series. He hit 29 points in the final game and the Lakers won, four games to two.

Mikan had the reputation of being a brute under the basket. As the lights glinted off his glasses, he would get the ball, whirl toward the hoop and heaven help the poor guy who dared to be in his path. Down on the floor would go the bloody opponent and into the basket went the hook shot. Field goal, Mikan! But George received punishment too and the broken wrist was just one example. One tally showed that in his pro career—from his first game when he lost four teeth to his last game in 1956—George suffered a broken leg, a broken nose, a broken wrist, two broken feet, four broken fingers and cuts and scratches that needed 166 stitches (three to sixteen stitches at a time). Not counting cuts under his eyes from his eyeglass frames jamming against his face.

"Those elbows banging your teeth from each side take a toll," he said. "I've lost my share of teeth. . . . But it's worth it."

A writer once entered the Laker locker room after a game and told Mikan the players on the other team had been complaining about his rough play. George pulled off his jersey, revealing bruises and welts all over his upper torso.

"What do they think these are?" he asked. "Birthmarks?"

The Lakers had a lucrative exhibition-game series with the Harlem Globetrotters in the Mikan era. Early in 1948, before Minneapolis switched to the BAA, the two teams played before 17,823 fans in Chicago Stadium. The Lakers were leading the National Basketball League at the time and the 'Trotters' record for the season was 101 and 0 (built mostly against teams acting as stooges for their gags). The 'Trotters won 61–59 but tried only one stunt the whole game, rolling the ball between a startled Laker's legs to Reece (Goose) Tatum, the nutty center.

One of the best games was in Chicago Stadium before 21,866 fans. The Globies were on a 113-game winning streak, but Minneapolis got off to a 40–29 lead and won handily 76–60. "Sweetwater" Clifton fouled out trying to guard Mikan, who scored 36 points. Goose Tatum sobbed in the locker room.

"This is the next best thing to winning the national championship," said Big George.

The Lakers' bitterest rivals in Mikan's years were the Rochester Royals, with good players like Arnie Risin, Bob Wanzer and Bob Davies. In fact, the Royals once beat out Minneapolis for the NBA title, in 1950–51. Minneapolis won the Western Division over the Royals but lost to them in the second round of the playoffs when Mikan had to play on a fractured ankle sprayed with ethyl chloride.

Mikan was not a welcome guest in Rochester. After he scored 61 points against the Royals in the 1951–52 season (on 22 field goals and 17 free throws), Royals' owner Les Harrison couldn't contain himself. "A monster!" he said. "That's what he is, a monster!"

That same year a Rochester fan threw an opened pocketknife at Mikan after George had fouled out. Harrison was not apologetic, at least not in public.

"A knife?" he said. "More likely it was a double-edged woodsman's ax. Rochester people just don't throw little things like knives."

Fans and players in Rochester had reason to feel frustrated by Mikan. In 1949–50, when the BAA changed its name to the National Basketball Association, he led in scoring again with 1,865 points and a 27.4 average. The two teams tied for the Central Division title, but the Lakers beat the Royals 78–76 to break the deadlock and marched through the playoffs to the championship. In 1951–52, 1952–53 and 1953–54 it was always Minneapolis blocking the way in the division or the league playoffs, and sometimes in both.

Of course, Mikan did not win five NBA championships in six seasons by himself. Mikkelsen, who fouled too much and didn't have a great shooting touch, nevertheless played tenacious defense, rebounded well and scored more than enough. He played in six All-Star Games. Pollard earned about half as much money and scored about half as many points as Mikan, but he averaged better than thirteen points in four All-Star Games. Red Auerbach called 5 foot-10 inch Slater Martin "the greatest defensive little man in basketball today because he's also the greatest competitor." Martin once held Rochester's Bob Davies without a field goal in a game. Mikan claimed Slater could stop Boston's Bob Cousy ". . . every time. Cousy never ran wild against us. He could never compare with Martin on defense."

Still, it was for Mikan that Philadelphia owner Eddie Gottlieb once offered his entire team (leaving out Paul Arizin, who was in the Marines at the time). Mikan was not a springy leaper and was far from being a sprinter up and down the court, but those two weaknesses helped opponents only slightly. He was the overwhelming force, the Babe Ruth of pro basketball. In January of 1951 the Associated Press polled 380 writers and broadcasters to find out who was considered to be the finest basketball player in the first half of the 20th century. Alex Groza finished fifth in the voting, Chuck Hyatt was fourth, Nat Holman third, Hank Luisetti second and—sixteen votes ahead of Luisetti—Mikan first. It was a nice honor, although the fact that he was the sport's reigning star at the time of the voting obviously helped him win.

In 1953–54, Minneapolis won its fifth NBA championship, but George slipped to fourth in scoring. He had his law degree and had passed the Minnesota bar examination, so he decided it was time to hang up his eyeglass guard and give his battered body a rest.

"It wasn't a sudden decision," he said. "I've been thinking about it for some time. I've got three boys and they scarcely know they have a father."

In April of '54 the NBA Board of Governors met at the Biltmore Hotel in New York City and made an important rule change. So important, in fact, that many people believe it saved the league from going out of business, as so many pro basketball ventures had. This was the 24-second rule, whereby a team had to take a shot within 24 seconds of gaining possession of the ball.

The main proponent of the idea was Danny Biasone, owner of the Syracuse Nationals (and a notorious referee-baiter). The purpose was to speed up the game and eliminate stalling. Biasone noted that in the previous season NBA teams had averaged more than 75 shots a game. One shot every 24 seconds would be 120 shots, only 60 per team, so it would not be a hardship on anybody.

Still, some owners were "bitterly opposed to it," according to present NBA Commissioner Walter Kennedy, and Milton Gross in the New York Post lamented the loss of the "strategic freeze" and complained that "ballhandling now becomes a liability." He said the game had become an exercise for "mathematicians, statisticians, clock-watchers and coaches who are afraid to attack their problems" at their sources.

Bob Cousy and most others disagreed, especially after a few tests.

"Before the new rule, the last quarter could be deadly in a pressure game," Cousy said. "The team in front would hold the ball indefinitely, and the only way you could get it was by fouling somebody. In the meantime, nobody dared take a shot and the whole game was slowed up."

There was a companion piece of legislation passed at that same April meeting. Each team was limited to six fouls a period. Any beyond that would mean the opponent would get a "bonus" free throw.

Wilt Chamberlain drives against Cincinnati. Wilt joined the Philadelphia Warriors as a rookie in 1959–60 and won Player of the Year trophy. He moved to San Francisco with the team.

This effectively prevented teams from fouling on purpose and giving their opponents a chance for only one point rather than a chance for two.

The 24-second clock, along with steadily improving shooting skill, noticeably increased scoring in the NBA. In 1953–54 only one player, Neil Johnston of Philadelphia, averaged 20 points a game or better. In 1954–55, four guys did it. Two years after that, eight did it. Boston averaged 101.4 the first season with the clock and only one team (also Boston) had been above 90 before.

With Mikan gone in '54–55, the Lakers finished second to Fort Wayne in the Western Division and also lost to the Pistons in the semifinals of the play-

offs. Attendance in Minneapolis went down, too. Syracuse, featuring a load of future college and pro coaches (6 foot-9 inch rookie Johnny Kerr, Paul Seymour, George King, Red Rocha, Dolph Schayes), won the championship. In the first year of the clock, the Nats played such tough defense during the regular season that their opponents averaged less than 90 points a game. They beat Fort Wayne in a final playoff that wasn't decided until the last twelve seconds of the seventh game, when King put in a free throw to make the score 92–91, then stole the Pistons' subsequent inbounds pass.

The Syracuse coach, a tough 5 foot-11 inch Italian from Buffalo named Al Cervi, was a high-

school dropout who had been going through the semipro and pro basketball wars in upstate New York since 1937. He went back to the days of St. Stanislaus Hall in Rochester, where players had to leap up on a stage after driving to one basket (they presumably did a snappy soft-shoe routine to entertain the customers and then quickly returned to the game). At one time he played in a gym in Oil City, Pennsylvania, that had "a red-glowing coal stove in the middle of the court" with a protective railing around it. In 1947–48, when Syracuse was still in the NBL, Cervi was both coach of the year and a member of the All- Star team.

"Al was one of the great players," said Dolph Schayes. "Most people didn't see him until he was in his 30s, but he was a fellow who could do everything on the court. And competition was Cervi's life, on and off. Why? Maybe because he wasn't a college man and we all were and he was out to show us something. He showed it to us, all right."

It was Schayes who was the star of the '54–55 championship team. A 6 foot-8 inch forward who could dribble, pass, drive, defend, rebound and hit consistently with a two-handed set shot from the corners, Dolph was an NBA All- Star twelve times in sixteen seasons. He once played in 765 consecutive games (a fractured right cheekbone ended the streak), and his career totals of 6,979 free throws and 1,059 games are NBA records. Dolph had joined Syracuse in the NBL days when he was just a nineteen-year-old kid out of New York University. The New York Knicks had offered him 5,000 dollars and a guaranteed 700 dollars in playoff money even if the club didn't make the playoffs, but Syracuse, which had obtained the rights to him from Tri-Cities, had offered 7,500 dollars. In the championship year he made .833 percent of his free throws and averaged 18.8 points and 12.3 rebounds.

In January of 1956 Mikan made the mistake of trying a comeback, the same mistake Joe Louis and so many other sports champions have made. Big George was slowed down by excess fat, couldn't rebound well and averaged only 10.5 points in 37 games. Coach Kundla started him ahead of Clyde Lovellette anyway, and the ex-Kansas All-America (no svelte model himself) resented it. Philadelphia, led by jump-shooting Paul Arizin, Neil Johnston and Jack George, won the title. Mikan retired for good after the 1955–56 season, just missing the arrival of the man who would take his place as the dominant force in the NBA.

Bill Russell, who was to lead the Boston Celtics to eleven championships in thirteen years, actually should have gone to the St. Louis Hawks. He finished his college career as the University of San Francisco romped through an undefeated season and took its second-straight NCAA title. The Harlem Globetrotters offered him a reported 32,000 dollars for his first pro year, but Bill, an intensely proud man, resented it when the 'Trotters' representative hardly acknowledged he was there and made the sales pitch to USF coach Phil Woolpert instead. Another nomadic group, the Harlem Clowns, offered him a part ownership, and some AAU teams chimed in with promising career opportunities. The Hawks said they would wait until after the Melbourne Olympics to approach him.

Just before the U.S. team left for Australia the press announced what was undoubtedly the most important trade in the hopscotch history of professional basketball. Boston, having only seventh pick in the 1956 draft, had traded "Easy Ed" Macauley and Cliff Hagan to St. Louis for the rights to Russell. Because a first-round draft choice was involved, the trade had to be approved by the other NBA clubs. Somehow the Celtics' Walter Brown and Red Auerbach got the approval.

Not long after, late in August, the touring Olympic team reached Washington, D.C., Auerbach's home, giving the Celtics' majordomo a chance to see this West Coast kid in action. Russell was rotten in the game and was almost too embarrassed to meet with Red later.

"Mr. Auerbach," Bill said, "I'd like to apologize for that miserable exhibition. I hope you don't think I play like that all the time."

Russell returned from Australia and in mid-December married his sweetheart, Rose Swisher. Celtics owner Walter Brown was a guest at the wedding, which gave a fairly strong clue as to the bridegroom's intentions. Bill went to Boston on his honeymoon and signed for a first-year salary of something between 19,000 and 24,000 dollars, highest ever for an NBA rookie but quite a bit under the Globetrotters' offer.

It was a bargain for Brown, generally recognized as one of the finest and fairest owners in pro sports. He and a partner had taken complete control of the foundering club in 1950 for 2,500 dollars, which wasn't such a good deal because it had lost 100,000 dollars a year for four years. Before he signed Russell, he had lost 500,000 dollars and had literally mortgaged his home. Eddie Powers, assistant treasurer of the Celtics in those threadbare days, described one experience for *Sports Illustrated*'s Frank Deford:

"We used to have to spend all of the withholding tax. One day the IRS man finally gave up and came to my office and said that the government had taken enough [nonsense] from us and had to take us over. I stood up behind my desk and spread out my hands—you have to be an actor ·sometimes—and said, 'OK, you're going to have an auction sale of the Boston Celtics. How much do you think the government can get from a dozen T-shirts, some used jockstraps and a few beat-up basketballs?' Those were the assets of the Boston Celtics. He left, shaking his head, and Walter kept the thing going."

Before Russell, the Celtics had led the NBA in scoring for six years in a row but were always second or third in the Eastern Division and couldn't survive a division playoff series. With Bill, Boston always had numerous playoff games and approached respectable solvency. Apart from a fuller till, though, what did he mean to the team?

"He meant everything," said Bob Cousy. "We didn't win a championship until we got him in 1957 [actually late 1956], we lost it when he was injured in 1958 and we won it back when he was sound again in 1959. This is a team that has always been able to shoot. But when your offense is predicated on the fast break and you can't get the rebound, you haven't got a fast break."

Some people think Russell would have won championships even if he had been teamed with three midgets and an elf. Fortunately for him, he never had to prove it because he was always surrounded by excellent players. Probably the most talented was Cousy, who also came to the Celtics by a circuitous route—a route so circuitous, in fact, that it made Ulysses' odyssey look like a tightrope walk.

Cousy was a consensus All-America at Holy Cross in 1949–50, scoring 582 points and pretty much making the people in Worcester, Massachusetts, and Boston forget about the Crusaders' previous big star, George Kaftan. Naturally there was pressure on the Celtics from New England fans and sportswriters to draft him. When Auerbach was hired by Walter Brown in 1950, reporters immediately asked about Cousy. Red, ever the diplomat, turned to Brown and said:

"Am I supposed to win or am I supposed to worry about the local yokels?"

Brown obviously agreed with Red because Boston passed up Cooz and instead tabbed 6 foot-11 inch Charlie Share of Bowling Green. (As it turned out, Share never wore the shamrock. The St. Louis Bombers folded and, over the protests of the New York Knicks, the league gave the rights to 6 foot-8 inch Ed Macauley to the weak Boston team.

Two stars of the great Celtic teams of the '60s were K. C. Jones (below, driving for the lay-up). RIGHT: Bill Russell, who sometimes could be stopped only by a multiple foul.

Boston then had no need for Share, who ended up signing with Waterloo.) Owner Ben Kerner of the Tri-Cities Blackhawks drafted Cousy, then traded him to the deathly ill Chicago Stags for one Frankie Brian. Shortly before the 1950–51 season started, the Stags staggered after the Bombers into the franchise graveyard. There was a squabble over the rights to some Chicago players, so Commissioner Maurice Podoloff put the names of three, Max Zaslofsky, Andy Phillip and Cousy, into a hat and had a drawing.

Ned Irish of New York picked first and drew Zaslofsky, considered the prize. Irish was jubilant because in Max he not only had a fine player but a Jew, too—a nice attraction in New York. Eddie Gottlieb of Philadelphia then picked Phillip's name, and that left Walter Brown with the booby prize, Cousy.

"I thought I'd got stung," said Brown. "I'd had a bellyful of hometown heroes. We picked up half of that great 1947 Holy Cross team, including George Kaftan, Joe Mullaney and Dermie O'Connell. We tried Tony Lavelli from Yale, and Ed Leede from Dartmouth and half a dozen others. None of them made the grade. I was afraid Cousy would be just another of those home-grown phenoms."

As a rookie, Cousy was fourth in the league in assists and ninth in scoring. He was second in assists the next season and then led the NBA for eight straight years, until the arrival of Oscar Robertson at Cincinnati. His dipsy-doodle, behind-the-back passes and fancy dribbling caught the imagination of spectators all around the league and excited watchers on national television. Some booby prize.

"Bob made it because he worked hard and he was smart," said Auerbach. "People just don't seem to realize how much he has improved, especially on defense. . . . He listens to what I tell him, he gives all he's got and he learns every day."

As a kid playing basketball on concrete outdoor courts on Long Island, Cooz developed strong,

heavy legs which he considered his greatest asset. His behind-the-back dribble, which he popularized to such an extent that even high school players use it today, originally was a desperation measure.

"I picked that one up while I was at Holy Cross," he said. "We played Loyola one night and the only way I could get around a guy was by shifting the ball from one hand to the other. He had me so well guarded that I couldn't do it in front, so I did it behind my back."

It is hard to believe that he had never practiced the trick, but then a lot of things Cousy did were hard to believe.

The Celtics' other guard was Bill Sharman, a good minor-league baseball player in the off-season. Bill was a stubborn defender and a solid puncher when he had to be, but he was better known for his shooting ability. He once hit his first eleven shots against the Warriors, which stood as an NBA record for a while. He had consecutive free-throw streaks of 50 and 55, and in 1958–59 he made .932 percent of his free throws. His most famous shooting feat was in the first period of the 1957 All-Star Game.

Standing practically under the opponents' hoop, Sharman let go with a long pass to Cousy. It was badly overthrown, so badly that it went through the basket 70 feet away! Legend has it that Bill calmly turned to the man guarding him and said:

"You never could play defense."

Tom Heinsohn, a 6 foot-7 inch line-drive shooter from Holy Cross, broke in with the Celtics the same year Russell did and, playing on teams loaded with stars for nine seasons, seldom got the recognition he deserved as one of the league's best scorers and offensive rebounders (although he did beat out Russell for rookie of the year). He once had a fine game against the Minneapolis Lakers in Seattle, yet in the local newspaper's account of the game the next morning, he wasn't mentioned until the last line: "Tom Heinsohn also scored 38 points."

The undisputed boss of this troupe, of course, was Auerbach, called Arnold by Cousy and Red by almost everyone else. Like so many other members of the Basketball Hall of Fame, his first contact with the game was in the gymnasiums and playgrounds of New York City. He was reared in the Williamsburg section of Brooklyn, helping his father press pants, and was graduated from Eastern District High School. After playing ball for George Washington University and coaching high school teams for three years, he went into the service.

Norfolk Naval Air Station proved to be his springboard to the pros. Red heard that the BAA was organizing and went to see Mike Uline, who

LEFT: Hal Greer drives the base line. Greer, a career Philadelphia man, is now one of the top goal-getters in the NBA. BELOW: Jerry West poises to take his deadly jumper.

ABOVE: Driving left against Walt Hazzard, Oscar
Robertson controls game as only he can. OPPOSITE:
Pistons' Jim Fox (23) protects rebound as he lands.

had the Washington franchise and owned Uline
Arena. Red painted a beautiful picture of all the
good ballplayers hidden away at Norfolk and talked
himself into a one-year contract for 5,000 dollars.
He coached the Washington Capitols for three
seasons and Tri-Cities (Davenport, Moline and Rock
Island) for one before Walter Brown hired him to
run the Celtics for a salary of 10,000 dollars a year.

Auerbach was a fine coach who knew a thousand little annoying tricks to throw opponents off
balance. He recommended tugging at an opponent's
pants, having a scoreboard clock that was difficult
for visitors to read and any other sneaky trick his
Celtics could get away with. He was a good
strategist but considered the proper handling of
players to be more important. He described himself
as "a dictator with compassion."

"Strategy is something anyone can learn," he
said. "But not all coaches take the time to understand a man's personality."

Red was an incorrigible critic of referees. One
of his maxims was, "Question officials' decisions,
especially on the home court." He was so hot-
tempered and so anxious to win that he even got
kicked out of the 1967 All-Star Game in San Francisco for berating the refs.

"A club must feel its coach is supporting them,"
said Red. "If I think a ref blew one, it's my job to
argue. It gives my team confidence. When I get
clipped with a technical, it's right, but that doesn't
mean I'm sorry. . . ."

He believed in the fast-break, run-run-run game
and made sure his players were in the best of condition. People outside the game might think that
every professional player is in tip-top shape, and
some players themselves might think so, but it is
not true. Willie Naulls had played for St. Louis,
New York and San Francisco before he joined the
Celtics in 1963–64. He almost collapsed trying to
keep up with his new teammates at the first practice

session. However, Red's system didn't lead to championships his first few years at Boston because he didn't have the required big man to pull down the defensive rebounds and start the fast break.

"I've always been looking for that good big fellow to get me the ball," said Red. "I don't need shooters. Never did. But where can you get that big man?"

From San Francisco via Melbourne, Australia. Fresh from the Olympics and his honeymoon, Russell joined Cousy, Sharman, Heinsohn & Co. on December 22, 1956. The Celtics drew 64,000 people for his first five games. He held Philadelphia's Neil Johnston scoreless for 38 minutes one game and the next night he held him to four field goals.

"Nobody had ever blocked shots on the pros before Russell came along," said Auerbach. "He upsets everybody. The only defense they could think of was to dish out a physical beating and hope he couldn't take it."

Russell proved he could stand the punishment under the boards and dominate teams doing it. He grabbed 943 rebounds that season, an average of almost 20 a game, and Boston won the Eastern Division comfortably. In the playoffs they beat Syracuse 2 to 1 and St. Louis 4 to 3. It was Bill's third championship in one year—NCAA, Olympics and NBA! He had grown a goatee as a gag and said he wouldn't shave it off until the Celtics won the title. In the post-championship celebration, Auerbach, Cousy and Jim Loscutoff happily shaved it off for him. Later it came back to stay.

St. Louis got revenge in 1957–58. Boston won the Eastern Division easily and whomped Philly in the semifinals 4 to 1, but in the third game of the finals against the Hawks, Bill suffered a chipped bone in his right ankle and some torn tendons. He tried to play in the sixth game, but he was useless. St. Louis, coached by Alex Hannum and starring Cliff Hagan and Bob Pettit, won 4 to 2.

(It was the only championship that 6 foot-9 inch Robert Lee Pettit Jr. of Baton Rouge, Louisiana, was to enjoy in a ten-year NBA career with the Hawks. He was a fine all-around player, twice leading the league in scoring and once in rebounding. He was rookie of the year in 1954–55, most valuable player twice and MVP in the All-Star Game three times. Fellow pro Willie Naulls called him "the most graceful big man I've ever seen."

(In 1970 the NBA picked a ten-man Silver Anniversary Team, restricted to players who had retired. Pettit was on it with Paul Arizin, Bob Cousy, Bob Davies, Joe Fulks, Sam Jones, George Mikan, Bill Russell, Dolph Schayes and Bill Sharman. Russell was the only unanimous choice.)

K. C. Jones, Russell's teammate from the USF days, joined the Celtics in 1958–59 and he and Sam Jones (no relation) became an excellent backup pair of guards for Cousy and Sharman (and eventually their replacements). Boston won the East by twelve games, edged by Syracuse 4 to 3 in the semis and murdered Minneapolis in the finals 4 to 0.

Russell and the Celtics had a fresh challenge in 1959–60. Wilt Chamberlain, who had skipped his last season at the University of Kansas to tour with the Globetrotters, surprised nobody when he decided to sign with Philadelphia as soon as his class at KU was graduated. Warriors' owner Eddie Gottlieb had made him a territorial draft choice (a gimmick no longer allowed) when he was still at Philadelphia's Overbrook High School. 'Trotters' owner Abe Saperstein wasn't crushed when Wilt left. Abe really couldn't lose because he owned a chunk of the Warriors, too. A debate raged over who would prove best, Russell or Chamberlain, but there was little argument over the fact that Wilt would be an instant NBA star.

"He'll be great, that's all," said Red Auerbach. "He didn't need that year with the 'Trotters to learn anything. He'll take over this league anyway. The

Battling for a rebound, Cincinnati's Tom Hawkins tries to hold out San Francisco's Rick Barry (24). Barry later jumped to the ABA's Oakland Oaks, giving a boost to that league.

first time he meets Russell, we could fill Yankee Stadium."

They did fill Boston Garden for the first meeting, on November 7, 1959, even though a strike had shut down the Boston newspapers. Wilt was taller, stronger and had a two-inch reach advantage, but he was just a rookie. A rookie against the master of defense and psychology. Russ won the opening tap and blocked Wilt's first shot, a fallaway jumper. It is doubtful that that shot had ever been blocked before. Russ finished with 22 points, 35 rebounds and eight of eight free throws. Wilt, taking 19 more shots than Bill, had 30 points, 28 rebounds and six of 12 free throws. Boston won 115–106.

"He's the best rookie I've ever seen," said Russell afterward. "I wish I was that good when I started. You've got to keep your hands on him and bother him all the time. This guy's no freak. By the end of the season, he could be the greatest basketball player of all time. When you're that big and good—and, man, his potential is unlimited —there's no stopping him."

And there wasn't. Wilt was the league's most valuable player as a rookie. He beat out Russell for first team All-NBA and he accumulated startling statistics: 37.6 points and 26.9 rebounds a game. But his *team* could be stopped. Boston won seventeen games in a row in one stretch, finished ten games ahead of Philly in the Eastern Division and beat the Warriors in the playoffs 4 to 2 (before going on to beat St. Louis in the finals 4 to 3). It was a pattern that was to frustrate Wilt through most of the 1960s.

Whenever and wherever Russell and Chamberlain met in that decade, the crowds flocked in, the scalpers cleaned up and the partisans of one or the other player kept up the debate. Russell himself said it was no contest, although he might have been trying to "psych" his rival.

"Chamberlain is the greatest basketball player alive, no doubt about that," Bill said in the early '60s. "He has set the standards so high, his point totals are so enormous that they've lost their impact. There can never really be a rivalry when in my best year I averaged 18 and in his worst year he averaged 37. The highest total I've ever had for a single game is 37, and when Wilt is 'held' to 37, they say he's had a bad night."

One time Chamberlain most assuredly was not held was March 2, 1962, in Hershey, Pennsylvania, where the Warriors hosted New York. Starting center for the Knicks was 6 foot-10 inch Darrall Imhoff, a second-year pro from the University of California. But Imhoff played only 20 minutes and didn't deserve all the blame for what happened. Wilt scored 23 points in the first quarter, 18 in the second. At the end of the third he had 69 points and seemed a cinch to break his own record of 78.

He did better than that. With 42 seconds left he scored his 100th point. He had made 36 of 63 field-goal attempts and 28 of 32 free throws. That still stands as the NBA record almost ten years later. It was no wonder Russell called him "the greatest basketball player alive."

Oh, sure, said the Russell fans, but Bill's side always wins. He is simply a winner. Wilt is a loser. The Chamberlain fans always pointed to Russell's superior teammates—and Russ agreed, or at least he seemed to.

"I'm surrounded by a great collection of players," he said. "I may bring out the best in them, but they bring out the best in me. Can I perform the same function with another team?"

"It's a vicious, real feud on the floor," said Wilt. "It's a pretend feud when we're together after the game. And when Russell gets named to the NBA All-Star team—and I get left off—what am I supposed to do? Run screaming off into the night?"

Many of Russell's statements seemed calculated to keep Wilt from getting riled up, as: "I have a

Elgin Baylor, who once scored 61 points in a playoff game, keeps in perfect control against Cincinnati. Pros' desire to play no matter what is typified by Robertson in jaw guard.

three-part defense I use against him. One, I try to keep him from the ball. Two, if that doesn't work, I try to stay between him and the basket. Three is when everything else fails. I panic." At that he let loose with his high-pitched cackle. How he really felt was shown the night Wilt scored 49 points off him. Russ cried afterward.

"Pride has always been very important to me," he said.

The Celtics in the 1960s were devastating, building a tradition of winning that is unmatched in modern pro team sports. Season after season they had the most stamina, the best mental attitude, the best players and, when the buzzer sounded, the most points. Arrogant Auerbach, always in a sports jacket, never a suit, would infuriate fans in Philadelphia and elsewhere by lighting up a cigar when a game was clinched (at least once he had a lighted one thrown at him). Through the years he enjoyed a lot of stogies on the bench:

1960–61: Tom (Satch) Sanders, who was to develop into one of the best defensive forwards in the league, joins the team. Boston wins the East by eleven games over Philly, beats Syracuse and St. Louis in the playoffs. Afterward, owner Walter Brown gives Russell a three-year contract for more than 40,000 dollars a year.

1961–62: The Celtics win their sixth division title in a row, beat Philly 4 to 3 in the semifinals. The rivals in the finals are the Lakers, recently moved from Minneapolis to L.A. Series goes to the seventh game in Boston. Tie game at 100–100 when Laker Frank Selvy's shot in the last seconds barely misses. Celtics win in overtime 107–102. After the season Wilt and the Warriors move from Philly to San Francisco, giving the NBA two clubs on the West Coast.

1962–63: Bob Cousy's last season. John Havlicek joins team as an outstanding rookie whose ability to run up and down the court all night makes even his teammates seem out of shape. Boston wins East by ten games, beats Cincinnati and L.A. in the playoffs.

1963–64: Some people think the Celtics will not win again without the great Cooz. Nonsense. Boston wins the East by four games, strolls through the playoffs, beating Cincy 4 to 1 and San Francisco 4 to 1. Bay breezes haven't made Wilt a winner.

1964–65: Part way through the season, Chamberlain is traded to Philadelphia 76ers (formerly the Syracuse Nationals). Boston wins the East by fourteen games, beats Philly in semis 4 to 3, L.A. in finals 4 to 1.

1965–66: Upset. Philly wins the East by one game. Things get back to normal in the playoffs,

though. Boston beats Cincy 4 to 1, Philly 4 to 1, L.A. 4 to 3.

Eight straight NBA championships, and nine in ten years. With and without Cousy. With and without Sharman, Havlicek, Heinsohn, K.C. and Sam. Always with Russell.

Auerbach, with an NBA record of 1,037 victories, 548 losses and more than 17,000 dollars in fines, turned the coaching job over to Russ for the 1966–67 season, and perhaps that was a mistake. Maybe the days of a player-coach were past. Or maybe the Celtics were getting old. Or maybe Chamberlain finally reached his teamwork potential. Whatever the reasons, Philadelphia won the Eastern Division over Boston by a solid eight games, then knocked off the Celtics in the playoffs 4 to 1. In the last game of that playoff series, Wilt beat Russell in rebounds 36–21, points 29–4, assists 13–7. The 76ers trampled the once-proud Celtics 140–116. They went on to beat San Francisco 4 to 2 for the title.

Russell didn't quit as player or coach, though. He was back wearing both hats in 1967–68. Philadelphia won the Eastern Division by eight games and it looked as if a new dynasty was gathering steam under coach Alex Hannum, the only coach who had ever beaten the Celtics in the Russell era. But in the playoffs, Boston beat Detroit 4 to 2, upset the 76ers 4 to 3 and beat L.A. 4 to 2 for a tenth championship in eleven years.

The question of whether a Chamberlain team or any other club would ever again beat a Russell team seemed answered in 1968 when Jack Kent Cooke, the millionaire ex-Canadian owner of the Los Angeles Lakers, swung an amazing deal. He sent Darrall Imhoff, Archie Clark and Jerry Chambers to Philadelphia in exchange for Chamberlain. Actually, Wilt himself had as much to do with arranging the trade as Cooke. His family had moved from Philly to L.A. five or six years before, his father was seriously ill and he had several business interests in town, including a 32-unit apartment house, the Villa Chamberlain. Also, he had a bitter relationship with 76er president Irv Kosloff.

Here at last was the powerhouse center the Lakers had needed since Mikan retired back in the Minnesota days. Here was the man to complement the great forward Elgin Baylor, and the great guard Jerry West. Baylor—who started in the All-Star Game as a rookie—scored 71 points in one NBA game, rebounded with the giants up front (even though he was just 6 feet 5 inches) and came back again and again despite serious knee injuries. And West, skinny "Zeke from Cabin Creek," two inches and 45 pounds smaller than Oscar Robertson but, claimed Laker fans, better than Oscar because he was the finest clutch shooter in basketball. And now Wilt, too. How could even the Celtics stop such a team?

The Lakers' second-year coach Butch van Breda Kolff was happy with the deal—at first. Then he found out why Wilt—the man who once scored 100 points in a regulation NBA game, the man who once took down 55 rebounds against Boston—had been traded *twice*. Butch realized that if he didn't win the championship with all that talent, he would be the goat. He saw that Wilt was a sulker and a lackadaisical practicer. Wilt arrived with a beard and kept it, even though VBK preferred a clean-shaven team. Wilt wanted a private room on the road,

which meant the Laker management certainly had to give Elgin and Jerry the same privilege.

Butch was grumbling and gloomy, whereas the previous season he had been his usual exuberant self, while managing the difficult trick of being both buddy and boss to the players. The players were optimistic about the 1968–69 season, although nobody was doing any flip-flops of pure joy.

"We've always gotten along well and that's one reason the Lakers have always had good records in Los Angeles," said West. "Last year if we played well, we had a chance to win. Now if we play well, we're going to win."

Win they did, most of the time. Wilt was a new, intimidating factor on defense, enabling his teammates to gamble more. On offense, however, it was a struggle all season between Butch and Wilt. The coach wanted Wilt to play more at a high post, Wilt wanted to stay in his old, accustomed spot down low. Whichever place the big guy played, the Laker offense was not as free-wheeling and fast as it had been. Still, it was good enough for L.A. to win the West easily, by seven games over Atlanta. Then the Lakers beat San Francisco 4 to 2 and Atlanta 4 to 1 in the playoffs and braced themselves to face their old antagonists, the Celtics, once again.

That the Celtics were there to accept the challenge was something of a miracle. The aging champions finished only fourth in the East behind Baltimore, Philadelphia and New York, and it looked as if the Russell era was over. But in the playoffs they easily beat Philly 4 to 1 and, helped by an injury to the Knicks' Walt Frazier, beat New York 4 to 2. In the championship series, the Lakers had the vital home-court advantage should it go to the seventh game.

True to the usual final-playoff pattern, L.A. won the first two at home as Jerry West scored 53 and 41 points. The Celtics won the third game in Boston. In the fourth, Sam Jones, playing his last pro season,

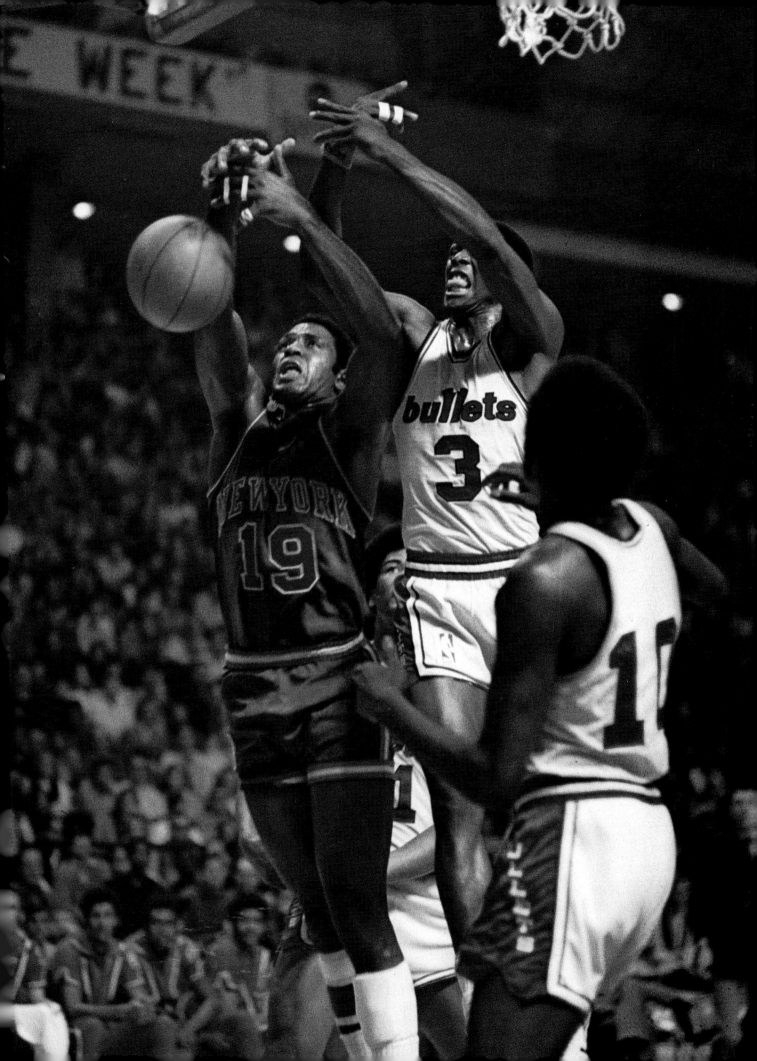

CLOCKWISE FROM TOP LEFT: New York guard Dick Barnett, formerly with the Los Angeles Lakers, gets set to make his move—but which way? Laker guard Jerry West fires one of his accurate jump shots, almost impossible to stop because he releases it so quickly (one instant he's dribbling and the next he's shooting); hitting the floor is old stuff to Dave Bing of the Detroit Pistons, who was an All-America at Syracuse before becoming one of the finest backcourt men in the NBA and the Pistons' leading scorer; the Virginia Squires and Denver Rockets battle for rebound in box-office success at Madison Square Garden. Bob Cousy, who was famous for his sensational passes and ballhandling when he played for Holy Cross and the Boston Celtics, crouches in front of his bench to get a better look at his Cincinnati Royals (who don't match Boston).

CLOCKWISE FROM BELOW: Bob Netolicky, part of Indiana Pacers' tough frontcourt trio, scores a lay-up versus New York Nets (including No. 24, the much-traveled Rick Barry); former UCLA backcourt star Lucius Allen gets a pass past the upstretched arm of Laker Happy Hairston; John Havlicek of the Boston Celtics, able to play either forward or guard as one of the finest "swing men" in the National Basketball Association, barrels his way through the Los Angeles defense and puts in an easy lay-up; dribbling against the legendary "Big O," Oscar Robertson, the Phoenix Suns' Connie Hawkins, something of a legend himself on the New York playgrounds and in two other pro leagues, tries to maneuver his way in close to the hoop.

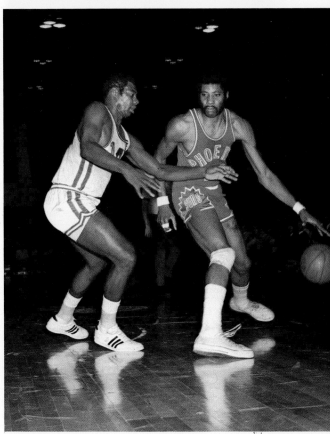

CLOCKWISE FROM FAR LEFT: Milwaukee's Lew Alcindor, chandelier-ducker that he is, still has to look up once in a while to follow the trajectory of a shot; hair flying in the manner of rebellious youth, Atlanta's Pete Maravich lets fly with a jump shot against the Bucks; Oscar Robertson, who starred for Cincinnati 10 seasons before being traded to the Milwaukee Bucks, scores an easy basket for the Royals—well, anyway, he makes it look easy; guard Dick Garrett of the Buffalo Braves (an expansion club new to the NBA in 1970–71) learned his basketball at Southern Illinois University as a forward, then played his rookie year as a starter for the Los Angeles Lakers; Archie Clark of the Philadelphia 76ers scores a lay-up over Don Kojis. Clark, who was a star at the University of Minnesota with the Hawk's Lou Hudson, teams with Hal Greer, Wally Jones and Matty Goukas to give Philly one of the strongest backcourts in the professional leagues.

scored on an 18-foot, off-balance jump shot with only seconds remaining. The ball hit the front rim, the back rim and, as Wilt blocked out Don Nelson and waited to gobble up the rebound, dropped through. Jones had been set up with a special play John Havlicek and Larry Siegfried remembered from their Ohio State days. Final score: 89–88.

L.A. won the fifth at home, Boston the sixth at home and the two teams flew across country for the decider. The Laker management was confident enough of victory to suspend a load of balloons near the ceiling of The Forum. The net would be opened after L.A. won and the balloons would cascade down. The Celtics couldn't help but notice the celebration trappings.

The final was played Monday, May 5, 1969, before a packed house and a national television audience. Everybody knew it was going to be Sam Jones' last fling. They didn't know it was the last for Russell, too. He didn't announce his retirement until later. No extra dramatics were needed anyway.

In the game Baylor was not the Elgin of old (he hadn't been for most of the series). West was bothered by an injured leg. And that left a lot up to Wilt. West and Havlicek had provided most of the heroics throughout the series. Wilt and Russell had neutralized each other, although Chamberlain did get 31 rebounds in the fifth game.

Boston used hot shooting to get off to a 17–9 lead and increase it to 24–12. L.A. got going and closed the gap to three points by the end of the first quarter, but the margin was the same at half time, the Celtics leading 59–56. In the third quarter the Lakers hit an incredible cold streak, scoring not one solitary point in a span of more than five minutes! (Chick Hearn, the frenetic Laker broadcaster who roots, coaches and referees while he's smoothly describing the action, must have felt the chill even in his booth.)

In addition, Chamberlain got his fifth foul. He had never fouled out of an NBA game, and he wasn't about to do so in this particular one, so he started playing more cautiously both on offense and defense. The Celtics led 91–76 at the three-quarter mark.

Jones ended his career by fouling out in the fourth period, and somebody removed the lid from the Lakers' basket—they came storming back. With 6:18 left it was Boston 103–94, an insignificant lead in the pros. But with 5:45 to go, Chamberlain fell and got up limping. He hobbled up the court once, then took himself out. Van Breda Kolff sent in Mel Counts. The Lakers closed it to 103–102 even without Wilt, but a couple of missed L.A. shots and a lucky basket by Don Nelson finally gave it to Boston 108–106.

West, with 42 points, 12 assists, 13 rebounds and a sports car for being the playoff MVP, said he couldn't understand how the Celtics had won again. The Lakers did seem to have the best of it in the statistics, but there had been that horrible cold streak, Wilt's knee injury and a little line on the stat sheet: Chamberlain—13 free throws attempted, four made.

As Celtics' general manager Red Auerbach headed toward the locker room, he was wearing one of his finest smirks and repeatedly asked reporters, "What are they going to do with all those balloons?" It was the fifth time the Celtics had been forced to go to the seventh game of the final play-offs. It was the fifth time they had won.

After the game, Wilt criticized van Breda Kolff for not putting him back in. Russell had a speaking engagement in Madison, Wisconsin, not long after the season and was asked about his old rival's behavior in that final game. Perhaps because he knew he wouldn't be involved in the NBA duels any more, Russ was unusually frank. He sided with VBK.

"Any injury short of a broken leg or a broken back isn't good enough," he said. "When he took

Playing despite a broken nose, Dave DeBusschere looks like a masked hero (or villain) from the comic books as he drives to the basket. The Knicks' best defensive forward, he also hits well from outside.

himself out of that final game, when he hurt his knee, well, I wouldn't have put him back in the game either, even though I think he's great.

"I never said Chamberlain didn't have talent," he added. "But basketball is a team game. I go by the number of championships. I play to bring out the best in my teammates. Are you going to tell me he brought out the best in Baylor and West?"

Is the widespread criticism of Wilt justified?

"I'd have to say yes and no. No, because people see his potential as greater than it is. They don't take human frailties into consideration. Yes, because he asks for it. He talks a lot about what he's going to do. What it's all about is winning and losing, and he's done a lot of losing. He thinks he's a genius. He isn't."

It became apparent as the 1969–70 season approached that Russell was not going to change his mind about retiring. The movie and television industries were opening up for blacks (Sidney Poitier, ex-football player Jim Brown and others) and Russ was going to try to build a career in Hollywood. Red Auerbach picked Tom Heinsohn to succeed Bill as coach. There was no one to succeed him at center.

It seemed like a perfect opportunity for Chamberlain and the Lakers: no Russell around, Nate Thurmond at San Francisco playing with a supporting cast inferior to Wilt's and Lew Alcindor just a rookie at Milwaukee. The Lakers, discounting their sad history as second-placers, were the logical favorites to win the title. Owner Cooke's royal color theme of purple and gold would now be most appropriate.

To no one's surprise, van Breda Kolff was no longer the coach. Butch moved on to Detroit, unhappy at having to leave California but thoroughly pleased at not having to work for Cooke and with Wilt. He turned down a national magazine's offer to publish his Laker memoirs. Cooke stayed with the policy of hiring college coaches and picked Joe Mullaney of Providence, who had produced such good NBA players as Len Wilkens, Jimmy Walker and Mike Riordan. Joe also had played in the backcourt at Holy Cross with Bob Cousy.

The hopes of Mullaney and the L.A. fans were punctured early in November when Chamberlain hurt a knee, his worst injury in 11 years of pro ball, and underwent surgery. Doctors predicted he would not be back until the following season, but Wilt insisted he would return before the playoffs. His replacement, 6 foot-9 inch Rick Roberson from the University of Cincinnati, was just a rookie.

Wilt diligently exercised the knee, got back in fair shape by playing volleyball and proved the doctors wrong. He didn't return in time to keep the Lakers from finishing two games behind Atlanta in the Western Division, but there was always a chance to correct things in the playoffs. Boston had proved that more than once. Sure enough, L.A. beat Phoenix 4 to 3 in a surprisingly difficult series, then stomped Atlanta 4 to 0. Only the New York Knickerbockers blocked the path to an NBA title at last.

The Knicks were a well-balanced, finely tuned team. Whenever anything got slightly out of adjustment, chief mechanic Red Holzman would do a little tinkering and get things running smoothly again. Center Willis Reed, 6 feet 10 inches and muscular as a blacksmith, was the rebounding and scoring leader with quick moves and a soft touch in and around the key. Dave DeBusschere had the responsibility of guarding the other team's best corner man and helping Reed with the rebounding. Forward Bill Bradley, the Rhodes scholar from Princeton, hit with his accurate jump shots and made the team move with his clever passes. Guard Dick Barnett, who once had teamed with West in the Laker backcourt, flipped in long-range jumpers. And Walt Frazier was the incredibly quick ball thief, the second-leading scorer and the dribbler in charge

Ignoring a forearm smash to the gut, Milwaukee's Lew Alcindor shoots a medium-range jump shot against San Francisco. He averaged 28.8 points a game in his rookie season for the Bucks.

of penetrating defenses and hitting the open man.

The New York reserves were the best in the NBA. Cazzie Russell was the most accurate shooter on the team (although poor on defense) and could come off the bench and fire up the team with point-scoring sprees. Dave (The Rave) Stallworth, recovered from a heart attack that had kept him out for more than two seasons, was a fine all-around forward, and Mike Riordan was the best driver on the team.

Apart from making wise draft choices, there were two moves that had made the Knicks into contenders for the NBA championship. Just after Christmas of 1967, when the club was doing badly as usual, management removed Dick McGuire and made Holzman the coach. McGuire, who had been too lenient with the players, took Red's old job as scout. Holzman cracked down from the very first day. Bradley, Howard Komives and Dick Van Arsdale were late for a meeting and got slapped with fines. There was emphasis on team defense, going over game films and unselfishness on offense. (Red ended the idea that more points meant better paychecks.)

The second important move came almost a year later. The Knicks traded Howard Komives and center Walt Bellamy to Detroit for DeBusschere. As a result, Reed moved back to center, his natural position, and was far better there than the up-and-down Bellamy had been. DeBusschere was a better forward than Reed had been, especially on defense. And Frazier, who moved into Komives' starting guard spot, became recognized as the finest defensive player in the league. In one stroke, New York had improved itself at three positions.

En route to the 1969–70 playoffs, the Knicks enjoyed a fabulous season. They won seventeen of their first eighteen games—the best start ever in NBA history—and set another league record by winning eighteen games in a row. Victory number eighteen came on November 28 versus Cincinnati

at Cleveland Arena. The Knicks were behind by five points with only sixteen seconds left. Reed made two free throws, DeBusschere intercepted a pass and drove in for a lay-up, Reed deflected a pass to Frazier, who was fouled in the act of shooting and made both free throws. Six points in sixteen seconds! Final score: Knicks 106, Royals 105.

"I've got ice water in my veins," said Walt.

Frazier was nicknamed "Clyde" by his teammates because his wild clothes and talent for theft reminded them of the Depression-era gangster Clyde Barrow in the popular movie *Bonnie and*

LEFT: Wheeling left, Baltimore center Westley Unseld hooks over defender. ABOVE: San Diego's "Big E," Elvin Hayes, gets ball inside Bullets' Jack Marin and stuffs it through.

Clyde. Frazier's extensive wardrobe includes such items as a wide-brimmed, cocoa-brown velour hat made in Italy, a yellow suit that matched his Cadillac Eldorado and four pairs of alligator shoes. And he was as good as he was flashy. In a 138–108 slaughter of the Hawks in his hometown of Atlanta, Clyde made twelve of sixteen field-goal attempts, scored 33 points, took eight rebounds and stole the ball fifteen times.

"I never saw a guy play a game like that," said Holzman.

New York, a basketball-loving town, was in a tizzy over the Knicks. The club had been in the NBA from the beginning but had never won a championship. It had not won a division title in sixteen years. The knowledgeable New York fans loved this team. They appreciated the team defense and instead of rooting for more points, they rooted for the Knicks to hold the opposition below 100. "DEE-fense, DEE-fense," they chanted.

As is usual with successful pro athletes in New York, the Knick players cashed in. Reed opened a hamburger joint close to the Garden. Frazier fronted for a fancy men's hair-styling salon where it cost $8 for a toenail trim. The advertising agency for Vitalis wanted the first six to do a TV commercial. Holzman said OK, but, still emphasizing team consciousness, insisted that the whole squad, including coach and trainer, take part and split the money.

To reach the final playoff versus L.A., New York beat Baltimore 4 to 3 and Milwaukee 4 to 1. A dash of spice was added to the L.A.-New York rivalry because the Lakers' Jerry West was bitter about not having been elected the league's most valuable player. NBA players themselves had done the voting and Reed out-polled Jerry 498–457. Lew Alcindor (rookie of the year) was third with 335 and Frazier a distant fourth with 50. The first time Reed appeared in The Forum after the results were

known, he was loudly booed by the spectators.

Because it had a better won-lost record, New York had the home-court advantage. The first two games were in Madison Square Garden and the seventh, if it came to that, would be there, too.

The teams split the opening two games. Frazier wanted the nearly impossible task of guarding West, and Holzman obliged him, but Walt was overanxious and overaggressive and got in foul trouble both games. West scored 33 and 34 points. From then on Barnett was assigned to him, which allowed Clyde more freedom to help others and to try for steals.

From this point, if each team won its remaining games at home, the Lakers would take the championship in game number six. So it was vital for the Knicks to win either the third or fourth game in The Forum. They did it in the third despite West's 55-foot field goal at the buzzer that forced the contest into overtime.

Game number five in the Garden turned out to be the crucial one in the playoffs. Reed fell and strained a hip muscle in the first half and wasn't able to return. At half time the Knicks were 13 points behind and knew they would have to play the third and fourth quarters without their captain and leading scorer and rebounder. Bradley proposed a 1-3-1 offense with himself in the middle, Frazier at the top of the key, Barnett and Cazzie Russell on the wings and DeBusschere on the base line. Without Willis they had less scoring and rebounding punch but more quickness, and this formation emphasized that advantage. It also was a good, time-tested formation for combatting what the Knicks felt was an illegal zone defense being used by the Lakers.

Given all the circumstances, most reporters, fans or coaches would have predicted that the Lakers and Chamberlain would annihilate the Knicks in that second half. After all, Wilt was being

guarded in turns by 6 foot-6 inch DeBusschere and 6 foot-7 inch Stallworth! Instead, the Knicks applied terrific defensive pressure, effectively closed off the passing lanes to Chamberlain and stole the ball continually. They swiped it eight times in the fourth quarter (Clyde alone had three steals in the last twelve minutes) and won the game going away 107–100.

Reed did not play in the sixth game at L.A. and Wilt went wild—45 points and 27 rebounds. West added 33 points and 13 assists, and the Lakers won by 22 points.

Would Willis be able to play in the seventh game? More important, how effective could he be? How much could he contribute?

The Garden was jammed with its 38th sellout crowd of the season (more than a million people attended New York home games in 1969–70), and it seemed as if each person there was craning his neck looking for Willis when the Knicks ran out on the court to warm up. He wasn't with them. A buzzing started in the crowd and it didn't take a mastermind to figure out whom they were talking about. Cazzie came out on the floor late. A cheer started in 19,000 or so throats but was stifled when the fans realized it wasn't Willis.

Finally, at 7:34 P.M., Reed came running out and was greeted by a tremendous, happy roar. He had waited in the locker room to receive injections of carbocaine and cortisone at the last possible moment. When he came into view, Dave the Rave clapped gleefully. Frazier slapped· hands with the captain. Reed then hit two or three of his practice shots and the Knick fans went crazy again. The Lakers warming up at the other end couldn't help but hear all the commotion.

"It gave us all about a ten-foot lift just to have him there," said Bradley.

"This was actually the turning point of the game," said Clyde, "*before* the opening tipoff."

Reed made his first two shots in the game, getting the Knicks off to an even more inspirational start, but he wasn't able to do much more in the 27 minutes he played. It didn't matter. To make up for his disability, every other Knick worked that much harder. Tenacious, gambling team defense thwarted Wilt, whose maneuverability was reduced because of his weak knee. He was in such a state with all the Knicks sagging in on him that he was afraid to put the ball on the floor.

New York led by 27 points at the half, faltered a bit in the third quarter and then ran off to an easy 113–99 victory. Dave DeBusschere scored 18 points and took 17 rebounds. Bill Bradley scored 17 and had five assists. Dick Barnett, the old man of the team at 33, scored 21 points, many of them on twisty, acrobatic drives to the basket.

Frazier played the greatest game of his life. He stole the ball five times, working his thievery even against the three Laker stars, Baylor, Chamberlain and West. He made twelve of twelve free-throw attempts, scored 36 points, took seven rebounds and made nineteen assists, tying the record for a final-series game.

For the seventh time Los Angeles had fought its way into the NBA finals. For the seventh time it had been frustrated. Cinch Hall-of-Famers Baylor and West were still without a championship in their careers.

The Knicks, exhausted from the long season, recovered quickly when time came to divide up the loot. They gave cuts of up to 2,000 dollars to secretaries, scouts, ball-boys and publicists, and a full share to the family of the team doctor, who had died during the season. The twelve players, coach Holzman and trainer Danny Whelan went home with 7,400 dollars apiece.

The NBA had known a Mikan-Minneapolis dynasty and a Russell-Boston dynasty. Would Reed-New York be the third? There were good reasons to think so. Youth, for instance. Willis was only 27, DeBusschere 29, Bradley 26. Clyde had just turned 25. Holzman was a good coach and disciplinarian. The Garden had large enthusiastic crowds and plenty of money.

Milwaukee would probably be the Knicks' biggest obstacle in the early 1970s. The Bucks' essential big man was Lew Alcindor, the most valuable player in the league the second half of his rookie season. New York easily beat them in the playoffs, but at that time the Bucks were still an inexperienced expansion team. In the off-season they strengthened themselves considerably by trading with Cincinnati for Oscar Robertson, who had been unhappy with the Royals.

Cincy had not won even a division championship in the 10 years Oscar was there, but somehow he never was tagged as a "loser" as Chamberlain had been. He was simply the master craftsman of the backcourt, averaging 30 points or better for six seasons and six times leading the league in assists. It seemed as though every new big guard who came along was tabbed as "the next Oscar," but none of them (with the possible exception of the Knicks' Walt Frazier) ever made that come true. "Hot Rod" Hundley once described what it was like to play against "Big O."

"You know the most helpless I've ever felt on a basketball court? Playing Robertson. Once Oscar intercepted a long pass downcourt and came dribbling back toward me. I was the only man back on defense and he had a teammate on either side to pass to. He came down on me with those 10,000 moves of his and I looked at him and I said, 'Oh, baby, this is the living end!' Did I stop him? Hell, no. He's the greatest! Who stops him? Not Rod, baby!"

The combination of Alcindor and Robertson on the Bucks was frightening, but perhaps no more frightening to the Knicks than Baylor, Chamberlain and West together on the Lakers. During the 1970–71 season Milwaukee had the best won-lost record of any club, was the first to clinch their division championship and with 20 consecutive victories broke the record the Knicks had set only a year ago. Yet significantly they did not play the Knicks during that 20-game streak and managed to beat the New Yorkers only once during the regular season.

The NBA as a whole had hopes in the '70s of emulating and even surpassing the National Football League, which prospered in the 1960s with fat television contracts, packed stadiums, lucrative endorsements, ad-filled magazines and orchestrated game films that were almost documentaries in themselves. It was difficult to open a newspaper or magazine, turn on the radio or TV, or even travel on an airplane without getting a dose of pro football. The NBA pictured itself doing much the same thing.

The man in charge of the effort was Commissioner Walter Kennedy, who, except for his years as a student and publicity man at Notre Dame, has lived in Stamford, Connecticut, all his life. He was the NBA's first press agent but left the league in 1951 to handle public relations for White Tower restaurants and the National Catholic Educational Association in Washington. He also broadcast football games with the famous Ted Husing and helped promote the Harlem Globetrotters' foreign tours.

In 1959 he ran for mayor of Stamford. He was a natural politician—smiling, affable—and the fact that he had suffered from polio as a child added a little drama to his life story. He won, enjoyed his term in office and was reelected in 1961. In January of 1962 the NBA owners decided to replace Podoloff as commissioner and approached Kennedy about the job. He said he wanted to finish some projects in Stamford and turned it down. One year later they offered it to him again. He accepted in April and took over the office in September of 1963.

Kennedy oversaw the NBA's rapid expansion. The Chicago Bulls were added in 1966–67 (despite the Windy City's historic refusal to support pro basketball). The San Diego Rockets and Seattle SuperSonics followed in 1967–68; the Milwaukee Bucks and Phoenix Suns in 1968–69, and, for 3.7 million dollars apiece, the Buffalo Braves, Cleveland Cavaliers and Portland Trail Blazers in 1970–71.

Over scrambled eggs at Toots Shor's (the Manhattan restaurant known for its host and sports-loving clientele rather than its food) Kennedy happily talked about the future. There were only three interruptions—by an old Notre Dame pal of Kennedy's, Toots himself showing off a gag gift, and gossip-columnist Leonard Lyons. Kennedy smoothly picked up the discussion after each visitor had left.

For one thing, the league was going to modernize its scheduling procedure, he said. With the recent expansion, this was a must. Making up the NBA schedule has been the "total headache" of old-timer Eddie Gottlieb since 1946. Each club sends in its "available dates," fitted around ice shows, ice hockey games, circuses, Globetrotter visits and whatever else the arena has booked. Eddie—who knows such things as what night the Catholic ladies in Oshkosh play bingo—then pieces together the complicated slate of games, doing his best not to have the San Diego Rockets, say, play ten nights in a row in ten different cities.

Kennedy said he had been talking to computer companies for three years, "but they throw up their hands and tell me that this guy is indispensable." As of this writing, a computer firm on the West Coast is trying to design a special machine using "all the knowledge in Mr. Gottlieb's head."

On the subject of future growth, Kennedy let his imagination loose.

"I think we're beginning to break through now like football did, with great TV exposure," he said. "I predict that by the end of the 1970s the NBA will be in Europe, Hawaii and the Philippines because basketball is the second most popular international sport [after soccer].

"I can visualize teams in at least two cities in Italy, one in Spain—Madrid, Barcelona or a combination—and maybe one in Athens. Mexico City, Honolulu and possibly Manila, too, because jet travel will be improved and cheaper. Satellite TV should have arrived in a big way."

Yesterday Fort Wayne. Today Portland. Tomorrow Barcelona. It was a rosy vision of the future. First, however, there was a problem here in the States—a little rival called the ABA.

Chapter Four / ABA
You can't tell the franchises without a program

The American Basketball Association was the brain-child of a onetime all-night disc jockey, a public relations man and a Madison Avenue promoter. It didn't have much in the beginning but a slogan ("The Lively League"), a brochure or two and, after almost a year of recruiting, a collection of approximately twenty prospective owners in the Louis XVI Suite of Manhattan's St. Regis-Sheraton Hotel. Most of the men were young Californians who knew little about professional basketball.

On the West Coast the idea of a second major basketball league started with Dennis Murphy, a PR man for an engineering firm. In July of 1966 he was busy trying to get various people interested in his idea and finally got around to John McShane. McShane had been a disc jockey for two radio stations owned by Gene Autry, an assistant to the president of Autry's baseball team, the Angels, and a self-employed PR man. He "reduced Murphy's idea to paper form" and the two of them went seeking would-be sports magnates.

On the East Coast, Constantine (Connie) Seredin, a lean, smooth Yaleman whose favorite words were "divine" and "concept," was trying the same thing through his Professional Sports Management Company, Inc. PSM's specialty was bringing together athletes and advertising agencies. The eastern and western operators heard about each other through the great ex-Laker George Mikan, whom both had contacted. They decided to combine their efforts. Murphy and McShane had most of the owner prospects, Seredin was experienced in pitching ideas to networks and agencies.

Several preliminary meetings were held. The promoters talked with Mikan and his brother Ed in Chicago. In New York an attempt to get some of the millionaire American Football League owners interested was a failure. Some well-heeled men represented at a 1966 Beverly Hills meeting—Bob Breitbard and Sam Schulman—soon wangled NBA franchises. California politician Jesse Unruh, approached about being commissioner, said he wasn't interested.

An incorporation meeting was held January 17 and 18, 1967, at the Beverly Hilton Hotel, but by far the largest part of the ABA foundation was laid at the St. Regis January 31, February 1 and 2. A publicity handout from PSM trumpeted "the first major sport to be founded on a platform of *Advanced Marketing*," "sportscard credit plan," "recruitment of present superstars *and* high area-preference draft policy" and an "anticipated twelve-city league" with only one team (New York) directly competing with the NBA.

Seredin had dreams of a big spread in *Sports Illustrated* on the birth of a league, so he invited SI to sit in the delivery room. SI pro basketball editor Jeremiah Tax, dubious but interested, sent the author over to the St. Regis for what turned out to be a few columns in the back of the magazine.

(There had been an earlier, embarrassingly feeble attempt to buck the NBA. Abe Saperstein, owner of the Harlem Globetrotters, organized the American Basketball *League* in 1961 and propped it up with his own wallet. It started play late that year with eight clubs: the Washington Capitols, Pittsburgh Rens, Cleveland Pipers, Chicago Majors, Kansas City Steers, Los Angeles Jets, San Francisco Saints and Hawaii Chiefs. The ABL had some interesting innovations, especially the awarding of three points for a field goal made from 25 feet or more.

(There was some good personnel, too. Ex-NBA players Bill Sharman, Neil Johnston and Andy Phillip joined up as coaches, and Dick Barnett, Ken Sears and several other active players jumped over from the established league. Phil Woolpert, producer of the Bill Russell-K. C. Jones teams at USF, coached the San Francisco entry. The ABL even broke the coaching color line and hired Tennessee State's John McLendon to handle Cleveland.

Holding the ABA's red, white and blue ball high, Spencer Haywood of Denver makes ready to move. In his one year in the league, as a young rookie, he dominated scoring and rebounding.

ABOVE: Outpositioning the Floridians' Tom Washington (14), Pittsburgh's John Brisker grabs the rebound. OPPOSITE: Here putting up a crazy lay-up, Kentucky's Darel Carrier has been the ABA's best three-point shooter.

(However, after slightly more than a season, the ABL folded. At the end late in December, 1962, it consisted of barely breathing franchises in Philadelphia, Pittsburgh, Chicago, Kansas City, Oakland and Long Beach, California. Mourning was minimal.)

At the St. Regis meeting there was one holdover owner from the ABL wreckage, Arthur Kim, who had operated in Honolulu and then Long Beach in the unsuccessful league and apparently hadn't learned his lesson. His ABA entry was to try its luck in the Anaheim Convention Center, across the boulevard from Disneyland.

Anaheim is in Orange County, the booming area south of Los Angeles, and so many people from there were involved in the ABA planning that the gathering in New York reeked of incest. Gary Davidson, part-owner of the Dallas franchise, had a law practice in the Orange County seat. One of his law partners, Donald J. Regan, was part-owner of the league's floating franchise, which was looking for a place to drop anchor. Dennis Murphy (Oakland) was a former mayor of Buena Park in Orange County (and so was PR man McShane). John Klug (Dallas) lived in Orange County; L. P. Shields and Fred Jefferson (Minneapolis) lived and ran a development company there; James Trindle (Denver) had an engineering office there which employed Murphy (Oakland), and so on.

The confusing meeting was run by McShane and Mark Binstein, an ex-West Point player connected with the New York franchise. On the first day, Tuesday, Houston did not show up. On Wednesday a representative was sent with the modest 6,000-dollar entry fee. The Indianapolis people did not arrive until just before the Thursday deadline, after which the tariff was supposed to shoot up to at least 25,000 dollars. Two men from Cleveland were there the first day, left that night, wired the next day saying they wanted in, were accepted by telegram—and never heard from again.

Sean Downey, son of singer Morton Downey, put in the 6,000 dollar check for the New Orleans franchise. A few weeks earlier he had been involved in trying to buy the NBA St. Louis Hawks for Louisiana and the deal seemed set until a check, not written by Downey, bounced. A good check was submitted, he said, but too late to save himself and New Orleans some embarrassing publicity. However, the other ABA owners accepted his latest check without apparent nervousness.

The commissioner-selection committee hardly considered anyone but Mikan, the 6 foot-10 inch Minneapolis lawyer who had been first-team All-NBA for six straight years with the Minneapolis Lakers and voted the top basketball player of the first half-century. Committee members phoned

Mikan right after the first session at the St. Regis and talked him into flying to New York. On Wednesday he asked for a three-year contract at 65,000 dollars per year and the owners countered with an offer of 50,000 dollars. The final figure was somewhere in between. Big George didn't give his answer until late Thursday morning, the very day of the press conference to announce the ABA's formation.

Mikan was staying at the St. Moritz and James Ware of the New Orleans group was in frequent contact with him by telephone.

"He phoned and said he had to see more people," said Ware. "I said, 'Possibly a prayer might help.' He said, 'All right, Jimmy, I'll call you or you call me—after eleven I should know something.' "

The climactic phone call, as described by Ware, was a model of polite avoiding the subject. Ware told Mikan who the new officers were. He boasted that an Indianapolis group was eager to join up. He asked Mikan's advice on where to place the floating franchise (Mikan suggested a look at Atlanta). Ware finally got to the point:

"Now I ask him, after all this. conversation—I didn't want to press him—'What is your decision?'

" 'James, I'm your new commissioner.'

" 'God bless you!' "

Ware hurried into the meeting and announced, "I'm happy to say he has accepted. George Mikan is our commissioner." About 30 minutes later Mikan walked in and shook hands with everyone. Pittsburgh owner Gabe Rubin, who had come into the

new venture after the NBA had turned him down, stood only as high as Mikan's tie clasp.

Despite the joyous back-patting and handshaking, there were still some details to be worked out. Mikan and the owners were actually negotiating up until ten minutes before the press conference, according to Dennis Murphy. George kept them sweating and finally agreed to some vague terms and prepared to go on stage as the new ABA commissioner.

The press conference was staged at the Carlyle Hotel, Harry Truman's and John F. Kennedy's favorite in New York and thus a logical choice for a league conceived by image-conscious press agents. The room was too small and cluttered by non-newsmen. Young owners like Davidson and Binstein did not field questions well. A TV cameraman tried to walk out with a basketball and got tough when he was caught at it. The atmosphere was so hostile that Jason Shapiro of Pittsburgh said, "I'm going to get a pad and pencil and pretend to be writing so I can get out of here *alive.*"

The whole thing was a fiasco until the TV lights and cameras were taken away and Mikan sat down in an adjoining room to talk quietly to reporters. His answers were straight and reasonably complete. He said there would be no raids on the NBA, but, "We hope, of course, that some big stars and others will be in a position to come to us; if they are free, we want to talk to them."

Of the first officers, Commissioner Mikan, vice-commissioner Arthur Kim, president Gary Davidson, first vice-president Gabe Rubin and second vice-president Max Zaslofsky, and of the two meeting chairmen, John McShane and Mark Binstein, only one was still around and had any importance (Binstein as Pittsburgh GM) when the ABA completed its fourth season in 1970–71.

Of the original eleven franchises, the Anaheim Amigos, Dallas Chaparrals, Denver Rockets, Houston Mavericks, Indiana Pacers, Kentucky Colonels, Minnesota Muskies, New Jersey Americans, New Orleans Buccaneers, Oakland Oaks and Pittsburgh Pipers, only four have stayed put. Three clubs have moved twice, four have moved once.

The ABA did indeed attempt to be as lively as its brochures and slogan, although just staying alive was really the problem. It picked up the three-point field goal from the extinct ABL and adopted a red, white and blue basketball, which one critic said would look good only on the nose of a seal. The fans liked the innovation, once they got over the ball's similarity to a beachball, and players for the first time could tell just what kind of spin they were putting on their shots. The patriotic ball became the symbol of the league and was used in various giveaway promotions (at gas stations in Indiana, for instance). However, not the official ABA leather ball made by Rawlings was offered but a cheap imitation made in Taiwan.

The pre-Mikan press release that said the ABA would directly oppose the NBA in only one place was incorrect. There were confrontations in three metropolitan areas: Los Angeles (Anaheim Amigos versus Los Angeles Lakers), New York City (New Jersey Americans versus New York Knicks) and San Francisco (Oakland Oaks versus San Francisco Warriors). Mikan himself said there would be no raiding. That also was incorrect.

Oakland hired Bruce Hale as coach. Hale had played college ball in the Bay Area at Santa Clara and had coached at the University of Miami (Florida). More important, his daughter had married his biggest star at Miami, Rick Barry, who had become an excellent player for the Warriors. It is unclear whether the Oaks latched onto Hale with the guarantee or merely the hope of also getting his son-in-law, but the strategy worked. Rick made a serious mistake and jumped to the ABA.

Rick is a handsome, 6 foot 7 inch blond who led the NBA in scoring as a second-year man in 1966–67, the first time in eight seasons a white man had led —the first time *anyone* but Wilt Chamberlain had led in that period. Good white players are scarce in the pros, and white players of all-star caliber—like Jerry West or John Havlicek—are collectors' items. Owners feel they need them to help at the gate. Advertisers pursue them to endorse hair tonic or swim suits. Barry's jump was a big boost for the new league—and for the legal profession, which proceeded to cash in nicely on the complicated series of suits, hearings, injunctions, etc.

Here is a capsulized version of Barry's odyssey through various courts, legal and ABA:

Warriors' owner Franklin Mieuli wasn't about to sit back and see his terrific tandem of Rick and

Paying no attention to that New York Net blocking his way, Dan Issel of the Kentucky Colonels fires a jump shot. Issel benefited nicely from the NBA–ABA war by landing multimillion-dollar contract when he joined pros.

center Nate Thurmond broken up, so he sued to get Rick back. He didn't accomplish that, but he forced Barry, healthy and in his basketball prime, to sit out the 1967–68 season. Rick played for the Oaks in 1968–69 and led the league in scoring average (34.0), but an injured left knee made him miss 59 games, including all the playoffs. Then into the stew jumped Earl Foreman, Washington lawyer.

Foreman had been owner of the Washington Whips soccer team and a part-owner of the Baltimore Bullets (basketball) and Philadelphia Eagles (football). He was vacationing in Maine when he heard about the deep financial trouble the ABA's Oakland franchise was in. He quickly made a visit to the Bay Area and agreed to buy the team, if "buy" is the right word. It is believed he took over the Oaks' debts and a 1.2 million dollar note held by the Bank of America. The other owners gave him permission to move the club to Washington for the 1969–70 season and rename it the Capitols.

That was more than Barry had bargained for (he thought). He had been reared in New Jersey and had played college ball in Florida, but San Francisco was his true love and he was horrified at having to leave. Late in the summer of 1969 he made up with Mieuli and signed a five-year, one-million-dollar contract with the Warriors. Nope, said the courts, he had to honor his previous Oaks-Capitols contract. Rick was forced into being a Cap that season whenever his ailing knee allowed him to suit up. Foreman lost an estimated 500,000 dollars in Washington, so for 1970–71 he moved to Virginia, and Barry balked once more.

"I have nó desire whatsoever to play basketball back there," he said. "Mr. Foreman will have one fat, out-of-shape, unhappy ballplayer in his training camp if I go there at all.

"I would never have considered going to the ABA if I had thought I would have to leave this area. Earl apparently thinks he can offer me enough

LEFT: *Ray Scott of Virginia Squires was one of several players who jumped from the NBA. BELOW: Playing for the East in ABA All-Star Game, Dan Issel comes down with the rebound and bumps into starry-pants Zelmo Beaty.*

money so that I'll be happy to go. I don't know if I'd be happier in Norfolk or wherever the hell it is even if he gave me one million dollars a year."

He continued to insult Virginia as often and as loudly as he could until Foreman finally traded him to the New York Nets (formerly the New Jersey Americans) for a future No. 1 draft choice and an estimated 250,000 dollars. Rick was overjoyed.

"If you're going to be any place in sports, New York is the place to be," he said. "My interest was at a low ebb when I thought I'd have to play in Virginia, and now my interest has been rekindled. All I want to do now is play basketball."

While Rick had been busy with his lawsuits and bad knee, others in the ABA had been playing basketball. Some of them had been playing it very well.

The Pittsburgh Pipers won the first championship. They had wisely followed the defunct ABL's lead and signed 6 foot-8 inch Connie Hawkins, a legend from Boys High of Brooklyn and the New York playgrounds. The NBA had refused to touch Hawkins because he had been implicated in the college point-shaving scandal of the early 1960s. Connie never was convicted of a fix, but he had admitted having contact with gamblers and subsequently was dumped by the University of Iowa before he ever played varsity ball. He was hired by the ABL, a league with a short, unhappy life, and his enormous talents were going to waste until Pittsburgh grabbed him.

Hawkins averaged 26.8 points a game in the regular season and was helped by Charlie Williams from Seattle U., Chico Vaughan from Southern Illinois and NBA-flop Art Heyman, an ex-Duke star. In the playoffs the Pipers beat Indiana 3 to 0, Minnesota 4 to 1 and New Orleans 4 to 3. With Barry idle, Oakland was last in the Western Division.

The game of musical chairs between the first and second seasons was difficult to follow. The NBA's Los Angeles Lakers had vacated the Sports

Arena in favor of The Forum in suburban Inglewood, so the Anaheim Amigos moved downtown from suburban Orange County and renamed themselves the Los Angeles Stars. The Minnesota Muskies went south and became the Miami Floridians. That meant there was no ABA team within 450 miles of league headquarters in Minneapolis. The Pipers had lost a lot of money despite their championship, so owner Gabe Rubin, with some urging from Mikan, foolishly moved them to Minnesota (he returned to Pittsburgh after one season). New Jersey's Americans moved to Long Island and became the Nets.

The players also were shuffled and dealt at a dizzying rate. Rookie of the year Mel Daniels went from Minnesota-Miami to the Indiana Pacers. Total-points leader Doug Moe and assists leader Larry Brown went from New Orleans to Oakland. Not only couldn't you tell the players without a program, you couldn't tell the franchises or owners either.

With Moe, Brown, a well-rested Rick Barry and Warren Armstrong, who was to be rookie of the year, Oakland was loaded for the ABA's second season, 1968–69. Bruce Hale concentrated on being general manager, and old NBA hand Alex Hannum, probably the finest coach in professional basketball, took over the team. The Oaks were never held below 100 points in 94 playoff and regular-season games and won in a romp. Rick was injured and missed the playoffs, but they still beat Denver 4 to 3, New Orleans 4 to 0, and Indiana in the finals 4 to 1 (two of the games went into overtime).

In January of 1969 the Houston Mavericks were bought by an ex-North Carolina congressman named James C. Gardner and some partners. Gardner had made a bundle of money in a chain of fast-food restaurants, Hardee's Hamburgers, and had a reputation as a fast mover. The reputation was justified. In April he transferred the Mavericks to North Carolina, renamed them the Carolina Cougars and announced they would play their home games in three different cities, Greensboro, Charlotte and Raleigh. In May he was elected president of the ABA!

The territorial franchise idea had first been suggested by Frank McGuire when he was coach at the University of North Carolina. Then it was brought up again by sportswriter Frank Deford in the October 21, 1968, issue of *Sports Illustrated*. In writing about the economics of pro basketball, Deford said that few cities could support teams on their own, and he put forth the notion that a state with a few medium-sized cities and good arenas could do well with a regional team. He cited North Carolina as the best prospect. Apparently, somebody took notes.

Up to this time the ABA had done poorly in signing its top draft choices. Minnesota had managed to outbid the NBA for Mel Daniels of the University of New Mexico, but that was an exception. Generally the new league suited up unknowns, second-raters and NBA rejects—a bunch of guys named Jones and Brown. Then UCLA's giant Lew Alcindor, the finest pro prospect since Chamberlain, became eligible for the drafts after the 1968–69 college season. The NBA's Milwaukee Bucks and the ABA's New York Nets picked him.

Here was a player who could make the ABA respectable overnight. With Lew dunking the red, white and blue ball around the circuit, people would forgive the Kentucky Colonels for once briefly putting a girl in a game. They would forget about games in the 6,500-seat Long Island Arena and the 6,425-seat quonset hut at Loyola University of New Orleans, home of the Buccaneers. They might even forget Dinner Key Auditorium, sometime home of the Floridians. (The "auditorium" is actually two end-to-end airplane hangars. It gets so hot inside during some games that the doors have to be opened and the players have to adjust their shots to the ocean breezes.) Alcindor had to be signed at all costs, and since he was from New York and loved the city, it was thought the ABA had a good chance.

Necktie tackles are not allowed in basketball, but that's what Denver's Don Sidle appears to be trying against Virginia's Ray Scott, as Wayne Chapman looks on. Sidle is a mere 6 feet 9 inches, 220 pounds.

"If Lew joined our league, it would be the equivalent of the Jets beating the Colts in the Super Bowl," said Mikan. "It would be showing the world that we had the most important college player to come along in years."

Lew went to New York in March with two UCLA alumni along as advisers. First they talked to NBA Commissioner Walter Kennedy and the Milwaukee owners, then to Mikan and Nets' owner Arthur Brown. Lew and his advisers emphasized to both groups that they wanted no bidding war, that they would listen to each offer and then decide. For the bidders it was a situation demanding the nerves of a sharp poker player. The ABA offer was lower and when Alcindor & Co. asked about a bonus for signing, Mikan said there would be none. Perhaps he figured Lew was using some sort of negotiating ploy and in the end would relent and allow a second ABA bid.

Lew stuck to his plan, however. He gave his regrets to Brown and announced he would play for Milwaukee. A group of ABA owners desperately tried to get in with another bid, saying their commissioner had not been given the authority to make the final offer. Sorry, too late.

"The ABA had had the inside track," said Alcindor later, "but they had blown it."

On July 14, 1969, Mikan resigned. In the ABA's infancy he had been one of the few people with a major-league aura about him, and he had come up with the idea for the multicolored ball, but he had failed to land any sort of national television contract and the owners felt he had messed up the Alcindor bidding. League President Gardner took over as acting commissioner and the headquarters were moved to New York City, where they should have been all along.

Gardner, alternately wearing his hamburger hat, his Cougar hat and his commissioner hat, was just as aggressive and fast-moving as ever. In August of 1969 the ABA and NBA announced the start of serious merger talks. However, it wasn't long before a series of ABA fountain-pen flourishes ended the marriage possibilities for a while. Gardner's Cougars signed Billy Cunningham of the Philadelphia 76ers to a future contract. According to the agreement, Billy, an ex-University of North Carolina star, would go back south when he had completed his obligation to Philly. Earl Foreman of Washington then

signed a similar contract with Dave Bing of the Detroit Pistons, a D.C. product. The Los Angeles Stars signed 6 foot-9 inch Zelmo Beaty of the Atlanta Hawks. In a situation similar to Barry's, he sat out the 1969–70 season in L.A. waiting until it was legal to play.

The most controversial deal of all was the Denver Rockets' signing of 6 foot-9 inch Spencer Haywood, hero of the 1968 Olympics, who still had two years of eligibility remaining at the University of Detroit. The Rockets claimed Haywood had approached them and said he was dropping out of school because of financial hardship. The club put him under contract and the league office okayed it. This was quite a departure from the accepted pro policy—keeping hands off college stars until their classes are graduated.

(There wasn't much the university or the NCAA could do to retaliate except yell loudly and refuse to give free tickets to ABA scouts. There were obvious scary implications for college coaches who were counting on talented athletes from poor families. Would Haywood's example be followed by Artis Gilmore of Jacksonville, Jim McDaniels of Western Kentucky, Ralph Simpson of Michigan State? Gardner said no, Haywood's case was unique. The following year Denver used the hardship rationale again and signed Simpson, who had two years of college ball left. The league disallowed the contract, but Simpson sued for the right to play and won.)

Haywood proceeded to rip the rest of the ABA apart in the 1969–70 season. With Connie Hawkins having switched over to the Phoenix Suns of the NBA, Haywood was not only rookie of the year but most valuable player, too. He led the league in points, scoring average (29.99), rebounds, rebound average (19.49) and playing time. He ended the year by scoring 59 points against the L.A. Stars. Denver, although still in the red, became the ABA's healthiest franchise and young Mr. Haywood went from poverty to a swank apartment on the 38th floor of Denver's Brooks Towers, overlooking the city. (The cozy arrangement didn't last long. Haywood left the team late in 1970, sat out for a while and then signed with the NBA's Seattle SuperSonics, thus setting off a nasty internecine struggle in the older league, where Commissioner Walter Kennedy and most owners opposed the signing.)

However, the Indiana Pacers—not the Rockets —won the ABA's third championship. Coached by ex-NBA guard Bob Leonard, the Pacers had an excellent front line of Mel Daniels, Bob Netolicky and Roger Brown. They finished 14 games ahead of the Kentucky Colonels in the Eastern Division, and in the playoffs beat Carolina 4 to 0, Kentucky 4 to 1, and Los Angeles 4 to 2. They also lost 80,000 dollars.

Hawkins was gone, Alcindor was lost and no team had bothered to stock any black ink yet, but there were some pluses for the ABA. The Greensboro-Charlotte-Raleigh Cougars attracted 120,637 people to their home games, a first-year record in pro basketball. And a new leader was found.

The ABA owners correctly figured they couldn't keep going without a full-time commissioner and some sort of national television contract. They wanted a man with the image of National Football League czar Pete Rozelle, someone equally at home at the bargaining table or the circular bar at Toots Shor's.

The man they picked was handsome Jack Dolph, director of sports for the CBS television network since 1959. Ironically, he was the same fellow who had once written a memo to his superiors at CBS advising them to forget the ABA. He must have relented a bit, though, because he was also in on the network's decision—in the ABA's first year—to offer to carry some of the league's playoff games. CBS would have paid nothing for the rights, but Dolph says that wasn't as stingy as it might have sounded. CBS figured it would not have been able to sell enough of the time to make a profit. Besides, said Dolph, "What the ABA needed then was exposure." Mikan, who was being advised by MGM's television division, turned down the offer.

(Which brings us to another corporate convolution: MGM's *merchandising* division later contracted with Commissioner Dolph to sell the ABA ball around the country.)

Dolph took office November 1, 1969, and within two months he had seen "some good friends at CBS" and sold the ABA's first national-TV package. Well, "sold" isn't exactly the right word. He proposed approximately the same deal Mikan had nixed, giving CBS the right to televise the ABA All-Star Game, plus the last three Saturdays of the playoffs. He received nothing in return but exposure, of which there was plenty. About six million people watched the All-Star telecast, more than had attended all the previous ABA games combined!

When Dolph took over he found the league had no bank, no accountant and a pension plan that wasn't funded. But those were piddling details compared to his main job of "franchise stabilization." That meant searching for fresh money and, in some cases, fresh cities. He didn't have to fret about the Kentucky Colonels. The same day he was named commissioner the franchise was sold to "five young guys" whose wallets were filled with money from Kentucky Fried Chicken and profitable rest homes. In March of 1971, they successfully unloaded some of that money by signing Artis Gilmore to a multi-year contract reported to be as high as 2.7 million dollars.

The L.A. Stars were playing before acres of empty seats, so they were sold and became the Utah Stars, with "a beautiful jewel of an arena," the Salt Palace. New Orleans moved up the Mississippi to Memphis. The Pittsburgh-Minnesota-Pittsburgh Pipers were sold to Haven Industries (sugar, airport services). They changed the nickname to Condors

Eyeing the basket greedily, Indiana's Roger Brown, a product of the New York City playgrounds, prepares to make his move. He, Bob Netolicky and Mel Daniels give Pacers one of finest front lines in the ABA.

and brought in NBA veteran Marty Blake to be general manager. Somebody cracked, "I don't know if they picked 'Condors' because they're birds of prey or because they're about to become extinct."

The Miami franchise failed and the league sold it to advertising executive Ned Doyle, who had once tried to buy the New York Jets pro football team. Doyle had left the famous Doyle Dane Bernbach agency in October of 1969 after helping create successful advertising campaigns for Avis, Clairol, Polaroid, etc. Creating a demand for the Miami Floridians was about as big a huckster's challenge as he had ever accepted.

He dropped the "Miami" and made the Floridians into a regional team à la Carolina, with home games scheduled in Miami Beach, Jacksonville, Tampa and West Palm Beach. No more games in the airplane hangars at Dinner Key or the north gym at Miami–Dade Junior College. He changed the team colors from aqua and orange to hot orange, magenta and black. He introduced ball-girls in bikinis. Best of all, he fired everybody except coach Hal Blitman, center Skip Thoren and two front-office people and acquired eleven new players and a new publicist. Yes, Ned Doyle had done what disgusted fans of inept teams had been urging for years, and he made a slogan out of it:

"We didn't fire the coach, we fired the team."

While Commissioner Dolph was ferreting out new owners and talking to CBS, he also helped get the merger talks going again. In separate meetings on June 18, 1970, the NBA voted 13–4 and the ABA voted 11–0 to start seeking legislation to allow, in Dolph's words, "a non-competitive agreement." The National and American Football Leagues had obtained just such an OK from Congress. One complication was an antimerger suit filed by the NBA Players Association.

"A merger would spread basketball throughout the country, it would make it a more popular game," said Sam Schulman, president of the NBA's Seattle SuperSonics. "I believe the majority of the ABA clubs have stability and many of the new owners are of high caliber. The money we would save through a common draft doesn't matter; that's the least of my reasons. I see an opportunity for basketball to become truly a national pastime."

The battle for the best players in the college class of '70 was an expensive one. The money flowed like spilled milk and the prospects lapped it up. The ABA got its checkbooks out of storage and signed big names Charles Scott of North Carolina, Dan Issel of Kentucky, Rick Mount of Purdue and Mike Maloy of Davidson. The NBA countered by laying lavish sums on Pete Maravich of Louisiana State, Bob Lanier of St. Bonaventure, Calvin Murphy of Niagara and Dave Cowens of Florida State.

It looked as if Schulman's pastime was going to become truly bankrupt before it became truly national. Surely a pro-basketball wedding ceremony would be held soon.

Instead, on November 20, 1970, NBA Commissioner Walter Kennedy announced an end to the joint effort to seek congressional approval of a merger. He gave no reasons, but at least three were apparent. Joe Caldwell had jumped from the NBA Atlanta Hawks to the Carolina Cougars. The ABA's Denver franchise had signed the college star, Ralph Simpson. And the ABA had not dropped its antitrust suit against the NBA.

"We'll fight them directly to the finish now," said one NBA owner.

If the NBA could finish off the ABA somehow, it could pick up the new league's promising franchises, perhaps Denver, Indiana, Kentucky and the New York Nets (who have Rick Barry and the soon-to-be-completed, 14,000-seat Nassau Coliseum). No doubt there already have been attempts to persuade some ABA teams to jump over, but each ABA team must put up a 100,000 dollar performance bond with the league office. That's a lot of money to leave behind.

Television revenue is the only thing that saved the American Football League from disaster when it was trying to survive, and the same probably will be true of the ABA. If the games on CBS in 1970–71 attract a reasonable amount of public interest and sponsor money, perhaps there will be a fatter contract the following season. Several teams including Indiana and New York had local TV contracts. And another possibility was the Monday-night sports slot on ABC. Monday night pro football was so successful in the ratings that the network was considering the same type of program with basketball and baseball.

Maybe the most fertile field of all was cable television. Bill Daniels, owner of the Utah Stars, made a good deal of money in cable TV in Denver and naturally decided to use it with his franchise. On Saturday night, October 24, 1970, the Stars played the Indiana Pacers before 11,163 people.

"The game went by cable TV throughout the Northwest," said Daniels. "About 300,000 people in over 40 cities in all of Idaho, all of Montana and half of Wyoming saw it.

"This was the first time in any professional sport this has been done. And it's just a start."

Meanwhile, Commissioner Dolph continued struggling with his franchise stabilization. In mid-December of 1970 the league had to assume financial control of the Memphis Pros, née New Orleans Buccaneers. An ex-Mississippi State football player named P. L. Blake had decided that owning a pro basketball team was not his meat.

"I was prepared to lose money in the first season," he said, "but not 200,000 dollars in the first two months of operation."

There was a chance the team would be renamed the Tennessee Riflemen and play its home games in Memphis, Nashville, Knoxville, Chattanooga and Buffalo Gap.

Science and scheming

"I'd do anything if it would give me an advantage," Al McGuire of Marquette once said. ". . . I can do two things in life—coach basketball and tend bar. I'm fighting to keep the apron off."

Basketball coaches are sufferers. Pete Peletta of USF developed ulcers and gladly accepted the job of athletic director when it was offered to him. Bob King of New Mexico sits on the bench and devours antacid pills by the pack. Lou Carnesecca of the New York Nets is up and down as if he were a marionette being jerked around by somebody up in the rafters. Ed Diddle, for years the head man at Western Kentucky, used to wring and fling a polka-dotted towel.

Jack Gardner of Utah drinks milk during a game to soothe his churning insides. It got to be such a trademark for him that he was once runner-up to Secretary of Agriculture Ezra Taft Benson as the dairy industry's man of the year. When Utah played in the Kentucky Invitational one year, a fan sent a fifty-cent piece to pay Gardner's milk bill. Jack wired back:

"Send another four bits. This is a two-quart game."

A tale of agony told and retold in the Atlantic Coast Conference concerns Horace (Bones) McKinney. Bones, an ordained Baptist minister, was known as the Barrymore of the Bench—yanking at his red socks, leaping up and down, dying with every opposition basket. When he was coaching Wake Forest in 1964 the Demon Deacons played Princeton in a holiday tournament.

During the game Bones kicked so hard that his shoe flew off and landed in the middle of the court. He ran out to retrieve it, but when he bent over his fountain pen fell out and he had to pick that up, too. When he straightened up he saw a Princeton fast break about to engulf him.

What did Bones do then?

"I did the only thing I could," he said. "I threw up my hands and started playing defense."

Most of the emotional outbursts are directed at the referees, who must not only concentrate on officiating a difficult, fast-moving game but try to tune out the constant crackle of abuse and advice from the coaches. Some of the outbursts are much more calculated than emotional. The coaches want to stir up the home crowd, rouse their own players or intimidate the officials.

". . . It's a little harder to win . . . if you're taking in the action like a fan who doesn't give a damn how the game ends," said Red Auerbach, one of the notorious ref baiters in the pros. "In our sport, the coach who takes a nap on the bench deserves to get the worst of the calls. Too much turns on the officiating in basketball, more peculiarly than in any other game, to take it lightly."

Two of Auerbach's hints for winning were, "Question officials' decisions, especially on the home court" and "A smart team will take advantage of the home court and the home fans. In fact, they may make moves to stimulate crowd reaction in their favor."

"A squeaky wheel gets the grease," says Don Haskins of Texas-El Paso.

Through experience and intuition, certain coaches have become artists at manipulating referees. One of them is UCLA's John Wooden.

Eddie Powell, a former assistant who moved with him from Indiana State to UCLA in 1948, learned a few psychological tricks from the master.

"Usually sometime during the first half he would choose one incident, a close call, and jump all over the referee," said Powell. "Just chew him out in a gentlemanly manner, if there is such a thing. But let him know that there was that side of Wooden. During the half he'd seek out the referee and apologize to him. He'd say 'I know I should have known it was a close call. I was wrong. It's just a job and you're doing the best you can.'

Philadelphia's Jack Ramsay stoops at the sideline, surrounded by his team, as he outlines play. Ramsay came from college ranks.

"And then they'd part, with Wooden walking away meek as you please. In the second half, if another close call arose, chances are the referee'd call the play in Wooden's favor."

To make his fullcourt press as effective as possible, Wooden wants referees to be acutely aware of the rule that gives a team only ten seconds to get the ball across the midcourt line. Sometimes he carries a stopwatch to the bench. He will not say a word about it and probably will not check it, but he will make certain that the officials notice it.

Wooden insists he knows what he is doing when he yells about calls. Often it is to show his players he is fighting for them. Of course, much depends on the personality of each official.

"I would think that any referee who does not command the respect of John Wooden can expect to be tested," said Al Lightner, until his retirement one of the toughest West Coast officials. "Personally, I never had any trouble at all with Wooden. I understand some referees have had trouble."

Lightner understands correctly, but Wooden feels his reputation as a ref baiter is "definitely undeserved."

"I don't say, 'You're a homer!' I'll say, 'Don't be a homer!' I'll say, 'See 'em the same at both ends!' I'll say, 'Watch the traveling,' or some such, but no profanity and not personal."

A sharp coach knows the fine print in the rule book every bit as thoroughly as the referees do. He can quote from it as if he were a preacher spouting Bible verses. For instance, there is a tricky bit of business called the "false double foul" which might not crop up more than once a season. If a foul is

committed while a free throw is in the air (usually by somebody jockeying too vigorously for position), the victim gets his free throw and then there is a jump ball, just as if there had been a double foul. The other team does not get the ball out of bounds as it would after a regular free throw, and sometimes refs must be reminded about the rule.

As if the referees don't have enough to worry about, they also have to contend with the expert fakers—the defensive man who is barely brushed by the dribbler but flies backward as if a car had hit him at 60 mph, the man who feigns injury merely to get a quick, unofficial breather.

The refs also have to try to keep the carnage under the backboards to a minimum, and sometimes it's very difficult to tell who is doing what to whom in the tangle of arms and legs and bodies. Wilt Chamberlain lost two front teeth his first season in the NBA. He claimed Clyde Lovellette elbowed him in the mouth and "hammered my teeth right up into my gums."

"As for the roughness under the boards, it's give and take," said Bill Russell. "You have to look at things realistically; competition here is at the highest level. There's always somebody ready to take your place. . . ."

There is much more for a coach to think about than just the officiating. If he is alert and experienced, he makes judicious use of his reserves, substituting not willy-nilly but with purposes in mind. Obviously, an injured or tired man should be replaced, but there are other times to substitute, too. Perhaps a player has disobeyed orders and needs to be disciplined or just is not playing well or needs some specific instructions.

When a team has clinched a game, it is wise for the coach to send in the subs rather than run up an eye-popping score. The reserves get game experience that might be valuable later and the other team is given less of a revenge motive.

LEFT: Boston Celtics celebrate NBA championship, with coach Red Auerbach (center) sucking on his victory cigar. ABOVE: Bill Russell drags Red away from refs after court battle.

A substitute must report to the scorer's table before entering the game. Failure to do so results in a technical foul, and more than one game has been lost by just such a seemingly small error. The player coming out of the game is often annoyed about it and would like to go down to the far end of the bench to sulk and grumble. Some even argue with the coach. Red Holzman of the New York Knicks put a stop to such behavior when he took over the club. He insisted that the replaced player sit next to him and perhaps get some instructions. However, when Auerbach was coaching Boston, he wanted the out-coming man to sit away from him until summoned.

An assistant coach or manager should keep track of fouls. If a player gets three on him in the first half, it is probably wise to take him out and save him for the second half. If a player in foul trouble plays too cautiously, though, it might be better to put in a man with less ability but also less inhibition.

Somebody on the bench also should keep careful track of time-outs. As with substitutions, time-outs should have a purpose, most often rest or instruction. When a player is trapped and about to be tied up by one or two opponents, it pays him to quickly call time. Another common reason is to stop a rally by the other team. The coach might not have any brilliant solution to suggest, but at least the pause might take some momentum away from the enemy. It is considered a mini-triumph if the other team is forced to call the first time-out.

The electronic age has provided another, mandatory, reason. Rather than settle for the regular time-outs and half time, the sponsors of TV broadcasts insist on being assured a certain number of extra breaks for commercials. Marquette coach Al McGuire got disgusted during his team's home-court victory over New Mexico State.

"The one-eyed monster governed the game, and it was like a marathon out there," he said. "Tel-

"What do I tell 'em to do now?" wonders Notre Dame coach Johnny Dee, who has called a time-out to slow down the other team. He had fewer problems when Austin Carr arrived.

evision kills the game with commercials. There is no continuity."

There is no standard way for a coach to talk to his players during a time-out. Wooden has his men gather around him in a semicircle with their hands on their knees, or sometimes he will have them sit down side by side and he'll crouch in front of them. Henry Iba used to have his men lie down on the floor on their bellies in a semicircle while he sat above and shook a finger in their faces.

There are thousands of little tricks that a coach can use to help his team win, some of them legal. In the NCAA Tournament one March, Duke was in a close battle that went right down to the last seconds. An opponent was fouled and the two teams lined up along the lane. Duke coach Vic Bubas called time-out. When time was in the two teams lined up again and again Bubas called time. When play resumed the rattled opponent blew the foul shot. Character building—that's what it's called.

Boston's Red Auerbach advocated holding on to an opponent's pants to aggravate him and slow him up. He taught his players that on out-of-bounds plays they should step right up and *assume* the referee would hand them the ball. He was delighted to have a difficult-to-read scoreboard clock in Boston Garden on the off-chance that a visiting player or coach would have a difficult time reading it at a crucial point in a game.

Hot dog in one hand, cup of Pepsi in the other, program and pencil balanced in his lap, the busy fan at a basketball game tends to concentrate on watching the man with the ball and the opponent guarding him. What else happens on the floor either leaves just a faint impression in the back of the fan's mind or isn't noticed at all. Yet in a college game there are 40 minutes, ten players and only one ball, which means that if possession could be divided equally, each man would have the ball just

Gesturing to emphasize his point, Bill Sharman dictates strategy to his players. RIGHT: As Seattle players converge on him from several directions, little Hal Greer of the Philadelphia 76ers passes to an open teammate. The ability to quickly see and hit "the open man" is not common.

four minutes. Obviously, nine guys must be doing some things *without* it—passing, cutting to the basket, setting picks, blocking out under the backboards, rebounding, playing defense.

Perhaps the best strategical move of all for a coach is to convince his players that basketball is a team game. They must help each other on defense and pass unselfishly on offense. They should shoot when they are free—but only from close in or medium range, not the third balcony.

Getting these lessons across is not easy because the big idol in most arenas, pro or college, is still the guy who scores the most points. Very seldom does a news story begin, "Tom Sanders led the Boston Celtics to a 110–105 victory over the Chicago Bulls last night by holding Chet Walker ten points below his season average and setting tough picks for teammate Jo Jo White." No, the glory and the fattest pay envelopes usually go to the shooters. Somehow a coach must find ways to reward and motivate the players who contribute in other ways.

With the possible exception of having a giant center, the star system does not lead to wins in basketball. Pete Maravich, coached by his father at Louisiana State and given carte blanche to shoot as he pleased, won three straight national scoring titles and got a huge pile of money from the Atlanta Hawks. But Pete's shooting percentage was not outstanding and LSU won no national championships, no league championships and lost three straight years to Kentucky. Oscar Robertson also won three scoring titles, but the University of Cincinnati didn't win an NCAA championship until after he left.

"Everybody can put the ball through the hole today," says Cincinnati Royals' coach Bob Cousy. "It's much more of an art to make the right pass to the right place to set up the score."

". . . I hope I never have the nation's leading scorer," says UCLA's Wooden.

There is little doubt that Lew Alcindor could

BELOW: Using his arms, back and rear end, John Havlicek of the
Boston Celtics "blocks out" Wilt Chamberlain of Los Angeles,
who has a decided height advantage but probably won't get
this rebound. RIGHT: Rudy LaRusso exhibits a good follow-through
on his jump shot and keeps his eyes on the target despite
the big hand in his face.

RIGHT: Since the defensive men in the NBA seem to get away with almost anything—holding, shoving, grabbing jerseys—it's only fair that the poor guys trying to score should be able to foul a little bit once in a while. Here, Dave (The Rave) Stallworth of the Knickerbockers fends off his opponent with his left arm, dribbles with his right and thinks about that sure basket that lies just ahead if no one trips him. BELOW: One of the fundamentals in any sport that demands quick stops and starts is that you can't come to a quick stop straight-legged. You have to lower your center of gravity, i.e., get your rear end down and bend your knees (not necessarily in that order). FAR RIGHT: Nate Thurmond of the San Francisco Warriors learned a long time ago that playing center in the NBA was no lark in Golden Gate Park. Here, he merely endures a forearm shove to the kidneys, but there are worse occupational hazards, such as elbows in the bridgework, twisted ankles, losing.

156

TOP LEFT: San Francisco's 6 foot-11 inch Nate Thurmond waves the ball around as he decides which teammate will get the pass. Maybe it will be Bob Portman (No. 33). TOP RIGHT: Denver Rockets' Lonnie Wright (No. 42) prepares to hit teammate breaking free from the man guarding him. So many plays start with a guard-to-forward pass that some teams drill on denying that pass. RIGHT: Under the basket is where the action is; even tiny San Diego Rockets' guard Calvin Murphy knows that. In this episode, it looks as if Detroit's Erwin Mueller will get the rebound. He's No. 51, the fellow hoisting himself up on an opponent's arm as if it were a tree limb. Did we hear a whistle? Ah, yes, that referee on the opposite page saw the infraction and called it right away. Raise your hand, Mueller! OPPOSITE: San Diego's Murphy seems in control despite banging into a foe.

have piled up amazing personal statistics in his three years at UCLA. Instead, the Bruin *team* piled up an amazing total in the win column. Wooden convinced Lew that he should pass off when he was double- and triple-teamed, and the other members of the squad were sold on the idea that they would get better shots with Lew being surrounded in the middle. That is not to say there was no resentment of Alcindor's publicity or special treatment, but Wooden did a good job of keeping it to a minimum.

Picking a starting lineup does not always mean sending the five most talented players out for the tipoff. The coach is putting five gears to work and he wants them to mesh, not grind. He must also consider defensive abilities. A good shooter isn't much help if he gives up more points than he makes.

At center the coach puts his best rebounder, a man with either great leaping ability or height or both. The center does not have to have great shooting range because he's going to be working close to the hoop. Playing in the corners, the two forwards should be from 6 feet 4 inches to 6 feet 8 inches (for major colleges and the pros), better shooters and ballhandlers than the center and good enough jumpers to help with the rebounding. In the backcourt, the two guards need quickness and outside shooting ability but not so much height. At least one of them should be able to dribble well enough to drive to the basket and elude pressing defenses.

Sometimes, when a team has two good centers, a coach will use a double-post offense, with the two big men playing high and low in the key or across the key from each other. There are two wings and one guard, or point man, who plays at the top of the key and directs the attack.

Single post and double post are the two basic formations, but there are dozens of variations and a few radical departures. Notre Dame had success with a "double stack," which started with the players lined up on either side of the key. The idea was

LEFT: There's not much you can do when leaping Johnny Green and two Cincy teammates come down on a three-on-one fast break—except turn and shut your eyes. INSET: Knicks' Red Holzman plots strategy with his world champions. ABOVE: "You play closer to the base line, you block out that #$%&," instructs Baltimore coach Gene Shue during a time-out.

to clog up the middle with all sorts of picks and screens and allow relatively short Austin Carr to dart in and out among the taller players like a rabbit in a redwood grove.

A team can use various tempos of attack within a season or a game. Perhaps the most popular and successful offensive tactic is the fast break, used by UCLA, Kentucky and other college teams that give themselves names like the Runnin' Redskins and Hurryin' Hoosiers. Virtually every pro team uses the fast break.

The first requirement is to have a big man to dominate the defensive backboard. When the Boston Celtics had Bill Russell, the other four starters could "cheat" after an opposition shot was taken because Russ would nearly always get the rebound if the shot missed. The four would race for the other end of the court, Russ would fire a quick "outlet pass" to one of them and often they would catch the defense with only one or two men back. They'd have a two-to-one, three-to-two or three-to-one advantage.

Ideally, on the fast break the man with the ball should race up the middle of the court and two teammates should "fill the lanes" on either side of him. That way the dribbler has four options: take a jump shot or lay-up himself, pass left, pass right, or stop, pivot and hand off to a "trailer." When the break does not result in a good shot opportunity, the team should be able to resort to a "set offense."

This sort of basketball is not universally popular, however. Stanford's great player Hank Luisetti once wrote a magazine article entitled, "Racehorse Basketball Stinks!" Plenty of coaches still feel that way. The advocates are equally adamant.

"I can't understand why a boy would want to go to a place where they don't want to play," said Adolph Rupp. "We think that a ball with seven pounds of air in it should be made to move."

162

*LEFT: Conduct unbecoming a Princeton man is Butch van
Breda Kolff's exhorting a ref. BELOW: UCLA's Lew Alcindor leans
close to get every pearl of wisdom from coach John Wooden.*

"We want to make the game interesting for the people who watch," said the late Branch McCracken of Indiana. "Sure we make mistakes when we're running and firing the ball up. But we get the people yelling and throw off the patterns of the teams we're playing. That's why my clubs are always in shape—we'll run the other guy right into the floor."

The best way a team can defend against the fast break is to make most of its shots, thus forcing the opposition to take the ball out of bounds and bring it upcourt the conventional way. The next best thing to do is harass the rebounder trying to make the outlet pass. Don't allow him time or room and perhaps he'll throw inaccurately or too far and have the ball intercepted.

The antithesis of the fast break is the stall, also known as slowdown, modified slowdown, freeze, delay game, conservative style, letting the air out of the ball and, most euphemistic of all, deliberate and selective attack. Whatever name is used—it is an attempt by a team to make up for some horrible disadvantage, such as having no talent. Or having a dwarf center against Wilt Chamberlain. The coach orders his underdogs not to shoot unless they have a safe-conduct pass to the basket. He hopes that in the last two or three minutes the game will be close and his team will have a chance to luck through.

"It's a case of the haves and have-nots," said longtime Kentucky assistant Harry Lancaster. "You're not going to see a team with the horses holding the ball. But there are too many have-nots who think the only way they're going to beat a better team is by using the stall."

Such hide-and-seek tactics can be exciting, with clever dribbling, chasing and attempts at stealing the ball. The trouble comes when the defensive team decides not to seek. Then the players stand around like figures in a sculpture garden, the fans scream for refunds (when they're not booing) and the cry goes up for a collegiate version of the 24-second clock. Of course, everyone considers it perfectly acceptable for a team to stall at the end of a game to protect a lead.

One of the famous, or infamous, stall games was in the L.A. Sports Arena late in the 1966–67 season. UCLA had Lew Alcindor and 14,417 people showed up to see him play against crosstown rival USC. Trojan coach Bob Boyd spoiled the party for Bruin fans by ordering his team into a game-long stall. USC led at half time 17–14 and forced the eventual national champions into overtime before falling 40–35. The fans saw Alcindor standing around most of the time looking bored and occasionally bending down and touching his palms to the floor.

As a group of policemen escorted Boyd to the USC dressing room, he was cursed and spat upon. But he was stubborn. Two years later, in Lew's last season, USC stalled again and won 46–44.

Boyd's strategy was nothing new. In fact, back in 1932 USC froze the ball for the last fifteen minutes of the first half against UCLA. The Bruin band played a funeral dirge, fans tossed pennies on the floor and Trojan star Jerry Nemer read a newspaper. The second half was played normally (for those poor-shooting days) and USC lost that game 19–17. That same year Kansas and Missouri players *sat* at either end of the court and stared at each other in the first half. Those two thrillers prompted a new rule for the next season requiring the offensive team to get the ball across the halfcourt line within 10 seconds.

The professionals have had stall games, too. In 1951 the Fort Wayne Pistons froze the ball in Minneapolis and beat George Mikan and the Lakers 19–18, then had to fight their way to the dressing room. (It takes a considerable amount of nerve to stall, when you are employing your delaying tactics on the other team's court.) With the 24-second clock ticking away in the NBA these days, such tactics are obsolete.

Going right as he almost always does, Elgin Baylor of the Los Angeles Lakers still is a hard man to stop. Almost every player favors one hand over the other.

LEFT: "Keep your hands up" is an old defensive axiom in basketball, and here Sidney Wicks talks at the same time.
BELOW: Coach Arad McCutchan of Evansville ponders next move.

Most college coaches do not want a clock. Many go along with Jack Gardner of Utah, who says, "A 24-second clock makes a robot out of the coach."

"The pro teams play so much alike," said Houston's Guy V. Lewis, "that a player can be traded from one team to another between halves and never miss a pass."

"If a 24- or 30-second law was adopted, I imagine everybody would play a zone defense," said Steve Belko of Oregon, "and force the offense to take the 20-foot shot. When everybody adopts a zone to force more outside shooting you have then taken the driving shot out of basketball. You can't drive against a good zone."

Some claim that it would be impossible to stall if referees enforced the rule that says, "A team shall not delay the game . . . by allowing the game to develop into an actionless contest." A team must be "reasonably active" in trying to get the ball, or, on offense, in trying to advance it. However, the college rules do not require anybody to *shoot*.

"It's perfectly possible to stall by moving the ball from the midcourt area into the frontcourt area and then back out," said a Missouri Valley Conference official. "No rule violation is involved. But the lack of action rules do enforce movement of the ball. A man can't just stand out beyond the free-throw line, holding the ball or dribbling it. So a team may not do much shooting, but it can't refuse to move the ball."

The tempo is up to the coach. He has his hand on the gear shift and can put it in overdrive, drive, low or even park. Of course, the other coach is usually no dummy and can come up with things to force a shift or perhaps even cause a dropped transmission. Pete Newell had his teams practice at fast and slow speeds and several gradations in between when he was coaching at the University of San Francisco, Michigan State and California.

"We want to use tempo as a weapon, make the other team play the game we can play better," said Newell. "We make them play at a speed they're not used to."

Newell's own preferred pace was slow and careful. His teams had extraordinary patience and confidence. They could be twelve points behind, but they would methodically take the ball up the floor, set up their offense and work tirelessly for a good percentage shot. They seldom got panicky, seldom tried to step up the pace.

"The eastern fast-break system emphasizes speed and shoot, shoot, shoot," said Newell. "Scoring situations are ideally developed in one or two passes downcourt against a fall-back zone defense, many shots being made close-in because the scoring area is not jammed.

"Our western system principally embraces a good regard for the value of the ball. We'll fast break when the floor is open, of course, but we're willing to work against a congested defense, four or five passes to get the shot we want."

The classic master of pattern basketball is Henry Iba, former coach at Oklahoma State. His theory is that when his team is controlling the ball, there is no way the other team can score. His boys "work a set play or pattern until the good shot comes," he says. "It may come early or it may come late.

"I'm not against shooting. I'm against bad shooting. I want my boys to shoot. I love my boys to shoot. But, glory be, make it a good shot."

For some coaches defense becomes a passion, even an obsession. Such men as Bob Boyd of Southern California, Dick Harter of Penn and Dean Smith of North Carolina sell their teams on the idea that every player eventually will have an off-night

shooting but that if they learn their lessons well, they need not ever have an off-night on defense.

"Either a boy has the scoring touch or he doesn't," said Pete Newell. "But defense—you can teach any good boy defense!"

"An awful lot of people give lip service to defense in basketball, but we work at it in Stillwater," said Iba before his retirement. "Here is our chief contention: airtight defense will get you a win more often than a high-geared offense."

When it came to giving up points, Iba was one of the stingiest. His ex-players who have become coaches—such as Don Haskins of Texas at El Paso and Jack Hartman of Kansas State—have carried on the tradition. However, Iba's son Moe was the Memphis State coach for a couple of years and wasn't too successful. In one game Memphis State lost to North Texas State 96–69. Afterward, Moe

discussed the game over the telephone with his dad but continually avoided the little matter of the score.

"I'll tell you what the score was," Iba finally yelled. "I listened to the game. Ninety-six damn points, that's what the score was. Bret and Greg [Moe's sons] are in the will, but you're out."

And he hung up.

Almost without exception, the college teams with the best talent play man-to-man defense in preference to zone defense (in which the players are responsible for an area rather than a man). Wooden, Rupp, Iba—most of the great coaches have been man-to-man advocates. But even the masters have had to resort to a zone in certain situations, although they hated to admit it. Phog Allen of Kansas called his a "stratified, transitional, man-to-man defense with a zone principle." His pupil, Rupp, altered this to a "transitional, shifting man-to-man with a hyperbolic paraboloid."

The man-to-man takes longer to learn and requires better conditioning, but coaches like it because it assigns specific responsibility and allows sensible match-ups. A player can be stirred up to stop a certain opponent. It is a good defense to use when either behind or ahead, whereas a trailing team usually has to abandon a zone because it's too passive.

A zone is effective when the defensive team wants to sag in on a particularly good or tall center, or when the opposition cannot shoot well from outside. It is easier to learn and there is less chance of fouling. It is difficult to drive against. And sometimes a zone is a coach's only choice because he has a tall, slow team – or a short, slow team.

The zone is weak against the fast break because the team often can't get back and set up in time. The opposition can whip the ball around the perimeter and spread the defense until there are wide-open shots available. Or the opposition can overload on one side and force a defender to worry about two men in his area.

"It is impossible to cover all the areas adequately on a regulation-sized floor against a good team," says Wooden.

Some coaches have good luck in a game by going back and forth from a zone to a man-to-man, keeping the opposition off balance and confused. Or a team can have four men playing a box- or diamond-shaped zone while the fifth man sticks with the opponent's big scorer. UCLA did that against Houston and Elvin Hayes in the 1968 NCAA semifinals.

When Butch van Breda Kolff was coaching at Princeton in 1967, the Tigers had a tough game versus Brown at Providence, Rhode Island. With 59 seconds left Brown was behind by one point and had possession of the ball. Brown stalled and called time out with eighteen seconds left to decide on one final play. If it worked, Princeton would probably have no time to retaliate.

Van Breda Kolff instructed his team to fake a man-to-man defense just for a moment to induce

Brown into the wrong course of action, then quickly shift into a zone. It worked beautifully. A Brown guard saw the man-to-man, drove into the middle intending to pass off to one side to his team's best shooter, but suddenly found himself entangled in Princeton's brier-patch zone. He lost the ball and the game.

At one time the fullcourt press (either zone or man-to-man) was a desperation measure used by the trailing team in the last minutes of a game. Today, due to UCLA's success with the Gail Goodrich-Walt Hazzard teams of the late '60s (they pressed all game, every game), many teams blessed with quickness and good bench strength use the press as a tactical weapon—usually against a slow opponent or one with five-thumbed guards. Another weapon is the halfcourt press, in which the defensive men pick up their opponents crossing the DMZ and try to hound them into mistakes.

The most common antidote for the fullcourt press is to get the ball up the court via quick, accurate passes (a basic tenet of basketball being that a thrown ball travels faster than a man). It is usually a mistake to try to dribble through a press, but exceptional ballhandlers can get away with it and give the audience a show at the same time.

Coaches generally devote more of their precious practice time to offense because it is more complicated (and more fun). Very few let a practice end without several hard defensive drills, however. Newell used to have his Cal players shuffle up and down the floor for 20 minutes at a time with knees flexed, one hand up and one hand down, looking something like Groucho Marx trying to hail a taxi.

"The hand should be in the shooter's face to disconcert him," said Pete. "The other arm should be extended almost parallel to the floor to deflect passes. We condition arm muscles so that the arms can be held up over protracted lengths of time. In boxing, it is fatal to drop your hands. The same is true in basketball."

Because of the high scores and accurate shooters in pro basketball, the pros are occasionally accused of not playing defense. But they do play it, most of them very well. The main reason New

ABOVE: Houston's Guy V. Lewis is one of many coaches who wring a towel during games. RIGHT: Syracuse's Dave Bing has gone for the fake. When he comes down, the Davidson man will hit.

ABOVE: *Frank McGuire won a national championship while coaching at North Carolina, but most of the time he found it hard to get past the Atlantic Coast Conference tourney.*
OPPOSITE: *John Austin of Boston College, dribbling against UCLA's Edgar Lacey (54) and Gail Goodrich (25), loses race to base line.*

York won the NBA championship in 1970 was the team defense taught by coach Red Holzman. The battles of such fine defensive forwards as Tom Sanders and Dave DeBusschere against scorers Billy Cunningham and Elgin Baylor are sometimes more entertaining to watch than the games as a whole.

The pros are not allowed to play a zone defense, but they are allowed to blatantly shove and grab, which is much more useful anyway. "Hand-checking" it is called. Often the NBA refs have started off a season calling fouls for doing it but soon became more permissive. The result is that often a mongoose-quick guard like Jerry West will get a step on the defender, only to have the villain hold him until he can catch up.

"You have to show them you're not going to let them push you out of the league," said Bill Sharman back in his Boston days. "So you square off and somebody runs in between. I could name some players who were pushed out of this league because they wouldn't fight back. . . ."

Of course, the most tenacious defense, the most imaginative offense or the sneakiest trick ever devised might not help if the opposition is lucky enough. When Everett Dean was coaching Indiana, his team got involved in an overtime battle against Minnesota. Ten seconds to go and the score tied 36–36. An Indiana guard took a shot and the ball hit the hoop and bounced straight up to the backboard's top edge—and stayed there.

"I liked to die," recalled Dean. "That ball poised on the edge for a while, then started to roll. Slowly it went along the narrow edge. The players stared open-mouthed. I prayed. It seemed hours that we waited for that cursed ball to make up its mind."

Seconds before the overtime ended, the ball finally rolled off and dropped through the hoop.

"I fell right off the bench," said Dean, "the winner on the luckiest basket I ever saw."

"We'll scout 'em—you play 'em"

There was once a coach in the South who excelled at the game of Blue Chip. He would be sitting around at a clinic or convention and some colleague would challenge him.

"You'll never get this one," the challenger would say. Then he'd give out the clues: "Back-court man, six-one, two-time runner-up in state scoring, brown hair."

"Sandy Swisher, Enid, Oklahoma," our coach would answer without hesitating.

"Right. How about 6 feet 7 inches, good left-handed hook, father a fire chief."

"Ruffy Boardman, Pierre, South Dakota—but he's just a junior."

"Right again. Try 6 feet 5 inches, straight A's, wants to be a doctor, also a major-league baseball prospect."

At this, the Blue Chip expert would stop and quickly riffle through the index cards in his brain, and finally he'd say:

"No such player."

"Right, damn it."

College coaches learn of blue-chip prospects from a number of sources, including out-of-town newspapers, alumni, high school coaches and tip sheets. One of the latter is "Cage Scope," put out by Dave Bones Publications in Toledo, Ohio. It rates players as AA ("big time"), A ("major"), B ("low major-high medium"), C ("medium") and D ("small college"). Not great literature, but thoroughly read nevertheless. Another is Bill Bertka's semiannual list of the top junior-college players in California. The price is 35 dollars, which he considers "very cheap actually." In addition to basketball information Bertka publishes such facts as the kind of college wanted by the prospect, what he hopes to study and how much financial help he needs.

Such reports are especially helpful to out-of-the-way schools, but the NCAA takes a dim view of the practice and has notified all coaches and ath-letic-department employees to cancel their subscriptions. (But there are few coaches who haven't been able to find an alumnus or fan to subscribe for them.)

It might make an interesting court case if one of the enterprising publishers sued the NCAA for trying to harm his business. It is hard to see anything horribly unethical about the tip sheets. Too bad, really, that there is no demand for similar reports on blue-chip scholars.

Although high school basketball is popular in most parts of the country, the most and best talent is found in the big population centers (New York City, Philadelphia, Washington, D.C., Detroit, Chicago, Los Angeles and San Francisco-Oakland) and in the swath of states that includes New Jersey, Pennsylvania, Ohio, Indiana, Illinois and Kentucky. Eight of the ten men on the NBA's Silver Anniversary Team and six of the ten men on United Savings-Helms' all-time college team are from those cities and states.

The best gold mine is probably the New York metropolis, from which high-grade ore is shipped as far away as South Carolina (John Roche of Manhattan), Texas at El Paso (Willie Worsley of the Bronx) and UCLA (Lew Alcindor of Manhattan). There are years when every starter at Boys High of Brooklyn can get a grant-in-aid from some college and be a starter his sophomore year. Three members of the 1966–67 Weequahic High team of Newark (across the Hudson River from Manhattan) were starring for widely scattered major-college teams four years later: Bill Mainor of Fordham, Dana Lewis of Tulsa and Dennis Layton of Southern California.

Frank McGuire, who grew up in Greenwich Village, has used almost nothing but New York-area players in his successful coaching stints at St. John's, North Carolina and South Carolina.

"Just riding a subway takes more moves than

Bob Lanier, Detroit Pistons' top draft choice, tries to rebuild leg after operation on knee injured during NCAA tournament. Rehabilitation is a long, hard process.

I could ever teach a kid," he said. "A boy's got to be quick just to survive crossing a New York street. A New York cabdriver isn't happy unless he tags at least one pedestrian a day."

Coach Ted Owens of Kansas says his annual recruiting budget is 20,000 dollars, mostly for travel. Most high schools do not film their games, so some college staff member has to watch the prospects in person, usually more than once. Owens says that colleges in heavily populated areas can get by for less. However, that 20,000-dollar figure does not include the cost of a big, fancy recruiting brochure (disguised as a press guide) or the salary of an assistant who may do nothing but beat bushes for talent. For instance, Purdue "assistant coach" Bob King is actually a full-time recruiter. His job is to find the Rick Mounts, wherever they might be hiding, and sell them on the advantages of continuing their education—basketball and otherwise—at his school.

One of the first things a recruiter must do is find out a player's grades. The NCAA requires a prospective scholarship athlete to take one of two tests, the ACT (American College Testing) or SAT (Scholastic Aptitude Test). Using a formula that differs from school to school and conference to conference, his test score and rank in high-school class must "predict" at least a 1.6 average on a 4.0 scale. In other words, his record must indicate he can do D + or C − work at the college of his choice.

However, all is not lost if a boy does not qualify. Schools have all sorts of evasive gimmicks, the most legitimate of which is to "farm out" the kid to a junior college, where he can make up his grades for one or two years and play top-grade basketball at the same time. In 1969–70 Indiana University took in as freshmen two "non-predictors" from Indianapolis, George McGinnis and Steve Downing. They ostensibly paid their own way and were not allowed to play frosh ball, but they passed

enough courses to be eligible for the varsity as sophomores and get grants-in-aid, i.e., athletic scholarships. Kentucky did the same thing the same year for its first black player, Tom Payne.

Once it is known a prospect has the moves, the shots and the grades, the sales campaign begins. He receives questionnaires from schools all over the nation. If he fills them out—and often even if he doesn't—the assistant and head coaches start coming around, the propaganda brochures flood in, he is invited for a campus visit (round trip paid by the school) and his parents are sweet-talked.

"Before they allowed expense-paid trips, you could be almost certain a boy wanted to play for you if he paid his own way to your school," said Kentucky's Adolph Rupp. "Nine times out of ten a boy today still knows where he is going to college before he graduates from high school. But he's not going to be crazy enough to tell anybody."

The cinch future All-Americas, such as Jerry Lucas and Wilt Chamberlain, are practically hounded into insanity. Wilt was contacted by 200 colleges.

"So many people come and see me," he said when he was still playing for Overbrook High in Philadelphia. "I'm so confused I don't know what I'm doing. I just wish everybody would leave me alone. But I go home now and I know there'll be phone calls and letters and people. I just wish they'd leave me alone."

When Chamberlain finally announced for Kansas, a reporter excitedly phoned KU coach Phog Allen to give him the news.

"Well, isn't that nice," said Phog. "I hope he comes out for the team."

Lucas, an A student who scored 2,466 points in three years at Middletown High in Ohio, had to be protected by a special guard at the school's front door. Too many recruiters were chasing him down the halls and disrupting classes. Said his mother:

"One scout promised that my husband would

get a 15,000-dollar-a-year job, the mortgage on our home would be paid off, Jerry's brother Roy would get a scholarship to the same school and Jerry would get a new car, an expense account and everything."

Expense accounts are rare perhaps, but one cynical Missouri Valley Conference coach says flatly, "Any kid who goes more than 100 miles away from his home to go to school is getting a deal." If a prospect is good enough, the deal might be a scholarship for his girl friend, or he and his high-school coach might be taken as a package.

(The NCAA says a student athlete can receive only "commonly accepted educational expenses," meaning tuition, fees, room, board and "required course-related supplies and books." The school can pay for an athlete's incidental expenses up to 15 dollars a month.)

Les Cason, a 6 foot-10 inch high school star in East Rutherford, New Jersey, got the rush act so early and so hard that he announced his choice—Long Beach State, way out in California—*before* his senior season.

"I used to feel funny when I came out of a classroom and there was a scout waiting for me," said Cason. "How could I tell them, 'I'm sorry, but I don't want to play for your school.'"

Even if a prospect publicly announces he is going to School X and signs a "letter of intent," he could end up at School Y when fall rolls around. Few talent hunters will take no for an answer, and many schools, including Long Beach State, don't recognize letters of intent. Nothing is really certain until the athlete shows up at school to enroll.

A good guard prospect named "Poo" Welch told Kansas that he would be ready to sign just as soon as coach Ted Owens got back from coaching in an All-Star Game in Hawaii. When Owens returned he found out that Welch had changed his mind and signed with the University of Houston.

Owens got razzed about it by his fellow coaches, notably Dean Smith of North Carolina, who asked, "Was that trip to Hawaii worth it?"

But Smith had the same misfortune strike him in the most publicized switch of recent years. Tom McMillen, a 6 foot-11 inch A student from Mansfield, Pennsylvania, announced for North Carolina although there had been terrific family pressure on him to go to Maryland, where his older brother had played. Smith was in Europe when news reached him that Tom had changed his mind and was going to Maryland after all. Owens said he didn't have the heart to ask Smith if the trip to Europe was worth it.

Once the highly prized recruits are safely in school, the coach faces another problem. He must change from buddy to taskmaster because a successful team needs discipline and hard work as well as raw talent. It is often difficult for players to accept criticism and punishment from a man who was buying them steak dinners not long before.

The pros rely much less on chance and personal selling in acquiring talent. They hold a draft at the end of each college season, determining the picking order merely by turning the standings upside down and letting the weaklings go first. Balance is the objective. The hope is that a bad team of this year—such as the Cleveland Cavaliers of 1970–71—will become a contender in a few years, and a dominant team, not getting a regular infusion of high-quality rookies, will eventually sink down in the standings. The system doesn't always work because poor clubs sometimes draft as poorly as they play, and the kind of players who can turn a franchise around—the Bill Russells and Lew Alcindors—don't come along every year.

Most of the produce being squeezed and picked over consists of players who have completed their college eligibility, but the pros must also be alert for men in a second category. Sometimes an athlete will sit out a season because of injury, poor grades or some other reason. NCAA rules allow him to stay in school a fifth year and play his senior season, even though his original class has been graduated. But if the pros like him, he is fair game. Both Elgin Baylor of Seattle U. and Walt Frazier of Southern Illinois, for example, skipped their senior seasons and signed pro contracts.

When two leagues are warring, draft rules are about as rigid as Silly Putty. Sometimes a league will conduct a secret early draft by telephone before the college season is over, so its members can get a head start signing up players. Or a league itself can sign a prospect to a contract and later assign him to a team. The ABA's Denver Rockets added a new twist, signing up two "hardship cases," Spencer Haywood of Detroit and Ralph Simpson of Michigan State, each of whom had two years of college competition left. ABA Commissioner Jack Dolph tried to void the Simpson contract, but Ralph sued for the right to play pro ball and won.

Clubs do not just mosey into the draft meeting room clutching lists of the various All-America teams. Each of them has a scout or scouting staff that has been crisscrossing the country seeing Evansville versus Kentucky Wesleyan at Owensboro, Kentucky, one night, Jacksonville versus Florida State at Tallahassee the next. Men like Jerry Krause of the Chicago Bulls and Max Shapiro of the Phoenix Suns live out of suitcases almost the entire college season.

Their job is to evaluate the available talent and help prepare a draft list. They are particularly good at finding potential pros at the underpublicized Negro colleges—Willis Reed of Grambling, Earl (The Pearl) Monroe of Winston-Salem State, Bob Love of Southern U. One of their big problems is the "in-betweener," the forward who is too small to play that position in the pros and might also be too slow to switch to guard, or the small center who might not be able to play forward.

Once a top prospect has been drafted, the pro club still has work to do. Until a merger or the collapse of the ABA—most insiders feel one or the other is inevitable—a club must outbid some team in the rival league that also has its heart and pocket-book set on capturing the prize. Since the ABA came into existence, the prices have escalated rapidly, not only for rookies but also for veterans who have managed to jump from one league to the other. Some of the war profiteers: Zelmo Beaty of the Utah Stars, reportedly getting 650,000 dollars; Dan Issel of the Kentucky Colonels, 1.4 million dollars; and Pete Maravich, Atlanta Hawks, 1.9 million. In each case, of course, the money is spread out over a number of years.

"There's going to be a bunch of rich young men this year," said a top pro scout early in 1971. "This war is so crazy the figures are ridiculous. Now they're talking hundreds of thousands of dollars for kids who five years ago would have signed for 20,000 dollars."

Two men eligible for the '71 draft, seven-footers Artis Gilmore of Jacksonville and Elmore Smith of Kentucky State, each said they were seeking contracts worth two million or more. Such fat packets of money being waved at basketball players have brought agents swarming around college campuses like sharks around a bleeding tuna. Sports attorneys Arthur Morse of Chicago and Robert Woolf of Boston, both of whom hate to be called "agents" and insist they do not solicit business, have been joined by dozens of competitors, including Athletes Advisory Group, Sports Plus, Sportsworld, Sports Management, Sports Headliners, Uni-Managers and Pro Sports.

Their fond hope is to negotiate the initial contract for a first-round draft choice and collect a fee, which ranges from five percent (for some agents) on up to whatever the client will allow (for the greedy). Some are honest and earn their percentage by getting the player a better contract than he could ever have swung himself. ("Boys are very naive and don't have any idea what they're worth," says Norman Blass of Athletes Advisory. "There is a great need for responsible representation," says Bob Woolf.) Others are accused of overcharging or taking money under the table from one league or the other to "deliver" their clients.

If the truth about what has been going on ever comes out, basketball could be hit by another bomb almost as big as the point-shaving scandals of the early 1950s and early 1960s. Agents say that it is not too uncommon for coaches to demand, or at least hint around for, a cut of the player's contract or a cut of the agent's fee. Coaches say agents hound their players until the players can't concentrate on their studies or remaining college games. Dozens of star college seniors have reached agreements with agents before their eligibility is up, violating the NCAA rule which says:

"Any student athlete who agrees or has ever agreed to be represented by an agent or an organization in the marketing of his athletic ability or athletic reputation no longer shall be eligible for intercollegiate athletics."

A school would have to forfeit "any game in which an athlete participated after reaching an agreement." If the violators of the last three or four years were discovered, *hundreds* of games would have to be forfeited.

"Bring up your son to be a basketball player," advises lawyer Robert Woolf, who also negotiates contracts for athletes in football, baseball and ice hockey.

On the average, players in the National Basketball Association are the highest paid men in professional team sports, the plutocrats of the locker room. In 1970 the owners and the players association agreed to a three-year contract which boosted the minimum salary from 13,500 to 15,500 dollars. For the 1972–73 season it will jump to 17,500 dollars. The average salary is probably 35,000 to 45,000 dollars, and on some clubs, notably the New York Knicks, even the sixth and seventh men get that kind of money. A newspaperman covering the Philadelphia 76ers in 1969–70 estimated that the team's player payroll averaged out to 70,000 dollars per man.

For the best players, especially those in the big cities, there are numerous opportunities to make money endorsing products and fronting for businesses. Boston's John Havlicek has endorsed hair cream, L.A.'s Jerry West has his own TV show and has plugged swim suits, New York's Willis Reed has a basketball camp and a restaurant, New York's Walt Frazier has endorsed socks, sweaters and automobiles and L.A.'s Elgin Baylor fronts for a fried-chicken chain.

Prize money is hot fudge topping on the sundae. In 1969–70 the NBA put up 400,000 dollars in extra loot and the Knicks won 118,000 of it, broken up this way: 5,000 for finishing the regular season with the best winning percentage in the league, 20,000 for winning the Eastern Division championship, 20,000 for participating in the division semifinals against Baltimore, 25,000 for winning the division finals and 48,000 dollars for winning the NBA championship.

The amount in the playoff pool grew to 700,000 dollars in 1970–71, so if a team had the best winning percentage in the regular season and then won the playoffs, it would receive 212,000 dollars. Split up evenly among 12 players, the coach and the trainer, that would be more than 15,000 apiece. Just to keep up with inflation, the pot will contain 725,000 dollars in 1971–72 and 750,000 in 1972–73.

At least a few of the players are worth every penny they can wheedle out of the owners. In 1957–58 the Minneapolis Lakers lost 53 of 72 games and, what was worse, dropped more than 100,000 dollars. Robert Short, a Minnesota businessman who had bought the team not long before, desperately needed a star-player drawing card and decided Elgin Baylor of Seattle U. was the man. Baylor had a season of college ball left, but his original class had been graduated. He made a statement on national television that he was going to finish school, but Short thought he could be talked out of it.

"I also knew that Seattle was on the verge of being slapped down by the NCAA for recruiting practices and that the coach might be fired," said Short. ". . . I concluded it was only a question of how high we had to go to get the boy."

They went high enough and, with Elgin as a great rookie in 1958–59, Minneapolis moved 30,000 dollars into the black. Short shipped the team to Los Angeles and acquired Jerry West. Seven years after signing Baylor, he sold the club to Jack Kent Cooke for 5,175,000 dollars.

Even before Oscar Robertson finished his senior season at the University of Cincinnati, everyone in town knew he would be the Cincinnati Royals' territorial draft choice (legal then), and the club's advance ticket sales had increased by 40,000 dollars. Cincy couldn't sign him until after the 1960 Olympics. When it finally did, it paid Oscar 100,000 dollars for his first three years as a pro, plus a percentage of the gate.

Lew Alcindor had the biggest impact on Milwaukee since the arrival of the German brewmasters and the departure of the baseball Braves. The *Wall Street Journal* reported that for the fiscal year ending May 31, 1969, Milwaukee Professional Sports & Services, Inc.—the Bucks to you—lost 371,894 dollars. Milwaukee finished last in its division and another expansion team, Phoenix, was last in the other division. The two new clubs flipped a coin for first draft choice and Bucks owner Wes Pavalon won. He didn't need scouts to tell him to draft Lew.

For the fiscal year ending May 31, 1970, the Bucks increased their attendance 50 percent and made a profit of more than a million dollars.

The basic source of income for clubs is, of course, ticket sales. NBA prices for the best seats range from $8.50 in New York to $5 in Portland and Seattle. Most clubs charge $6. Perches in the rafters cost from $4.50 in New York to $1 in Chicago. In both the NBA and ABA, the home team keeps all gate receipts, the visiting team gets nothing. In each league, six percent of the gate goes to the commissioner's office and is used to pay for such things as the salaries of the commissioner and his staff (assistants, consultants, publicist, secretaries), referees' salaries and expenses, office rental, statistical service and league awards.

Ticket prices are hiked for the playoff games, which often help put a money-losing club into the profit column—or at least siphon off a few gallons of red ink. The Knicks, for instance, upped their premium-ticket prices to $12 for the 1970 playoffs and still jammed the Garden with 19,500 fans for each game. The Garden was scaled for about 140,000 dollars for the playoffs, so the club grossed about 1,540,000 dollars for the 11 games. It is easy to see why the pros ignore the critics' complaint that "it is ridiculous to play a long season of 80 games or so merely to determine which eight teams will get in the playoffs."

Counting both regular-season and playoff games, the ABA in 1969–70 averaged slightly less than 4,000 fans a game, the NBA averaged slightly less than 10,000 a game.

Many of those ticket buyers must pay to park their cars and at some arenas, such as The Forum outside L.A., the club gets all or part of the parking profits. Inside the turnstiles, the club gets a cut of the considerable profits from sales of programs, yearbooks, pennants, hot dogs, ice cream, beer and other things fans put down their gullets or cart home.

Of the other income sources, the most lucrative is radio-TV. In 1970 the NBA signed a three-year contract with ABC worth a reported 17 million dollars. That was a nice, round one million per club. Commissioner Kennedy estimates that the Seattle SuperSonics' local radio-TV contract might be worth as much as 250,000 dollars, and he thinks the Los Angeles Lakers have an even better deal. The Atlanta Hawks in 1969–70 had a network of eighteen radio stations in five states and six TV stations in four states.

The New York Knicks not only have local radio and TV arrangements, but *every* Knick home game is seen on cable television in Manhattan. Kennedy says that cable TV has the potential of being a better source of revenue than gate receipts "by the end of the '70s."

Each time the NBA expands, which it has done four times since 1966–67, the league office ladles out savory gravy to each of the clubs. On the last occasion, the entrance fee for Buffalo, Cleveland and Portland was 3.7 million dollars apiece, which meant that each of the "established" fourteen clubs collected close to 800,000 dollars.

A relatively new revenue producer is NBA Properties, modeled after the highly successful NFL Properties. The idea is to peddle the league imprimatur to various businesses who want an identification with pro basketball. The Licensing Corporation of America runs it for the NBA and the result has been "official" NBA clothes and table games, plus a hookup with a prominent publisher to publish a line of books called the NBA Library.

A pro club's outgo is considerable, too. The ABA, before it opened for business, "made a survey which set the cost of operating a franchise at 650,000 dollars a season without the sale of a single ticket." That cost is considerably higher today. It includes travel (planes, buses, taxis, hotels, meals), player salaries, arena rental (it cost the Indiana

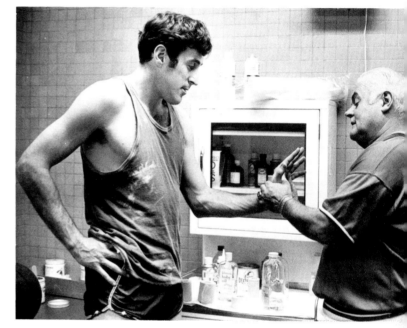

Knick trainer Danny Whelan looks at Mike Riordan's injured left hand. Although not a doctor, Whelan is invaluable to the club. He received a full share of playoff monies.

Pacers 1,350 dollars a game in 1970–71 to rent the 9,147-seat Fairgrounds Coliseum), equipment, promotion and advertising, taxes, insurance and office staff.

The most important man in the office is the general manager, who is just what his title says. His duties might include hiring and firing, promotion, supervising scouts and perhaps scouting himself, searching for a new arena site, making trades (presumably after consulting with the coach) and negotiating contracts (with players, radio-TV, concessionaires, arena owners, coaches). One of the brightest young GMs, or at least one of the fastest moving, is Mike Storen of the ABA's Kentucky Colonels, who was hired away from the Indiana Pacers. In his first two months in Louisville he made four trades, changed the club's logo, uniforms and colors, hired a new staff and announced three-year contracts with local radio and TV stations. Eddie Donovan, now with the Buffalo Braves, deserves part of the credit for the Knicks' title team in 1970 because of his successful trades and draft picks.

The publicist, sometimes sporting the title of "director of public relations" or even "press services director," puts out each season a handy-sized press guide containing all pertinent information about the club including player biographies and records. Often this guide doubles as a yearbook and is sold to the fans. The publicist also churns out press releases and aids writers and broadcasters at each home game, furnishing pre-game notes, half-time and final box scores and a "running"—a score-by-score account of the action hot off the ditto machine after each quarter.

With all the income and outgo, just what is an NBA franchise worth? That depends on the city, the arena and whether or not there is a Lew Alcindor or Jerry West on the squad, among other factors. In 1952 the estimated value of the lowliest NBA club was 50,000 dollars. In 1957 it was 250,000.

As we have already seen, the L.A. Lakers were worth more than five million to Jack Kent Cooke in 1965 and are worth much more today. Yet the San Diego Rockets, a couple of hours' drive down Highway 101, reportedly were on the market in 1969–70 for 4.5 million dollars and had no takers.

Colleges have many of the same income sources and expense headaches as the pros. In most cases schools have their own gyms or arenas and don't have to pay rent. That is balanced somewhat by the fact that they have to let at least some of their students in at reduced rates (usually through some sort of activity-book plan). They don't have to pay hefty salaries, but grants-in-aid account for about a quarter of the expenses.

An NCAA study of 118 large schools showed that in 1969 the cost of the average basketball program was 130,000 dollars—64,000 higher than in 1960. The largest amount any school spent was 257,000 dollars. The average basketball revenue for these 118 schools was 131,000 dollars, which means that in many an athletic department there wasn't much profit from basketball to buy foils for the fencing team or racing shells for the crew.

When the pro basketball training camps open for business early in September—the start of an exhausting season that will last *eight* months for the two playoff finalists—very few players show up out of shape. They have the obvious motive of wanting to be ready to go all out from the first day and impress the coach, but there's more to it than that. Basketball players enjoy playing basketball and tend to keep at it even in the off-season (when many football and baseball players are out on golf courses). If they're in New York, they'll probably play in the outdoor Rucker Tournament in Harlem. In all the big cities—Chicago, Detroit, L.A.—there are gyms or playgrounds where the pros and the best collegians gather to test each other: one-on-

one, halfcourt, fullcourt and shooting contests.

Another factor is the growing number of summer basketball camps. Willis Reed has a highly successful one in upstate New York. Walt Frazier has one in the Berkshires near Pawling, New York. Elvin Hayes conducts clinics at the San Diego camp run by Phoenix Suns' scout Max Shapiro. UCLA coach John Wooden, Jerry West, Richie Guerin, Bob Leonard—the list of camp operators goes on and on. If a pro player doesn't have his own, he can make the rounds as a guest lecturer. And there is time during the day for the pros to work out against each other.

Most clubs conduct a rookie training school (or camp or tryout) during the summer, inviting all their draft picks and anybody else who seems promising. The coach gets an advance look at the rookies, who are under less pressure because they are playing against their peers and not the veterans. The coach can also teach them something and give them a bit of a head start.

Pro clubs usually hold their training camps at a nearby college. The Knicks use the State University of New York at Farmingdale, Long Island. In 1969, for instance, their rookies reported to the Garden for physical examinations September 10 and had their first workout at Farmingdale the next day. Some of the veterans showed up early, too. They had their physicals at the Garden September 14. Picture day was September 15. Photographers, TV cameramen and reporters could pose and interview players all they wanted.

The entire club started two-a-day workouts under Red Holzman on September 16, drilling for an hour and a half in the mornings and two hours in the late afternoons. The Knicks played ten exhibition games in such places as Bangor, Maine; Salem, Virginia, and Grand Rapids, Michigan. The first regular-season game was October 14, less than a month after the veterans had to report.

The established players find the camp and the exhibition games boring, but the coach needs the time to get the teamwork clicking again (if it ever clicked in the first place) and evaluate the rookies under practice and game conditions. Very few rookies survive until opening day, which is not surprising considering that there are only 204 jobs in the NBA (12 per team). Because the big-name All-Americas usually have no-cut contracts, an impressive but unheralded rookie might be cut undeservedly. Perhaps he can catch on with an ABA team or go down to the Eastern League for a year and then try out again the following September.

College teams start workouts in the middle of October, about six weeks before the first games. They usually can't have two sessions a day, so the coach conducts longer practices than he will once the season begins. Six weeks is a long time to go without playing a game and a coach risks having a bored, listless team if he feeds them nothing but a steady diet of drills, drills, drills. The answer is to have a few full-dress scrimmages using officials and perhaps admitting fans.

Wooden of UCLA tries to give each candidate 20 minutes of scrimmage time a day for the first two weeks, in all sorts of combinations. At various times he wants each player to be with a strong group, an average group and a weak group. His managers keep careful statistics, which he uses as a guide for cutting the squad. Very few non-scholarship athletes make the varsity at any major school.

Methods of conducting practices differ widely, but with few exceptions the winning coaches are highly organized disciplinarians. They know that under pressure in games, players will revert to habits they've developed in practice. Most teams do very little fullcourt scrimmaging once the season starts. However, the coach usually will let the non-playing subs work off their frustrations with a 30- or 40-minute scrimmage at the first practice session.

There are a number of gadgets that a coach can use to improve player skills. One of the most popular is the *rebound ring,* which can be quickly locked onto a regular hoop with a thumb screw. It is considerably smaller in diameter, so only a perfect shot will go in. A player stands underneath and time after time leaps up and tips the ball, improving his fingertip control and getting into the habit of making a second, third and fourth effort. Another commonly used gizmo is the *rebound standard,* which can be set at a height just barely within a player's reach at the top of his leap. The ball is either attached to a cord of some type or is sitting on a spring-held rack so that the player not only has to reach it but grip it tightly and yank it down with some strength.

All a coach really needs, though, is a hoop and a ball and a few players who can put the latter in the former a good percentage of the time.

Harv Schmidt, the skinny, crewcut coach at the University of Illinois, is an ardent believer in scouting. If Iowa's center dribbles to his left 51 percent of the time and to his right 49 percent, Harv wants to know. If Purdue's star guard loves to shoot from a certain spot on the floor, parts his hair in the middle and puts ketchup on his French fries, Harv wants to know. He is hungry for every scrap of information he can get on his opponents' patterns, defenses and, if possible, personalities.

"We can't scout enough," he says.

Harv divides up the Big Ten among his staff and expects each man to become an expert on three or four teams, although league rules allow a team to scout an opponent only twice. Harv does not want to be surprised, and if the other team does something new against the Illini, "it damn well better not be smoothly done."

In Schmidt's first year as head coach, Illinois had to play vastly superior Houston, which had Elvin Hayes, Don Chaney and Ken Spain. From the scouting reports, Harv knew that the ball often went to Spain at a high post and Spain then would feed it to Hayes underneath or out on a wing. The Illini played Spain belly button to belly button and made it difficult for him to complete that pass. Hayes was held below his average and Illinois was beaten by only eight points. Houston guards Chaney and George Reynolds were so frustrated by Illinois defensive maneuvers, said Harv, that they had to be taken out of the game.

Usually there are a number of big and little flaws that a sharp scout can see and a sharp coach can exploit. Do most of Duke's plays start with a guard passing to the right forward? North Carolina can try to "influence" the guard to his left as he dribbles upcourt. Are Utah's guards poor ballhandlers? Arizona can work on a fullcourt press.

Most of the time the head coach is too busy to do much scouting himself, so the chore falls to his assistant or assistants. On some staffs, the scouting specialist is on the road looking at other outfits so much that he seldom gets to see his own team.

Another possibility is to use a professional scouting service, perhaps the Mid Atlantic Basketball Scouting Bureau of Parkton, Maryland, or the biggest, Bertka Views of Santa Barbara, California. ("We'll scout 'em—you play 'em—anywhere in the U.S.A.") One disadvantage of the services is that they don't know the *client's* team very well, or, more likely, they don't know it at all. Said Brooks Gracie, owner and sole employee of Mid Atlantic:

"Since most of my reports are for coaches in other parts of the U.S., where I don't get a chance to see the teams, I try to give them just what an opponent likes to do. The coach knows his players and I leave the coaching to him. If I told him to press and he had five slow players, he would get killed. My reports are aids to the coach, but *he* must make the right moves."

Gracie, who scouts only in the Baltimore-Philadelphia-Washington area, charges 30 dollars a report, which is cheap, but he says he usually has two or more schools paying him to cover the same game. Bill Bertka (the same fellow who lists California JC talent) charges between 55 and 65 dollars, depending on expenses. He has "associates" all over the country, many of them ex-coaches. He was a head coach himself for four years at Kent State University but is much happier as a scout.

"I have a family and I have basketball, that's it," he said. "No other hobbies. Scouting and the game have been fascinating things to me. I enjoy it, I get a vicarious pleasure out of analyzing a team. It used to hurt so much to lose. In scouting, you don't have a won-lost record."

One of his boasts is that Kansas State won the Big Eight championship in 1969–70 while using Bertka Views to scout every opponent. Bertka's smart Swedish wife handles most of the paperwork while he does much of the West Coast scouting. Naturally, he has been paid many times to look over UCLA—without it doing the clients much good. The Bruins execute so well, he says, that "other teams can know exactly what they're going to do, yet not be able to do anything about it."

Some coaches, including UCLA's John Wooden, like to have their *own* teams scouted, just as if the reports were for opponents. Bertka will do it, reluctantly. He once was hired to give a coach an extensive critical analysis of his team, but when the coach read it he became furious. He thought Bertka was insulting him.

It would be a waste of time and money for pro teams to scout opponents the way colleges do. What could a scout tell Walt Frazier about stopping Baltimore's Earl Monroe? Frazier has already been cursed with the Monroe assignment dozens of times. There might be an exception—two teams in different divisions that had not played each other for some time and were going to meet in the playoffs.

The visiting team has some extra headaches. Everybody has a theory as to why teams have better records at home than on the road. For the visitors the crowd will be hostile, the shooting backgrounds will be slightly different, the beds at the hotel will be strange—a hundred little things that add up to perhaps a three- or four-point advantage for the home team. A coach's familiar boast is:

"We not only beat them, we beat them at *their* place."

Except for giving up the home-court advantage, travel is not too much of a problem for a college team. Modern transportation makes it possible to zip in and out of a town so quickly that a minimum of classwork is missed. And little whistle-stop college towns such as Starkville, Mississippi, and Fort Collins, Colorado, nowadays have a clean, new motel or two, so that the decaying downtown hotels can be avoided. (Kentucky coach Adolph Rupp recalled that on Southeast Conference road trips in the old days, the Wildcats had to stay in some awful "rat holes." "I used to stay awake all night with a list of the boys' rooms by my bed in case there was a fire," he said.)

A college team usually arrives the day before a game and goes through a light practice at the gym, just loosening up and getting the feel of the place. Often the players will see a movie that night—a shoot-'em-up or war epic is favored by most coaches.

(Players get a little free time on trips, but coaches are very strict about incoming and outgoing phone calls. Gamblers are always on their minds. They remember that from 1947 through 1950, 86 games in New York City and 22 other cities were contaminated by point-shaving or outright dumping, that 32 players at seven schools were involved and 13 fixers were convicted. They remember that another wave of gambling scandals hit in 1961. They know that if they are not careful it could happen to them just as it happened to such fine coaches as Adolph Rupp, Nat Holman, and Clair Bee.)

Travel is far worse in the pros. The clubs bounce around the country each winter, popping in and out of cities, airports, buses, hotels, arenas and time zones until the players don't know Boston from Phoenix except for the sunshine or lack of it. Such travel is seldom broadening.

"It's too much of a rush," said Ken Sears, who used to play for the Knickerbockers. "Why, people back in California ask me what Boston is like and I have to tell them I've never even seen the place in three years. All I know is the road between the airport and the hotel, which is right beside Boston Garden. We fly in, go to bed, get up, play ball and leave. It's like that in almost every city we visit."

"Whenever you get a chance to sleep, you just got to close your eyes and do it," said Oscar Robertson.

"The game itself is the easiest part of the whole NBA season," said Bill Russell. "The traveling and the hours are the toughest part."

The Knicks have to take an extra-long road trip every season when an ice show takes over Madison Square Garden, but the club's most wearying trip of 1969–70 was a western swing.

"We beat Detroit in the Garden by one point Christmas night, then caught a midnight flight to Los Angeles," recalled Walt Frazier. "We arrived at L.A. International Airport at 3:30 A.M. (6:30 New York time). We lost by 12 points that night at The Forum. We were up at 6:45 the next morning for a flight to Vancouver that arrived at 11:15 A.M. That night we beat Seattle by two. We were rousted out of bed at 5:45 A.M. for a six-hour, three-stop flight to Phoenix and beat the Suns that night by nineteen. How, I don't know. We flew home, finishing off a trip of more than 7,000 miles. We changed our name from the Knicks to the Zombies."

Obviously, pro basketball is no place for someone who is afraid of flying. In 1965 the Celtics' Red Auerbach could have drafted either Gus Johnson of Idaho or Bill Green of Colorado State. He had not seen either one play but, to his eternal regret, picked Green. It turned out that Green would not go up in an airplane even if Charles Lindbergh and Billy Mitchell were the copilots. Red bought him a train ticket and sent him home. Gus Johnson became an All-Star.

In 1947 Eddie Gottlieb of the Philadelphia Warriors traded Jerry Rullo to Baltimore because Rullo refused to fly. The Bullets had not traveled by plane much the previous season.

"No sooner had Rullo joined Baltimore when they decided they were going to fly a lot more," said Gottlieb. "So he retired."

Horror stories abound. The Warriors once arrived in Rochester after midnight and found that the hotel had not held their rooms. The management curtained off a section of the lobby and set up five cots, but the rest of the team had to sleep in lobby chairs. Another time they were trying to get to Rochester after a game against the Knicks, and their plane was held on the runway at Newark Airport because of heavy fog. They managed to convince the pilot to let them off the plane, and they hired taxis to drive them all the way upstate.

The nearest pro basketball has come to a tragic airplane accident was in January of 1960. The Minneapolis Lakers lost to the St. Louis Hawks on a Sunday, then boarded a twin-engine DC-3 which was to carry them home. There were 23 people on board, including some children. Forty-five minutes out of St. Louis the plane's electrical system conked out and the cabin became very cold. The pilot and copilot had to lean out the windows to see anything, but that wasn't much help because they were caught in a heavy snowstorm. They had to use a flashlight to read their instrument panel.

"I believe most of the fellows were thinking more of the youngsters aboard than of themselves," said Jim Pollard. "They tried to keep as quiet as possible and not arouse fear."

Elgin Baylor got up and went to the rear of the plane but couldn't fasten the safety belt on a stewardess seat, so he wrapped himself in a blanket and lay down on the floor.

Finally, with ten minutes worth of fuel left, pilot Vernon Ullman landed in a cornfield near Carroll, Iowa.

"I didn't even know when we came down," said Baylor. "It was the smoothest thing you ever felt."

College teams usually have a "training meal" four hours before tipoff. UCLA's John Wooden, a stickler for detail, favors this menu: a ten- to twelve-ounce steak (cooked medium), small baked potato, green vegetable, three pieces of celery (there is probably a student manager in charge of measuring stalks and doling them out), four small slices of melba toast, honey, hot tea and fruit cocktail. Dick Harter of Penn, another detail man, allows some sherbet for dessert. The pros eat whatever and whenever they want.

After the training meal, college players usually take a walk, then get off their feet in their rooms. Wooden goes so far as to insist on a darkened room —no reading or watching television.

Pros and collegians report to their dressing rooms early enough so that 40 minutes to an hour before tipoff they have had their ankles taped and have been otherwise ministered to by the trainer. They're in their uniforms ready to go. The uniform is simple: supporter, pants, jersey, two pairs of sweat socks, shoes and warmup jacket and pants. The coach usually talks to the team for ten minutes, perhaps emphasizing the highlights of the scouting report, quickly going over the defensive assignments and giving the starting lineup. Many coaches use a

A music lover (not a man from outer space), Dick Barnett of the Knicks relaxes in the locker room before a game without disturbing his teammates, who perhaps don't dig.

chalkboard, but Butch van Breda Kolff of the Detroit Pistons says, "The only time I use chalk is to throw it at somebody."

Warmup procedures differ greatly from team to team. Jacksonville's players make up their own razzle-dazzle routine, and Niagara let Calvin Murphy put on a pre-game Globetrotter show. UCLA and Kentucky, as might be expected, are all business. Penn's players take turns standing near midcourt watching the other team go through its drills, but Walt Frazier of the Knicks thinks it is better not to even acknowledge the other team's presence.

"As soon as the tipoff comes, I'll see more than enough of them," he says.

Looking down on the court from up in the stands, fans think players such as Mike Riordan of the Knicks, Freddy Crawford of the Bucks and Dick Van Arsdale of the Suns look smaller than their 6 feet 4 inches. This is because of perspective and the players' proximity to so many men 6 feet 7 inches and up. However, the fan can't always rely on his program for accurate measurements either. The "official" listed heights of basketball players are almost as unreliable as listed weights in football. For various motives, players, coaches and publicists sometimes like to add on or chop off a fraction or even an inch in a silly attempt to fool the opposition or the public. Oklahoma A&M only fibbed a little about the altitude of All-America Bob Kurland.

"Actually I'm as close to 7 feet as 98 cents is to a dollar," said Kurland later. "The school 'stretched' me a little because the idea of a 7-foot basketball player caught the fans' imagination. They probably sold a few more tickets that way."

Bill Russell was stretched slightly, too.

"When I first came to college I was 6 feet 7 inches, and that year I grew an inch to 6 feet 8 inches," he said. "The next year I grew another inch to 6 feet 9 inches. For my junior year I grew only

ABOVE: Clyde Frazier, like many of today's pros, spends coin on the latest in clothes. RIGHT: A common added source of income is the basketball camp.

half an inch, but the publicity department just assumed I'd keep going up a full inch at a time and sent out 6 feet 10 inches—and that's what it's been listed as ever since."

Jerry Lucas was "very carefully measured at 6 feet 9½ inches in high school," according to a 1960 issue of *Sport,* but either the measurer was misreading the yardstick or Jerry has shrunk, because he has been listed at 6 feet 8 inches through his college and pro careers. Elgin Baylor shrank an inch after going

from college to the pros. Westley Unseld of Baltimore wasn't hurt so badly. He lost only half an inch.

Players, of course, are not the only people needed to put on a game. In fact, there are critics who charge that players are not even the most important people, that the referees have taken over. In college ball there is a referee and an umpire. The ref is the boss. He is in charge of making sure that the court is playable, the backboard is secure, the basket is ten feet from the floor. He tosses the ball

up to start each half. During the game, there is no difference between the ref and the umpire. The Big Ten has experimented with three referees, but the idea has not spread.

A basketball referee's job is one of the least enviable in the world, roughly comparable to being mayor of New York City or selling shoes to ladies. He can't please everyone and seldom pleases anyone. The game is ten large men moving quickly in a confined space. Sometimes it seems that all ten want to be in the same spot—underneath the hoop—at the same moment. While the crowd, the coaches and sometimes the players scream at him, the referee has to make difficult instant judgments: Was it charging or blocking? Was the man hacked just as he shot or a half-second after?

Some of the coaches' histrionics are just gamesmanship, but they do have some legitimate gripes. Most college referees are not full-time professional officials, and coaches resent it when a part-time worker can seriously affect games for which teams have prepared so diligently. Suggestions for improved officiating have included hiring three refs, hiring National Football League officials (many of whom have had basketball experience) and dividing the court so that a ref could not call fouls at the other guy's end.

The "homer" referee is another problem. Even the most purely impartial officials cannot avoid being influenced by a howling home crowd. At many schools, "split crews" are the answer. If Penn plays at Ohio State, one of the refs will be from the East. Coach Harv Schmidt of Illinois doesn't care for that system because it sometimes turns into "better competition than the game itself." He suggests that when, for instance, Stanford visits Michigan, two Pacific Coast refs work the game and vice versa.

"Let them try to homer you in your place," says Schmidt.

At the end of every season Big Ten coaches rate the referees for the commissioner's office. The scale is one to seven, seven being incompetent. One season Ralph Miller, then at Iowa, gave every ref in the league a seven. The NBA used to have a similar system under Commissioner Maurice Podoloff in which coaches rated the refs after every game—that is, until Boston's Red Auerbach found out that the men in striped shirts had access to the rating cards. He told Podoloff that he would not fill them out anymore. Podoloff said he would be fined five dollars for each game he didn't comply.

So wily Red instructed his secretary to fill out the cards for him and give every referee the top grade for every game. That ended the ratings.

The NBA's supervisor of officials is John Nucatola, a college referee for 25 years and an NBA ref for seven. He operates with a 20-man crew with, as elder statesman, Mendy Rudolph from Wilkes-Barre, Pennsylvania. Rudolph followed his dad and started refereeing in the Eastern League, was hired by the NBA in 1953 and has worked every championship playoff series since.

Pay for an NBA ref ranges from 10,000 to 25,000 dollars a year, plus playoffs. The league claims its pension plan for officials is the "most elaborate" of any pro sports organization.

Nucatola succeeded Dolph Schayes as supervisor, which is ironic because it was a play involving Schayes years before that led, in part, to Nucatola's leaving the NBA and blasting it in a national magazine.

In the mid-1950s Nucatola was officiating in a game at Syracuse, where Nationals' owner Danny Biasone sat on the bench under the pretext of being an assistant coach. John called a charge on Schayes with four seconds left and Biasone and coach Al Cervi rushed onto the court after him. The fans grabbed whatever objects were handy and used the striped shirts for target practice. There were four delays before Nat (Sweetwater) Clifton of the Knicks took his foul shot. Nucatola and his partner were mobbed by the fans after the game, had to take refuge in the Knicks' dressing room and were sneaked through a back door and out of town by a police detective.

Nucatola recommended that Cervi and Biasone be fined a thousand dollars each, but, according to him, Commissioner Podoloff didn't so much as reprimand the club.

Nucatola complained out loud, stopped getting assignments and quit, subsequently writing an article for *Sport* accusing the league of "rowdyism." He charged that the owners were influenced by "petty politics, suspicion, animosity and the belief that the fast buck is the best one."

"It hurt this league tremendously when it lost Nucatola," said Bob Cousy. "John is the personification of everything a referee is supposed to be. In character, in judgment and integrity."

Since Commissioner Walter Kennedy hired him back, Nucatola has been busy with a recruiting program. About 90 men applied for positions as NBA officials for the 1970–71 season, and 45 were invited to three rookie camps. The best eight worked some exhibition games and only three were hired.

In running the game the referee is helped by a scorer, timer and, in the pros, a man who operates the 24- or 30-second clock (24 in the NBA, 30 in the ABA). The scorer records the names and numbers of all players and keeps track of field goals, free throws, fouls and time-outs. His job is pretty cut and dried except for "assists," which are passes that lead directly to baskets. (Some college scorers keep track of assists, but the NCAA's statistical service does not. It is generally a pro category.)

The distinction between an assist and a plain old pass is not always clear. If Seattle's Lennie Wilkens flips a clever pass to Tom Meschery, and Meschery makes a basket, Wilkens gets an assist. If Wilkens hits Meschery and Tom maneuvers on his own to get free and score, there is no assist. The trouble comes on all the kinds of plays in between. Assists have become an important part of the stats in pro ball, especially to the playmaking guards who can't brag about their points or rebounds at contract time. Nearly every one of the playmakers feels that when he's away from his home arena he doesn't get a fair shake from the scorers. It is similar to the situation in baseball, where batters and fielders want every batted ball to be a hit and pitchers want every batted ball to be an error. The official scorer in the press box must make the decision, bear the gripes.

The college timer keeps track of two 20-minute halves and the 15-minute half time, starting and stopping the scoreboard clock at the referee's signal or on all violations. He keeps a spare clock and/or stopwatch at the table in case something goes haywire with the scoreboard. The pros have twelve-minute quarters, 90 seconds between quarters and a 15-minute half time. The greatest pressure on a timer comes at the end of a close game. The team behind wants the clock to crawl, the team ahead wants it to sprint. The timer cannot please both and, of course, shouldn't try to please either. He should sound the buzzer when time has elapsed regardless of who is leading or trailing or who is about to take a shot.

One of the well-known clock controversies came in the fourth game of the NBA's 1965 Eastern Division playoffs. Boston led by two points with one second left on the clock. Philadelphia had possession out of bounds, Red Auerbach recalled, and the ball was thrown in to Hal Greer, "35 feet away and with his back to the basket." Auerbach said Greer took a step, made a full turn and took a jump shot. It went in.

"Now that happens to be impossible to do in one second," complained Red.

Nevertheless, the basket counted, the game went into overtime and Philly won.

The man operating the 24- or 30-second clock starts it when a team gets possession of the ball. If the offensive team does not attempt a shot within the time limit, it loses possession. The referee has the right to order the clock reset "to cover any special situation that he thinks warrants such action," according to the NBA rules. Each 24-second clock in use at Madison Square Garden is manufactured by General Indicator Corp. and costs about 670 dollars.

The home team supplies the game ball, and even this can lead to controversy. Each year Notre Dame plays Kentucky in Louisville's Freedom Hall before a big crowd. In December of 1970, Notre Dame coach Johnny Dee complained loudly and at length before the game about the ball provided by Kentucky, which carried the signature, "Adolph F. Rupp." Rupp insisted it was a Spalding ball of exactly the same type used in South Bend, but Dee would not accept it. Before the arguing was over the Kentucky athletic director and both referees were involved.

The refs finally decided to go ahead and use the Rupp signature model. Not long afterward a different ball mysteriously appeared at the scorer's table.

"That's Notre Dame's ball and I'm not playing with it," said referee Ben Dunn. "Get it out of the way."

"During warmup, my kids told me they thought the Rupp ball was a bit lighter than the one we usually use," said Dee. "Oh, there probably wasn't much difference, but this is a sensitive game, the shooting aspects of it, and you want everything to be just right.

"This is supposed to be a neutral court and we are co-hosts. I told Kentucky that if they were determined to use that ball they should send us four or five to practice with, and they refused."

Anyway, Notre Dame's players were stirred up

(which was probably Dee's idea in raising the fuss) and won the game 99–92.

Half time's main purpose is to provide a period of rest. The players sit around and perhaps suck on oranges and think about what they must do in the second half. The coach takes advantage of the time to correct mistakes and introduce any new strategy he might have for the rest of the game. If the team has played poorly, he might choose this time to stomp and swear and threaten. If the game is close, he might try a Knute Rockne pep talk. Outside the dressing rooms, the concessionaires take advantage of the hiatus to sell food and drink as fast as they can. TV and radio squeeze in interviews between the commercials.

After the game the players go directly to their dressing rooms. Some take their showers and get dressed right away. Others, like Dave DeBusschere of the Knicks, prefer to sit down, lean back and relax. They gulp down beer or soft drinks, answer reporters' questions and look over the final box score. It might be 20 or 30 minutes before they have unwound enough to stand up and take off their sweaty uniforms.

In the losing team's locker room, the dejected coach is likely to be telling the press how the referees "jobbed" him and how so-and-so on the opposing team was "drawing blood" without getting a foul called. In the winner's locker room there is good-natured kidding and horseplay. The Knicks used to have a ceremony to honor the player who made the worst shot of the night, perhaps an "airball" or "brick" that missed everything—rim, backboard, the works. The prize was known as the Scumball Award. The Detroit Pistons improved on the idea with their Silver Brick Award (a brick wrapped in tinfoil).

It was one of the few awards in sports the recipient would not accept willingly.

Chapter Seven / Olympics

Strike up the band

A barefooted palace guard from Ethiopia might win the marathon, the Pakistanis dominate field hockey and the Soviet Union even score highest in track and field, but no country represented at the Mexico City Olympics in 1968 was going to beat the good old U.S.A. at its own game, basketball. That was the common opinion in America a year or so before the Olympic torch was lighted. There was good reason for this cockiness: the U.S. had won every gold medal in the six Olympics that had included the sport. In individual games the won-lost record was the U.S. 46, the rest of the world 0.

The Olympics is supposed to be a gathering of the best athletes on earth, upholding the ideals of sportsmanship and international goodwill while competing against each other for the sheer amateur thrill of it. In truth, of course, it is also a giant political arena (with embarrassing instances of drug abuse, commercialism and sex-test flunkouts). Whether Olympic officials like it or not, *countries* as well as athletes are competing. There is a pervasive feeling of nationalism, heightened each time a champion steps up on the winners' stand and gets chill bumps while his national anthem is played. The American public never gets tired of hearing "The Star-Spangled Banner" at such moments.

However, the U.S. began to lose confidence about basketball as the '68 Olympiad drew nearer. A teacher at San Jose State, Harry Edwards, was agitating for a black boycott of the Games, and at least two meetings of black athletes were held. Since Negroes dominate basketball, boxing and track and field in the U.S., a boycott's potential for lowering the precious medal count was obvious.

An outright boycott never materialized, but, for one reason or another—some of them awfully weak —a courtload of black and white basketball players turned down invitations to the tryout camp in Albuquerque. Lew Alcindor said he was going to stay at UCLA and study so he could be graduated

with his class. Bob Lanier of St. Bonaventure and Neal Walk of Florida also said schoolwork came first. North Carolina's Larry Miller had a groin injury. Elvin Hayes of Houston had signed a fat pro contract, saying, "I owe it to my family. Now—not a year from now after the Olympics." Westley Unseld of Louisville and Don May of Dayton were too tired. And so on, with Bill Hewitt of USC, Mike Warren and Lucius Allen of UCLA and even a California junior-college player, Sidney Wicks (later an All-America at UCLA).

Some people reacted to this as if Alcindor and his fellows had spat on Plymouth Rock. U.S. coach Henry Iba of Oklahoma State labeled the tryout spurners as "bad citizens." Lew received hate mail from self-anointed patriots who perhaps did not know—or care—that he spent part of the Olympic summer working with Operation Sports Rescue in the black slums of New York City.

Still, Iba and his aides managed to find 48 men willing to show up for the camp, and the candidates included some excellent black players. Calvin Murphy of Niagara (who didn't make the team), Charles Scott of North Carolina and Joseph (Jo Jo) White of Kansas were the best known.

"I make up my own mind," said White, "and I've decided to play. I don't care if I'm the only one. They can go ahead and boycott. I'm playing."

"I don't think the Negroes playing for us will be bothered by the boycott," said Iba. "The last Olympics I had five Negroes on the basketball team and they all did well."

Three of the men selected to wear America's colors in Mexico City's copper-roofed Sports Palace were obvious choices, or at least well known: White, Scott and 6 foot-7½ inch Wilmer (Bill) Hosket Jr. of Ohio State, whose father also had been a basketball player for the Buckeyes. The rest were relative unknowns: 6 foot-9 inch Ken Spain of Houston, no match for Elvin Hayes; Calvin

Stepping high after a basket, Yugoslavia's Trajko Rajkovic
helps his team beat Senegal 40–33 in Mexico City Olympiad.
The United States has won every basketball gold medal.

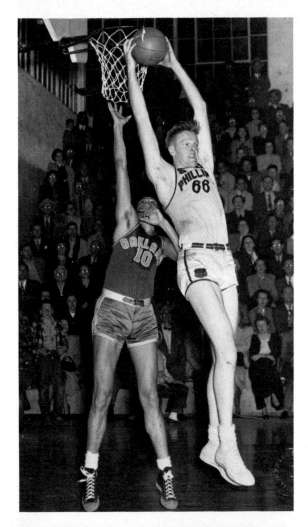

RIGHT: Easily outjumping a Russian rival, Bill Russell has an easy time of it as the United States beats the USSR 89–55 in the final Olympic game in Melbourne in 1956.

Fowler, an AAU standout for the Akron Goodyears; John Clawson and 6 foot-6 inch Mike Silliman of the U.S. Army; Mike Barrett of West Virginia Tech and the U.S. Navy, and two players from small colleges not recognized by the NCAA, Don Dee of St. Mary's of the Plains and Glynn Saulders of Northeast Louisiana State.

The *best* choice, as it turned out, was 6 foot-8 inch Spencer Haywood, only 19 years old. Haywood, called "The Claw" because "I've got four joints on my fingers," was a junior-college center in Colorado and pretty much known only to college talent scouts. His route to Mexico City was a circuitous one, typical of black players. Just as Bill Russell had moved from Louisiana to Detroit to San Francisco as a boy and Oscar Robertson had gone from Tennessee to Indianapolis, Haywood went from Mississippi to Detroit. He was a star at Pershing High School and led the Doughboys to the state championship his senior year. While most of his schoolmates stayed trapped in the Detroit ghetto, Haywood had basketball as a means of escape. His grades were not good, so his next stop was the JC out west, supposedly a stepping stone to the University of New Mexico. It led to the University of Detroit instead—after the Olympics.

"I wake up in the morning thinking Olympics, I dream Olympics, I write to my mother about the Olympics," said Haywood.

The pessimism grew, however. A U.S. all-star team toured Yugoslavia, the Soviet Union and Finland in the summer and was beaten four times in six games. Iba's assistant, Harry Vaughan, had a scary scouting report on the Russians, pointing out their 7-foot center, their 6 foot-8 inch and 6 foot-9 inch forwards and their familiarity with international rules. He said they "now have 12 solid players as against eight" in Tokyo four years before.

"Height isn't the whole of our problem," said Iba. "It's more than that. There's got to be some

TOP: Twice an Olympic hero for the U.S., AAU star Bob Kurland pulls down rebound versus Oakland Bittners. ABOVE: Kurland (left) and four Phillips mates played in Olympics.

kind of definite ruling on how long an Olympic team can be held together. The Russians, Yugoslavs and some of the others have been together for years, while our boys have played as a unit for only a few weeks.

"And another thing, America has been sending coaches, clinics and films abroad for over a decade. They've used our knowledge to build solid basketball programs. It's only natural they're catching up to us.

"We've done so well we think we can beat anybody on the block. We've got to get this out of our system—not just in basketball but in all sports."

There was dissatisfaction with Iba in some people's minds. Even some of his ex-players felt the sport had passed him by. Yes, his Oklahoma State Aggies had won back-to-back national championships in the mid-1940s, but in the last three seasons, 1965–66 through 1967–68, his college coaching record was 21 and 55. His defenders said the only thing that had passed him by was good material. And that went for this Olympic team, too.

The first good indication that the Olympians were better than expected came in Madison Square Garden when the New York Knickerbockers played an exhibition game against them. The Knicks had some handicaps. The game was only their second and it was played under international rules: 30-second clock, yellow ball made in Japan and strange, fan-shaped foul lanes, wide at the base line and narrowing at the free-throw line. Iba's team had

197

been in training at Adams State College in Alamosa, Colorado, to simulate the lung-straining, high-altitude conditions in Mexico City.

The exhibition game, watched by 10,029 fans, was extremely close. Mike Silliman, used to playing in the Garden from his college days at West Point, made a lay-up with 21 seconds to go to tie the score 56–56. In overtime Mike Barrett won the game for the amateurs with a set shot from the corner with 37 seconds left. Final score: 65–64. Teen-ager Haywood, said The New York Times, showed "poise, jumping ability and second-effort desire." He scored 17 points; Silliman had 12 and Jo Jo White 10.

When it was time to catch the plane for Mexico, Iba had his men ready. He had used the little time allowed him—he was famous for his discipline—to put together a running, hustling team with just enough of an inferiority complex to make it eager to prove itself. The U.S. had weak opposition the first three games in the Sports Palace, a modern arena near the airport. It started off beating Spain 81–46, with Haywood the dominant factor on both ends of the court.

"The game went about the way we thought it would," said Iba. "We have the fewest number of NCAA major-college players we have ever had. These small-college players make some errors, but all in all it was a good ball game for us."

Jo Jo White rested through most of the second no-contest, a waltz over Senegal. Haywood had 16 points and monopolized both backboards. In the 96–75 win over the Philippines, the first team saw little action in the second half. (The college no-dunk rule, put in because of Alcindor, was not in effect at the Olympics. Haywood often leaped up and stuffed the ball down through the hoop to "psych out" the opposition.)

The fourth game was surely going to be more challenging. Yugoslavia had beaten the U.S. touring team and was one of the favorites in the Olympic tournament. But in the first 11 minutes of the second half, the U.S. outscored the opponents 17–4 and ran away with a 73–58 victory. White scored 24 points, mostly on accurate outside shooting.

Panama fell 95–60 and Davis Peralta, the leading scorer in the tourney up to that time, was held to six points. Italy was massacred 100–61, Puerto Rico (coached by Lou Rossini of New York U.) did well but lost 61–56. Brazil was beaten in a tough game 75–63 before a crowd of 22,000. The Mexicans considered basketball one of the biggest attractions of the Games and seemed knowledgeable about the sport. They hissed rather than booed, but at least they hissed at the proper moments.

"This club has come a long way in a short time," said Iba after the Brazil victory. "They've got a lot of pride. If they didn't, we might have been out of this a long time ago." He said Haywood was potentially "the best basketball player ever."

Surprisingly, the opponent in the final was not the USSR. Yugoslavia had won a 63–62 thriller over the Russians to earn a rematch, which worried Iba. (With the championship at stake, he probably would have been worried about a team of Pygmies.)

"It's dangerous playing the same team twice," he said, "because they will come at us with so many changes."

"Coach Iba is the biggest asset we have," said Captain Silliman. "I don't think he'll let us lose."

He didn't. The Yugoslavs got off to an 11–6 lead and, to the delight of the underdog-loving Mexicans, trailed by only 32–29 at half time. But Iba made a few adjustments. At the start of the second half the U.S. guards picked up their Yugoslav counterparts at the halfcourt line and hounded them. The U.S. scored seventeen straight points in the first eight minutes and it was all over but the anthem playing. The U.S. won 65–50 and—even with Lew, Elvin and the rest at home watching—stretched its undefeated Olympic string to 55.

"They have the best defensive team we have ever seen," said losing coach Ranko Zeravica. "All of their five players are engaged in defense at each moment. We tried to slow down the game, but they came out in the second half and were too fast for us. . . . Spencer Haywood is the best amateur player in the world."

"Because everyone scorned us and downgraded us," said Spencer, "we just worked harder."

Henry Iba went back to Stillwater, Oklahoma, to begin his 35th year as a college coach.

The man most responsible for getting basketball into the Olympics was Forrest (Phog) Allen, who coached at Kansas for more than 38 years. Over the objections of AAU officials, with whom he had various feuds over the years, Phog pushed hard for the idea. As early as April of 1928, just before the Amsterdam Olympics, basketball was proposed as the "international demonstration sport" and turned down. Lacrosse was picked instead. It's hard to understand what the Olympic officials saw in the old Indian game of lacrosse, but it was picked over basketball again before the 1932 Games at Los Angeles.

Allen and others kept arguing and writing letters and finally got their message across. In October of 1934, Herr Fritz Sieweke of Germany informed them that the organizing committee had adopted a resolution to have basketball included in the 1936 Berlin Olympics. Not as a demonstration sport, but on the regular calendar!

Allen then had another bright idea: send Dr. James Naismith over to Germany to see the Olympic debut of the game he invented. This campaign succeeded, too, with the National Association of Basketball Coaches picking up most of the tab. Unfortunately Naismith was almost turned away at the gates.

"Dr. Naismith arrived in Germany without even a pass to see a game," charged Jim Tobin, a New York basketball official. "We managed to get him a pass for all games, but it was not through the American Olympic Committee's efforts. He was ignored and his name stricken from the pass list."

Everything turned out nicely, though. Naismith was honored at a ceremony in the Hall of German Sports and threw up the ball for the first game, between Estonia and France.

The U.S. team was made up of 13 AAU players —seven from Universal Pictures Corp. in Hollywood, six from the Globe Oil & Refining Co. of McPherson, Kansas, and one from the University of Washington. Universal placed the most players because it won a pre-Olympics tournament in Madison Square Garden in April. The Universal team included Frank Lubin, an AAU star for many years, and Sam Balter, an ex-UCLA player who later became a well-known broadcaster and sports columnist on the West Coast. The head coach was James Needles of Universal.

By 1936 the passionately anti-Semitic Nazis already had risen to power in Germany. The Jewish press in the U.S. tried to convince Jewish athletes not to participate, but Balter and some others went anyway.

"I was the first Jewish athlete selected for the Games and I was very conscious of being Jewish and going to Berlin," Sam recalled. "When we arrived we were driven through the streets in open-air buses and were greeted by several million Germans. Then we stopped at city hall, where Göring was to speak. The first sound I remember hearing was a rat-a-tat-tat and I actually thought it was a machine gun. It turned out that it was only the band striking up."

The basketball games were held on outdoor dirt courts, but that didn't seem to bother the Americans. They won the first game by forfeit when Spain's players had to leave the Olympic Village

and go home to fight in the Spanish Civil War. Then the U.S. raced through Estonia, the Philippines and Mexico.

It poured during the final against Canada, making the court more suitable for water polo. There was no dribbling because the ball would only splash, not bounce. There were no spectators except those who watched from their parked cars. The U.S. sloshed to victory over Canada.

"The final score was 19–8," said Balter, "so you can imagine what a travesty the whole thing was."

World War II interrupted the Olympics sequence—and much else—but when the Games resumed in 1948 in London, basketball was still on the agenda. The U.S. squad was again determined by a tournament in New York. The finalists were Kentucky's Fabulous Five—Alex Groza, Ralph Beard, Cliff Barker, Wah Wah Jones and Kenny Rollins—and the Phillips 66ers (or Oilers) of Bartlesville, Oklahoma, one the NCAA champion, one the AAU champion.

Phillips, year in and year out the top company-sponsored team in the nation, featured Oklahoma A&M's great seven-footer, Bob Kurland. A-student Kurland had passed up the pros for a basketball-business career in Bartlesville and that made lots of people suspicious of the team's amateur standing.

"We have investigated this situation from every angle and we have found nothing wrong," said a high AAU official. "It is our conviction, supported by long observation, that, although the Phillips Oilers players get their jobs solely because of their basketball-playing ability, they have to make good on the job, as well as on the team, to be retained." (Actually, Kentucky's amateurism deserved more scrutiny than the Oilers'.)

But it was ostensibly as pure amateurs that the 66ers and Wildcats met in the Garden. Phillips won 53–49 and Kurland, with advantages of height and experience over Groza, scored 20 points and held Alex to one field goal and two free throws. Omar (Bud) Browning of the 66ers thus became Olympic head coach and Kentucky's Adolph Rupp was named assistant, not an easy role for the egotistical Baron. All five Phillips starters were chosen, along with all five Kentucky starters. Four players from other tournament teams were added.

LEFT: Opening ceremony of the Olympic Games in Germany, 1936. This was the first Olympiad that included Naismith's game. BELOW: Brazil and U.S. players battle in Rome, 1960.

The U.S. had only one difficult game in London's Harrington Arena, a 59–57 squeaker over Argentina that was punctuated by two bitter arguments with the referees and many lead changes. America finally took the lead for keeps with just three minutes left. After that close call, Browning and Rupp used the Phillips and Kentucky units intact and marched through Egypt, Peru, Uruguay, Mexico and France. Groza scored 76 points in the eight games, Kurland 65.

Kurland was back again for the Helsinki Olympiad in 1952, which was spiced by the participation of the Soviet Union for the first time. The Russians lifted the Iron Curtain just enough to let a strong group of athletes travel next door to Finland. That was also the year Bing Crosby and Bob Hope teamed up for a telethon to raise money for the U.S. Olympic team.

Politics and bad sportsmanship abounded. When Red China accepted a spot on the roster of participating nations, Nationalist China withdrew. Then Red China arrived too late to participate. The U.S. and USSR engaged in a silly propaganda battle concerning athletic and ideologic superiority. And the Uruguayans topped them all with an abrupt breach of the peace.

Vincent Farrell of Newark, New Jersey, was refereeing a close game between the South Americans and France when he called a foul on a Uruguayan player. This offended Wilfredo Palaez so much that he slugged Farrell in the eye. Another player choked him from behind and a third kicked him when he was lying on the floor.

"The Uruguayans just got a bit too emotional, I guess," said Farrell. "I worked ten other games in the tournament and had no difficulty. Their coach apologized profusely after the attack and I was visited in the hospital by players from Brazil, Argentina, Cuba, France and several other countries."

The U.S. team, consisting mostly of players

from the Peoria Caterpillars AAU team and the NCAA-champion Kansas Jayhawks, was coached by John Warren Womble of Peoria, assisted by Phog Allen of Kansas. The Yanks had the usual easy time of it, beating Hungary, Czechoslovakia, Uruguay, USSR, Chile, Brazil and Argentina before reaching the championship game, a rematch with the Soviets.

Despite the Soviet strategy of slowing down the game to a crawl, the U.S. overcame a 17–15 half-time deficit and won 36–25. Clyde Lovellette of Kansas, a 6 foot-9 inch scoring machine, had a grand total of nine points. Kurland had eight. There were no ugly incidents, even after Lovellette fell on the USSR's 6 foot-8 inch Otar Korkiia while chasing after a loose ball. Otar and his teammates did surprisingly well in their first Olympiad.

"Wait and see," said Kurland. "In the next Olympics, Russia will have some outside shooters developed. They catch on quick."

At the end of the 16 days of competition, the U.S.A. had outpointed the Soviets 610–553½ and it was a happy American team that marched through the Marathon Gate into the stadium for the closing ceremonies. The Uruguayans, not mad at anyone by this time, were crying over the beauty of it all. Kurland had the honor of carrying the U.S. flag and getting his face smeared with lipstick by his proud wife, Barbara. It made an exciting end to his basketball career.

"I retired not because I was getting slower," he said later, "but because the kids coming up were getting faster."

One of the quick kids who came up in time for the 1956 Olympics in Melbourne was 6 foot-9 inch Bill Russell, who had just led the University of San Francisco to two straight NCAA championships. Bill could have gone to Australia as a high jumper as well as a basketball player. He finished ahead of Phil Reavis and Val Wilson in the Olympic trials but dropped out so they both could make the trip.

As usual, the U.S. basketball team had some Phillips 66ers—four of them, plus coach Gerald Tucker—in addition to Russell, K. C. Jones and Carl Crain from the college All-Stars, Dick Boushka of the AAU Buchan Bakers and four Armed Forces players. Russell might well have been enough by himself.

"We began practice on October 4," said Tucker. "From the beginning we knew everybody was a great shot, but we had to learn our defense. We didn't want to lose a game—ever. We figured if our defense was good it would take care of us when our offense was off. So right from the start we worked on that fullcourt press. It really paid off."

The U.S. beat Japan, Thailand, the Philippines, Bulgaria, Brazil, Uruguay and the USSR twice. The Melbourne Olympics was held not long after the Soviet Union invaded Hungary and suppressed a revolt, so the Soviets were the chief villains at the Games. The U.S. won the first meeting 85–55. The Russians were beaten almost before the tipoff. Along with everyone else in the place, they watched the Americans warm up and roared when Russell did some unofficial high jumping and stuffed the ball.

The second game, for the championship, was held before a standing-room-only crowd of 4,000 and the U.S. won 89–55. The Soviets were booed when they refused to step up the pace even when far behind. Their 7 foot-4 inch Jan Kruminsh (really closer to 7 feet 2 inches according to Russell) moved around less gracefully than a Red Army tank. He was taken out whenever Russell came in and he made no field goals in the game.

Russell called the victory his "proudest moment"—but not because the Russians had been embarrassed.

"It was pretty hard to hate the Russians," he said. "I couldn't talk to them on account of the language barrier, but I didn't find them obnoxious.

FAR LEFT: Jerry West and Oscar Robertson (middle) display their gold medals after victory in Rome. LEFT: Walt Hazzard (10) and Bill Bradley (5) fight for loose ball in 1964 Olympiad in Tokyo. U.S.A. beat Australia 78–45. ABOVE: Coach Henry Iba keeps coming back to Olympics with winners.

Maybe they were under instructions to make themselves agreeable. In any event, they smiled all over the place, and sort of nodded apologies whenever one of their boys fouled one of ours.

"The man who was covering me was taller than the others, but nowhere nearly as tall as I. He seemed sort of awed by my height. Between periods and at time-outs he kept looking at me, grinning and making measuring motions with his arms."

"This team is as good as any ever assembled," exaggerated coach Tucker, who was even more euphoric than Russell. ". . . They would be equal to any team in any league anywhere."

He should have seen the 1960 team that coach Pete Newell took to Rome: Oscar Robertson of Cincinnati, Jerry West of West Virginia, Darrall Imhoff of California, Bob Boozer of Kansas State, Walt Bellamy of Indiana, Jay Arnette of Texas, Adrian Smith of Kentucky and a pair of youngsters who still had two years of eligibility remaining in the Big Ten, Jerry Lucas of Ohio State and Terry Dischinger of Purdue.

Dischinger was the youngest man ever to represent the country in Olympic basketball. After a three-day tournament at the Denver Coliseum (the college All-Stars won), the selection committee met in an all-night session to pick the squad. Terry waited in the hotel lobby until his good news came at 4 A.M., then rushed to telephone his family in Terre Haute, Indiana. The committee made a wise choice—he finished third in scoring, behind Robertson and West.

Lucas, eight months older than Dischinger, started out as the fourth-string center behind Bellamy, Imhoff and Burdie Haldorson. He eventually fought his way up to the first team and made 84 percent of his shots in the Games.

"I never worked harder in my life," he said. "I knew if I was going to get to play I'd have to work and work, so I pushed myself harder than ever. The result was that when the Games in Rome began I was in the best shape of my life."

"Lucas is a marvel," said Newell.

The whole team was marvelous—or else the other teams were atrocious. Probably both. The U.S. won eight straight games by margins ranging from 62 points down to 24 (over the Soviet Union). The championship game was held the night of Ethiopian Abebe Bikila's barefooted victory in the marathon. The U.S. beat Brazil 90–63 for its fifth gold medal in basketball.

"We averaged over 100 points," said Newell afterward. "In only two of the eight games we played in Rome did we score less. And we played the entire squad of 12 in every contest. Had we been pressed we'd have gone with only six or seven of our best.

"The Russians are improving, but one thing they haven't acquired is the individuality of our American boys. They're not allowed to express themselves on the court. Conforming to regimentation, they haven't developed initiative. They go into a game with a set plan and stay with it. Our boys had a basic pattern, but we allowed them to deviate from it to exploit an opponent's weakness as it developed during a game."

However, things didn't go perfectly for Pete in every game. There was a Swiss referee, for instance, who seemed too quick in calling three-second violations (too long in the key). The ref didn't understand English and Pete was beside himself trying to convey his displeasure. He repeatedly pointed at his wristwatch and brought his finger down three times, but he wasn't getting through.

Hoping the Swiss spoke Italian, Pete went to an interpreter and learned quickly how to count three seconds in that language, "One thousand, one thousand and two, one thousand and three." Then he marched up to the ref, shoved the watch under his nose and emphatically counted in Italian. A

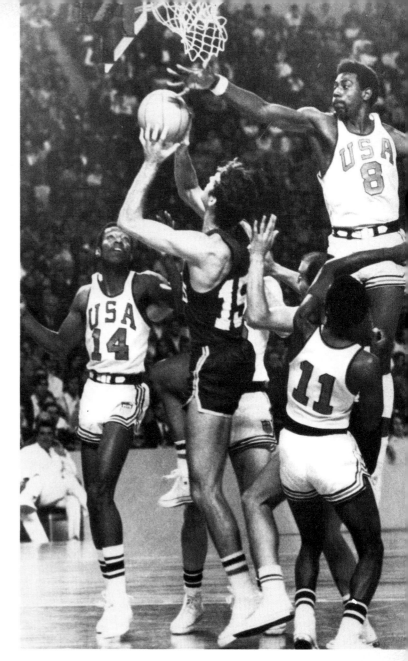

Going high to block a shot by Yugoslavia's Petar Skanski, Spencer Haywood shows why the United States continued its long unbeaten string in the Mexico City Olympic Games.

light dawned somewhere in the Swiss's brain and he grinned. He put his hand on Newell's shoulder in a friendly way.

"Nice vatch," he said.

Jerry Lucas did somewhat better in the field of international relations.

"We were going to play the Japanese team," he said. "Frank Evans, the sports editor of *The Ohio State Lantern,* who was traveling with us, taught me to say, 'How are you?' and 'Good luck in the game' in Japanese. Frank had been stationed in Japan when he was in the Army.

"Before the game, I shook hands with the Japanese center—he was 6 feet 2 inches, the biggest man on their squad—and I repeated the sentences Evans had taught me.

"The center looked at me with a surprised, happy smile and began to bow. He wouldn't stop bowing and the referee had to hold up the game. After the game finally started, he kept talking to me in Japanese continually, but I couldn't answer him. I couldn't keep saying, 'How are you?' "

The U.S. beat the Japanese 125–66, which wasn't too diplomatic.

The margins generally were much narrower at Tokyo in 1964, when coach Hank Iba had just a short period of time in Honolulu to mold a team out of such excellent players as Bill Bradley of Princeton, Walt Hazzard of UCLA, Joe Caldwell of Arizona State and Lucious Jackson of Pan-American. The U.S. beat Yugoslavia 69–61 (it was the Yugoslav team that was beaten by 62 points four years before) and trailed the Puerto Ricans at half time before winning 62–42. The championship game was a 73–59 victory over the Soviet Union.

"Names mean little," said Iba. "What counts is discipline and enthusiasm by the men on the day of the contest. We had the finest type of men on the U.S. Olympic basketball team."

Olympics officials were so pleased with Iba's coaching that, as we have seen, they tapped him again for the 1968 Olympics in Mexico City. At the 1972 Games in Munich, he will be the boss for the third straight time. One of these Olympiads, however, because of boycott or vast improvement in the Albanian team or whatever, the U.S. is going to lose a basketball game or maybe even a gold medal. Germany, where the winning streak began in 1936, could be the place.

But then Iba is likely to reach out to some ghetto or barnyard and find some "kids coming up" like Russell or Bradley or Haywood. He will fret about the lack of time and about that eight-footer from South Korea. Then he'll go to work to insure the correct national anthem gets played at the end.

Chronology

1891: Canadian James Naismith, an instructor at the YMCA Training School in Springfield, Massachusetts (later to become Springfield College), invents the game of basketball. His purpose is to provide interesting winter recreation for a gym class that is bored with gymnastics and calisthenics. Naismith has no idea his brainchild will become one of the most popular sports in the world. The first ball is borrowed from soccer, the first goals are peach baskets nailed to the lower rail of the balcony. The first teams have nine on a side, and the players are clumsy but enthusiastic.

1892: Naismith's original thirteen rules are first published in the Springfield school newspaper, the *Triangle*, on January 15 under the headline, "A New Game." The first public demonstration is conducted March 11. . . . Amos Alonzo Stagg, destined to become more famous as the patron saint of football, moves from Springfield to the University of Chicago and introduces Naismith's game. Other Springfield men introduce it at Geneva College in Pennsylvania, the University of Iowa and numerous YMCAs. . . . Lew Allen of Hartford, Connecticut, makes cylindrical baskets of heavy woven wire, a big improvement over perishable peach baskets.

1893: Allen's reign as a sporting goods magnate ends quickly as the Narragansett Machine Company of Providence starts manufacturing baskets with iron rims and braided cord nettings. Not only that, but backboards become required equipment, making it tough for the spectators who enjoy kicking away opponents' field-goal attempts. . . . Vanderbilt and Hamline organize teams. Vandy beats the Nashville YMCA in a high-scoring titantic 9–6.

1894: Soccer balls are replaced by basketballs manufactured by a bicycle company in Chicopee Falls, Massachusetts. Free throws are introduced.

1895: The Buffalo Germans, who will become one of the finest teams in the history of the sport, start playing as teen-agers at the Buffalo German YMCA. Two of the boys, Allie Heerdt and Eddie Miller, will still be on the team 30 years hence. . . . Minnesota State School of Agriculture beats Hamline 9–3 in the first game between college teams.

1896: The first professional game is played in a Trenton, New Jersey, Masonic hall. Trenton captain Fred Cooper is the highest paid new pro— he gets 16 dollars for the game, one dollar more than his teammates. . . . Chicago beats Iowa 15–12 at Iowa City in the first college game with five players on a side.

1897: Five-man teams are made mandatory. . . . The Amateur Athletic Union (AAU) holds the first basketball tournament ever, at the Twenty-third Street YMCA in New York City.

1898: The National Basketball League, the first pro circuit, begins play with such teams as Trenton and the Pennsylvania Bicycle Club. It will survive just five years. . . . James Naismith, finished with medical school in Colorado, joins the faculty at the University of Kansas.

1900: Dartmouth beats Boston College 44–0, an unusually high and one-sided score for the period. Yale completes "the longest trip ever taken by a United States college team."

1901: The Eastern Intercollegiate League organizes, and Yale wins the first championship over Princeton, Columbia, Cornell and Harvard. The New England League has Amherst, Dartmouth, Holy Cross, Trinity and Williams.

1903: Boundaries are now required to be straight lines. The first "suction-sole" shoes are advertised by Spalding—the birth of sneakers!

1904: A national tournament is conducted outdoors in conjunction with the Olympics, but it is merely a demonstration and includes only teams from the United States. . . . Spalding publishes the first book on technique, *How to Play Basketball* by George T. Hepbron.

1905: Wisconsin conducts the first state high-school tournament. . . . A committee of men from Columbia, Pennsylvania, Princeton and Yale meet in a marathon session to write the first set of college rules.

1906: Madison Square Garden conducts its first basketball tournament. This is the second Garden, which opened in 1890.

1908: The amazing Buffalo Germans start a string of 111 straight victories. They will not be beaten until sometime in 1910. . . . The fore-runner of the National Collegiate Athletic Association, founded 1905, takes control of college basketball rules. The double dribble is prohibited and players are now disqualified on the fifth personal foul.

1909: President Charles Eliot of Harvard recommends that colleges ban the sport because it is "even more brutal than football."

1910: To cut down on ungentlemanly play, a second referee is added for college games and players are sent to the bench on their fourth personal foul.

1912: Open-bottom nets, used in various places for six years, authorized for amateur championship play.

1915: Some confusion ends when Joint Basketball Rules Committee is formed.

1917: Texas loses to Rice after 44 consecutive wins, college basketball's first big victory streak. For the next 50 years or so, the Southwest Conference will be one of the weakest basketball leagues in the country.

1920: About this time "basket ball" becomes "basketball," perhaps a sign of acceptance and permanence. An even better sign: 10,000 fans show up at an armory to see New York University defeat City College.

1922: The New York Renaissance, or Rens, perhaps the greatest all-black team, organizes in Harlem. Bob Douglas, a native of the West Indies, will coach the team for 22 years, with a record of 2,318 and 381.

1923: A new rule states that the man fouled has to take the free throw. No more specialists.

1925: The winning streak of Passaic, New Jersey, High School, one of the game's several "wonder teams," ends at 159.

1926: Pasadena, California, hosts the first women's AAU tournament, which is won by a hometown team.

1927: A Chicago promoter named Abe Saperstein changes name of his Savoy Big Five to Harlem Globetrotters, even though none of the players has ever set foot in Harlem, and starts touring the Midwest in a battered old Ford. Abe is on his way to becoming a millionaire.

1928: Sporting-goods manufacturers introduce a concealed-lace ball. No more crazy bounces at unexpected times.

1929: The use of rope or chicken wire around courts is discontinued, but players are still called "cagers."

1931: A tournament in Peking attracts 70,000 fans in three nights.

1932: A new rule requires the team on offense to get the ball over the halfcourt line in ten seconds. This is in reaction to USC-UCLA and Kansas-Missouri games in which opposing players sat at opposite ends of the floor and stared at each other.

1934: Sportswriter Ned Irish starts big-time college doubleheaders in Madison Square Garden. A crowd of 16,188 fans see Notre Dame versus NYU and St. John's versus Westminster.

1935: Harold (Bunny) Levitt makes 499 free throws in a row in Chicago contest. It takes him seven and a half hours without rest to shoot 871 times with just one miss. Too bad the age of the free-throw specialist is long gone.

1936: The U.S.A. wins the gold medal at the Berlin Olympics, the first Olympiad to include basketball. James Naismith tosses up the first ball. Final game is played on an outdoor dirt court in a driving rainstorm; the U.S.A. beats Canada 19–8.

1937: Rulesmakers eliminate the rule requiring a tedious center jump after each field goal. Now, after Team A scores, Team B gets the ball out of bounds. Under the new system, the national two-team scoring average will jump more than six points the first season.

1938: Temple's Owls win the first National Invitation Tournament (NIT) in Madison Square Garden, beating Colorado 60–36 in the final.

1939: Oregon's "Tall Firs" beat Ohio State 46–33 to win first NCAA tournament at Northwestern's Patten Gym before 5,500 fans. . . . James Naismith dies at age 78. A free trip to Berlin is about all he ever earned from an invention enjoyed by millions of people.

1940: Basketball is televised for the first time, on Station W2XBS from Madison Square Garden. The video audience, what there is of it, sees Pittsburgh beat Fordham 57–37 and NYU beat Georgetown 50–27.

1941: Wisconsin, ninth in the Big Ten the previous season, wins last 15 games in a row, including the NCAA final versus Washington State 39–34. The event has grown in importance so that no "home" team is needed to make it a success. . . . Naismith's important *Basketball, Its Origin and Development* is published by Association Press. The late founder tells in detail how he came to invent basketball and how he turned down a student's suggestion that it be named "Naismith Ball."

1944: Because of a wartime shortage of talent, Utah, starting two sophomores and three freshmen, upsets Dartmouth in overtime and wins the NCAA title. Arnie Ferrin, a blond Mormon from Ogden, Utah, scores 22 points and is named the tourney's most valuable player. Pretty good for his first year in college. . . . The rulesmakers impose a five-foul

limit on players regardless of the number of overtime periods. Unlimited substitution is allowed for the first time. Another new rule forbids a defensive player to interfere with a shot on its descent toward the hoop (this was aimed at DePaul's George Mikan and Oklahoma A&M's Bob Kurland).

1946: The National Basketball Association starts play as the Basketball Association of America. . . . Bob Kurland leads Oklahoma Aggies to their second-straight NCAA title, but the astounding feat of the year is a 55-foot field goal by Rhode Island State's Ernie Calverley in the semifinals of the NIT.

1947: Eddie Gottlieb's Philadelphia Warriors beat the Chicago Stags 4 to 1 in the playoffs to win the first NBA championship. The star of the Warriors is jump-shooting Joe Fulks from Murray State in Kentucky.

1948: The U.S.A. team, featuring the best players from the Phillips 66 Oilers and the University of Kentucky's "Fabulous Five," wins the gold medal at the London Olympics. France is beaten in the final 65–21.

1949: Kentucky, led by Alex Groza and Ralph Beard, wins its second-straight NCAA title.

1950: City College of New York, which lost five games during the regular season, wins both the NCAA and NIT championships. Coach Nat Holman, formerly a mainstay of the Original Celtics, saluted as the coach of the year.

1951: A point-shaving scandal shakes college basketball. There are more than 30 arrests involving 49 games in seventeen cities between 1947 and 1950. Such great players as Alex Groza, Ralph Beard, Sherman White of Long Island U. and Ed Roman of CCNY are implicated. LIU coach Clair Bee calls it the "worst scandal in the history of sports." . . . The Harlem Globetrotters play before 75,000 people at Berlin's Olympic Stadium.

1952: The U.S.A. wins the gold medal at the Helsinki Olympics, beating the Soviet Union in the final 36–25 as Bob Kurland stars. This is the USSR's first Olympiad.

1953: Clarence (Bevo) Francis of tiny Rio Grande College in Ohio averages 50.1 points a game, but because of junior-college opposition on the 39-game schedule, the NCAA throws out his records.

1954: The NBA introduces the 24-second clock, thus speeding up the pro game. A team has to take a shot within 24 seconds after gaining possession of the ball. Most of the credit for the idea goes to Danny Biasone, owner of the Syracuse Nationals. . . . Bevo gets his revenge by averaging 46.5 against four-year schools. Far more impressive is Frank Selvy's 41.7 average against somewhat better competition. Furman's flash scores 100 points against Newberry.

1955: George Mikan of DePaul and the Minneapolis Lakers is named the all-time greatest player in *Sport* poll of 123 coaches. . . . Rubber-covered balls approved for high-school use, and for college or AAU games if both teams give approval.

1956: The University of San Francisco takes its second-straight NCAA title and extends its winning streak to 55. Fans hail Don star Bill Russell as the greatest defensive center of all time. Russ joins Olympic team and leads it to a gold medal at Melbourne. The Boston Celtics trade Ed Macauley and Cliff Hagan to St. Louis for the rights to Russell, probably the most important personnel deal in pro basketball's history. . . . Kansas coach Forrest (Phog) Allen retires. His record for 46 years: 771 and 233.

1957: Even though Kansas has giant sophomore Wilt Chamberlain, it loses NCAA final to North Carolina in triple overtime. Frank McGuire's Tar Heels finish with a 32 and 0 record.

1958: Oscar Robertson from Indianapolis becomes the first soph in history to win the NCAA scoring championship (his average: 35.1).

1960: The U.S.A. team, featuring Jerry West and Oscar Robertson, wins the gold medal at the Rome Olympics. . . . The Minneapolis Lakers move to Los Angeles, making pro basketball a coast-to-coast game for the first time. The nickname is kept despite the scarcity of lakes in southern California.

1962: Cincinnati wins its second-straight NCAA championship, again beating Ohio State and Jerry Lucas in the all-Ohio final.

1964: The U.S.A. wins still another gold medal at the Tokyo Olympics. Americans beat the USSR in the final 73–59.

1967: The American Basketball Association is organized by a group of promoters and public-relations men and selects George Mikan as its first commissioner. Mikan comes up with the idea for a red, white and blue ball, which one critic insists would look better on the nose of a seal. . . . Giant Lew Alcindor, only a sophomore, leads UCLA to undefeated season and the NCAA championship.

1968: The Naismith Memorial Basketball Hall of Fame is opened in Springfield, Massachusetts. . . . The UCLA Bruins lose to Houston before 52,693 fans in the Astrodome, then come back to murder the Cougars 101–69 in the NCAA semifinals in the Los Angeles Sports Arena. . . . The U.S.A. wins the gold medal at the Mexico City Olympics despite the absence of Alcindor and many others who decline to try out for the team. An unknown junior-college kid named Spencer Haywood leads the Americans to their 55th straight Olympic victory without a loss. . . . The Pittsburgh Pipers win the first ABA championship.

1969: UCLA wins its third NCAA title in a row. Alcindor is the tournament MVP for the third-straight time.

1970: UCLA wins fourth-straight NCAA title, and sixth in seven years, all under coach John Wooden. The Bruins beat Jacksonville and 7 foot-2 inch Artis Gilmore 80–69 in the final at College Park, Maryland.

Records

NATIONAL COLLEGIATE ATHLETIC ASSOCIATION TOURNAMENT CHAMPIONS

UCLA's six titles in seven years were won on the court, not in mythical wire-service polls à la college football. No football team has been able to accomplish anything close to it, yet football has fewer participating schools than basketball and fewer championship contenders.

YEAR	TEAM	COACH	RUNNER-UP	SCORE
1970	UCLA	John Wooden	Jacksonville	80–69
1969	UCLA	John Wooden	Purdue	92–72
1968	UCLA	John Wooden	North Carolina	78–55
1967	UCLA	John Wooden	Dayton	79–64
1966	Texas Western	Don Haskins	Kentucky	72–65
1965	UCLA	John Wooden	Michigan	91–80
1964	UCLA	John Wooden	Duke	98–83
1963	Loyola (Chicago)	George Ireland	Cincinnati	60–58
1962	Cincinnati	Edwin Jucker	Ohio State	71–59
1961	Cincinnati	Edwin Jucker	Ohio State	70–65
1960	Ohio State	Fred Taylor	California	75–55
1959	California	Pete Newell	West Virginia	71–70
1958	Kentucky	Adolph Rupp	Seattle	84–72
1957	North Carolina	Frank McGuire	Kansas	54–53
1956	San Francisco	Phil Woolpert	Iowa	83–71
1955	San Francisco	Phil Woolpert	LaSalle	77–63
1954	LaSalle	Ken Loeffler	Bradley	92–76
1953	Indiana	Branch McCracken	Kansas	69–68
1952	Kansas	Forrest Allen	St. John's	80–63
1951	Kentucky	Adolph Rupp	Kansas State	68–58
1950	CCNY	Nat Holman	Bradley	71–68
1949	Kentucky	Adolph Rupp	Oklahoma A&M	46–36
1948	Kentucky	Adolph Rupp	Baylor	58–42
1947	Holy Cross	Alvin F. Julian	Oklahoma	58–47
1946	Oklahoma A&M	Henry Iba	North Carolina	43–40
1945	Oklahoma A&M	Henry Iba	New York U.	49–45
1944	Utah	Vadal Peterson	Dartmouth	42–40
1943	Wyoming	Everett Shelton	Georgetown	46–34
1942	Stanford	Everett Dean	Dartmouth	53–38
1941	Wisconsin	Harold Foster	Washington State	39–34
1940	Indiana	Branch McCracken	Kansas	60–42
1939	Oregon	Howard Hobson	Ohio State	46–33

NCAA TOURNAMENT MOST VALUABLE/OUTSTANDING PLAYERS

This award was changed from MVP to outstanding player after the 1965 tournament as a result of the Bill Bradley-Gail Goodrich voting. Most people agreed that Bradley was the best player, but some contended Goodrich of UCLA was more valuable in terms of what everybody was there for, winning the national championship. Bill won the vote, after which the NCAA's public relations committee changed the name. There is an oddity in this list: the MVPs for 1957–58–59, Chamberlain, Baylor and West, were all on second-place teams. All three men became stars in the NBA and ended up on the same pro club, the Los Angeles Lakers, in 1968–69 and 1969–70. Both seasons they were runners-up.

YEAR	PLAYER	SCHOOL
1970	Sidney Wicks	UCLA
1969	Lew Alcindor	UCLA
1968	Lew Alcindor	UCLA
1967	Lew Alcindor	UCLA
1966	Jerry Chambers	Utah
1965	Bill Bradley	Princeton
1964	Walt Hazzard	UCLA
1963	Art Heyman	Duke
1962	Paul Hogue	Cincinnati
1961	Jerry Lucas	Ohio State
1960	Jerry Lucas	Ohio State
1959	Jerry West	West Virginia
1958	Elgin Baylor	Seattle
1957	Wilt Chamberlain	Kansas
1956	Hal (King) Lear	Temple
1955	Bill Russell	San Francisco
1954	Tom Gola	LaSalle
1953	B. H. Born	Kansas
1952	Clyde Lovellette	Kansas
1951	no selection	
1950	Irwin Dambrot	CCNY
1949	Alex Groza	Kentucky
1948	Alex Groza	Kentucky
1947	George Kaftan	Holy Cross
1946	Bob Kurland	Oklahoma A&M
1945	Bob Kurland	Oklahoma A&M
1944	Arnold Ferrin	Utah
1943	Kenny Sailors	Wyoming
1942	Howie Dallmar	Stanford
1941	John Kotz	Wisconsin
1940	Marvin Huffman	Indiana
1939	no selection	

HELMS NATIONAL-CHAMPIONSHIP COLLEGE TEAMS

The Helms Athletic Foundation in Los Angeles, founded in the mid-1930s by Bill Schroeder and Paul Helms, is a treasure house of sports memorabilia. Helms, a bakery owner, died in 1957, but the foundation kept operating smoothly until his heirs withdrew support in 1970. Late that year United Savings and Loan Association in L.A. became the new benefactor. This saved Schroeder the embarrassment of being evicted along with his vast collection of books, records, trophies and beloved junk. The Helms board of basketball experts checked the records carefully in retroactively picking the top teams back to 1901. From 1939, when the NCAA Tournament started, the Helms and NCAA champions have been the same except for 1939-40-44-54.

YEAR	SCHOOL	COACH	RECORD	POINTS	POINTS AGAINST
1970	UCLA	John Wooden	28 and 2	2759	2201
1969	UCLA	John Wooden	29 and 1	2539	1915
1968	UCLA	John Wooden	29 and 1	2802	2015
1967	UCLA	John Wooden	30 and 0	2687	1910
1966	Texas Western	Don Haskins	28 and 1	2260	1818
1965	UCLA	John Wooden	28 and 2	2589	2140
1964	UCLA	John Wooden	30 and 0	2666	2102
1963	Loyola of Chicago	George Ireland	29 and 2	2847	2110
1962	Cincinnati	Ed Jucker	29 and 2	2238	1707
1961	Cincinnati	Ed Jucker	27 and 3	2251	1823
1960	Ohio State	Fred Taylor	25 and 3	2532	1946
1959	California	Pete Newell	25 and 4	1854	1480
1958	Kentucky	Adolph Rupp	23 and 6	2166	1817
1957	North Carolina	Frank McGuire	32 and 0	2532	2098
1956	San Francisco	Phil Woolpert	29 and 0	2093	1514
1955	San Francisco	Phil Woolpert	28 and 1	1952	1511
1954	Kentucky	Adolph Rupp	25 and 0	2187	1508
1953	Indiana	Branch McCracken	23 and 3	2112	1808
1952	Kansas	Forrest C. Allen	28 and 3	2209	1807
1951	Kentucky	Adolph Rupp	32 and 2	2540	1783
1950	CCNY	Nat Holman	24 and 5	1993	1610
1949	Kentucky	Adolph Rupp	32 and 2	2320	1492
1948	Kentucky	Adolph Rupp	36 and 3	2690	1730
1947	Holy Cross	Alvin F. Julian	27 and 3	1826	1359
1946	Oklahoma A&M	Henry Iba	31 and 2	1661	1058
1945	Oklahoma A&M	Henry Iba	27 and 4	1677	1038
1944	Army	Edward Kelleher	15 and 0	874	521
1943	Wyoming	Everett Shelton	31 and 2	1959	1307
1942	Stanford	Everett Dean	27 and 4	1341	1083
1941	Wisconsin	Harold E. Foster	20 and 3	1004	835
1940	Southern California	Justin M. Barry	20 and 3	1099	827
1939	Long Island U.	Clair Bee	24 and 0	1320	815
1938	Temple	James Usilton	23 and 2	1121	884
1937	Stanford	John W. Bunn	25 and 2	1326	914
1936	Notre Dame	George Keogan	22 and 2†	1053	677
1935	New York U.	Howard Cann	19 and 1	740	489
1934	Wyoming	Willard Witte	26 and 3*	1097	737
1933	Kentucky	Adolph Rupp	20 and 3	1073	630
1932	Purdue	Ward Lambert	17 and 1	718	448
1931	Northwestern	Arthur Lonborg	16 and 1	560	372
1930	Pittsburgh	Clifford Carlson	23 and 2	940	660
1929	Montana State	Schubert Dyche	35 and 2	2236	1204
1928	Pittsburgh	Clifford Carlson	21 and 0	993	662
1927	Notre Dame	George Keogan	19 and 1	631	376
1926	Syracuse	Lewis P. Andreas	19 and 1	637	433
1925	Princeton	Albert Wittmer	21 and 2	777	433
1924	North Carolina	Norman Shepard	25 and 0	915	493
1923	Kansas	Forrest C. Allen	17 and 1	567	299
1922	Kansas	Forrest C. Allen	16 and 2	596	378
1921	Pennsylvania	Edward McNichol	21 and 2	651	353
1920	Pennsylvania	Lon W. Jourdet	22 and 1	735	393

YEAR	SCHOOL	COACH	RECORD	POINTS	POINTS AGAINST
1919	Minnesota	Dr. Louis Cooke	13 and 0	462	190
1918	Syracuse	Edmund Dollard	16 and 1	476	293
1917	Washington State	J. Fred Bohler	25 and 1	1037	515
1916	Wisconsin	Walter Meanwell	20 and 1	624	343
1915	Illinois	Ralph R. Jones	16 and 0	444	208
1914	Wisconsin	Walter Meanwell	15 and 0	520	226
1913	Navy	Louis P. Wenzell	9 and 0	481	187
1912	Wisconsin	Walter Meanwell	15 and 0	487	223
1911	St. John's	Claude B. Allen	14 and 0	608	312
1910	Columbia	Harry A. Fisher	11 and 1*	336	154
1909	Chicago	Joseph Raycroft	12 and 0	276	122
1908	Chicago	Joseph Raycroft	21 and 2	722	392
1907	Chicago	Joseph Raycroft	20 and 2	781	317
1906	Dartmouth	No Coach	16 and 2	575	326
1905	Columbia	No Coach	19 and 1*	526	358
1904	Columbia	No Coach	17 and 1*	478	228
1903	Yale	No Coach	15 and 1	372	178
1902	Minnesota	Dr. Louis Cooke	11 and 0	464	121
1901	Yale	No Coach	10 and 4*	328	153

† One tie game played by Notre Dame

* Undefeated against college competition

HELMS PLAYERS OF THE YEAR

YEAR	PLAYER	SCHOOL
1970	Sidney Wicks	UCLA
	Pete Maravich	LSU
1969	Lew Alcindor	UCLA
1968	Lew Alcindor	UCLA
1967	Lew Alcindor	UCLA
1966	Cazzie Russell	Michigan
1965	Bill Bradley	Princeton
	Gail Goodrich	UCLA
1964	Walt Hazzard	UCLA
1963	Art Heyman	Duke
1962	Paul Hogue	Cincinnati
1961	Jerry Lucas	Ohio State
1960	Oscar Robertson	Cincinnati
1959	Oscar Robertson	Cincinnati
1958	Elgin Baylor	Seattle
1957	Lennie Rosenbluth	North Carolina
1956	Bill Russell	San Francisco
1955	Bill Russell	San Francisco
1954	Tom Gola	LaSalle
1953	Bob Houbregs	Washington
1952	Clyde Lovellette	Kansas
1951	Dick Groat	Duke
1950	Paul Arizin	Villanova
1949	Tony Lavelli	Yale
1948	Ed Macauley	St. Louis U.
1947	Gerald Tucker	Oklahoma
1946	Bob Kurland	Oklahoma A&M
1945	George Mikan	DePaul
1944	George Mikan	DePaul
1943	George Senesky	St. Joseph's
1942	Stan Modzelewski (Stutz)	Rhode Island
1941	George Glamack	North Carolina
1940	George Glamack	North Carolina
1939	Chester Jaworski	Rhode Island
1938	Hank Luisetti	Stanford
1937	Hank Luisetti	Stanford
1936	John Moir	Notre Dame
1935	Leroy Edwards	Kentucky
1934	Wesley Bennett	Westminster (Pa.)

YEAR	PLAYER	SCHOOL
1933	Forest Sale	Kentucky
1932	John Wooden	Purdue
1931	Bart Carlton	E. Central Oklahoma
1930	Chuck Hyatt	Pittsburgh
1929	John Thompson	Montana State
1928	Victor Holt	Oklahoma
1927	Victor Hanson	Syracuse
1926	John Cobb	North Carolina
1925	Earl Mueller	Colorado College
1924	Charles Black	Kansas
1923	Paul Endacott	Kansas
1922	Charles Carney	Illinois
1921	George Williams	Missouri
1920	Howard Cann	New York U.
1919	Erling Platou	Minnesota
1918	William Chandler	Wisconsin
1917	Ray Woods	Illinois
1916	George Levis	Wisconsin
1915	Ernest Houghton	Union
1914	Gil Halstead	Cornell
1913	Eddie Calder	St. Lawrence
1912	Otto Stangel	Wisconsin
1911	Theodore Kiendl	Columbia
1910	Harland (Pat) Page	Chicago
1909	John Schommer	Chicago
1908	Charles Keinath	Pennsylvania
1907	Gilmore Kinney	Yale
1906	George Grebenstein	Dartmouth
1905	Chris Steinmetz	Wisconsin

CONSENSUS ALL-AMERICA TEAMS

At least thirteen publications (including College Humor, Literary Digest, The Sporting News and Pic), one foundation, three wire services, two syndicates and two associations have at one time or another picked All-America basketball teams. As in football, publicity counts a great deal, and many writers, coaches and other so-called experts blithely cast their ballots after having seen only a small fraction of the best players in the country. Still, the controversies and discussions stirred up by the selections have been good for the sport. And who could ever forget those All-America immortals Urgel Wintermute of Oregon and Bozie Berger of Maryland?

1969–70: Dan Issel, Kentucky; Bob Lanier, St. Bonaventure; Pete Maravich, LSU; Rick Mount, Purdue; Calvin Murphy, Niagara.

1968–69: Lew Alcindor, UCLA; Spencer Haywood, Detroit; Pete Maravich, LSU; Rick Mount, Purdue; Calvin Murphy, Niagara.

1967–68: Lew Alcindor, UCLA; Elvin Hayes, Houston; Pete Maravich, LSU; Larry Miller, North Carolina; Westley Unseld, Louisville.

1966–67: Lew Alcindor, UCLA; Clem Haskins, Western Kentucky; Elvin Hayes, Houston; Bob Lloyd, Rutgers; Westley Unseld, Louisville; Bob Verga, Duke; Jimmy Walker, Providence.

1965–66: Dave Bing, Syracuse; Clyde Lee, Vanderbilt; Cazzie Russell, Michigan; Dave Schellhase, Purdue; Jimmy Walker, Providence.

1964–65: Rick Barry, Miami (Florida); Bill Bradley, Princeton; Gail Goodrich, UCLA; Fred Hetzel, Davidson; Cazzie Russell, Michigan.

1963–64: Gary Bradds, Ohio State; Bill Bradley, Princeton; Walt Hazzard, UCLA; Cotton Nash, Kentucky; Dave Stallworth, Wichita State.

1962–63: Ron Bonham, Cincinnati; Jerry Harkness, Loyola (Chicago); Art Heyman, Duke; Barry Kramer, NYU; Tom Thacker, Cincinnati.

1961–62: Len Chappell, Wake Forest; Terry Dischinger, Purdue; Jerry Lucas, Ohio State; Billy (The Hill) McGill, Utah; Chet Walker, Bradley.

1960–61: Terry Dischinger, Purdue; Roger Kaiser, Georgia Tech; Jerry Lucas, Ohio State; Tom Stith, St. Bonaventure; Chet Walker, Bradley.

1959–60: Darrall Imhoff, California; Jerry Lucas, Ohio State; Oscar Robertson, Cincinnati; Tom Stith, St. Bonaventure; Jerry West, West Virginia.

1958–59: Bob Boozer, Kansas State; Johnny Cox, Kentucky; Bailey Howell, Mississippi State; Oscar Robertson, Cincinnati; Jerry West, West Virginia.

1957–58: Elgin Baylor, Seattle; Bob Boozer, Kansas State; Wilt Chamber-

lain, Kansas; Don Hennon, Pittsburgh; Oscar Robertson, Cincinnati; Guy Rodgers, Temple.

1956–57: Wilt Chamberlain, Kansas; Chet Forte, Columbia; Rod Hundley, West Virginia; Jim Krebs, SMU; Lennie Rosenbluth, North Carolina; Charlie Tyra, Louisville.

1955–56: Robin Freeman, Ohio State; Sihugo Green, Duquesne; Tom Heinsohn, Holy Cross; Bill Russell, San Francisco; Ron Shavlik, North Carolina State.

1954–55: Dick Garmaker, Minnesota; Tom Gola, LaSalle; Sihugo Green, Duquesne; Dick Ricketts, Duquesne; Bill Russell, San Francisco.

1953–54: Tom Gola, LaSalle; Cliff Hagan, Kentucky; Bob Pettit, LSU; Don Schlundt, Indiana; Frank Selvy, Furman.

1952–53: Ernie Beck, Pennsylvania; Walter Dukes, Seton Hall; Tom Gola, LaSalle; Bob Houbregs, Washington; Johnny O'Brien, Seattle.

1951–52: Chuck Darling, Iowa; Rod Fletcher, Illinois; Dick Groat, Duke; Cliff Hagan, Kentucky; Clyde Lovellette, Kansas.

1950–51: Clyde Lovellette, Kansas; Gene Melchiorre, Bradley; Bill Mlkvy, Temple; Sam Ranzino, North Carolina State; Bill Spivey, Kentucky.

1949–50: Paul Arizin, Villanova; Bob Cousy, Holy Cross; Dick Schnittker, Ohio State; Bill Sharman, USC; Paul Unruh, Bradley.

1948–49: Ralph Beard, Kentucky; Vince Boryla, Denver; Alex Groza, Kentucky; Tony Lavelli, Yale; Ed Macauley, St. Louis.

1947–48: Ralph Beard, Kentucky; Arnie Ferrin, Utah; Tony Lavelli, Yale; Ed Macauley, St. Louis; Kevin O'Shea, Notre Dame; Murray Wier, Iowa.

1946–47: Ralph Beard, Kentucky; Alex Groza, Kentucky; George Kaftan, Holy Cross; Sid Tanenbaum, NYU; Gerald Tucker, Oklahoma.

1945–46: Leo Klier, Notre Dame; Bob Kurland, Oklahoma A&M; George Mikan, DePaul; Max Morris, Northwestern; Jack Parkinson, Kentucky; Sid Tanenbaum, NYU.

1944–45: Arnie Ferrin, Utah; Wyndol Gray, Bowling Green; Walton Kirk, Illinois; Bob Kurland, Oklahoma A&M; George Mikan, DePaul.

1943–44: Bob Brannum, Kentucky; Audley Brindley, Dartmouth; Otto Graham, Northwestern; George Mikan, DePaul; Alva Paine, Oklahoma.

1942–43: Charles Black, Kansas; Harry Boykoff, St. John's; Andy Phillip, Illinois; Kenny Sailors, Wyoming; George Senesky, St. Joseph's.

1941–42: Price Brookfield, West Texas State; Robert Doll, Colorado; Robert Kinney, Rice; John Kotz, Wisconsin; Stanley (Stutz) Modzelewski, Rhode Island.

1940–41: Frank Baumholtz, Ohio U.; Gus Broberg, Dartmouth; Robert Kinney, Rice; Paul Lindeman, Washington State; Oscar Schectman, Long Island U. (only two All-America teams picked this season; this is the Converse version).

1939–40: William Hapac, Illinois; Jack Harvey, Colorado; Marvin Huffman, Indiana; James McNatt, Oklahoma; Ralph Vaughn, USC (Converse team).

1938–39: Robert Anet, Oregon; Banks McFadden, Clemson; Bernard Opper, Kentucky; Irving Torgoff, Long Island U.; Urgel Wintermute, Oregon (Converse team).

1937–38: Hank Luisetti, Stanford; John Moir, Notre Dame; Paul Nowak, Notre Dame; Fred Pralle, Kansas; Jewell Young, Purdue.

1936–37: Jules Bender, Long Island U.; Hank Luisetti, Stanford; John Moir, Notre Dame; Paul Nowak, Notre Dame; Charles Orebaugh, Drake.

1935–36: Vernon Huffman, Indiana; Robert Kessler, Purdue; Hank Luisetti, Stanford; Paul Nowak, Notre Dame; Wally Palmberg, Oregon State.

1934–35: Paul Birch, Duquesne; Claire Cribbs, Pittsburgh; Jack Gray, Texas; Lee Guttero, USC; Malcolm Wade, LSU (Converse).

1933–34: Claire Cribbs, Pittsburgh; Edward Krause, Notre Dame; Ed Mullen, Marquette; Fred Tompkins, South Carolina; Les Witte, Wyoming (Converse).

1932–33: Eddie Finnigan, Western Reserve; Edward Krause, Notre Dame; Elliott Loughlin, Navy; Forrest Sale, Kentucky; Don Smith, Pittsburgh (Converse).

1931–32: Bozie Berger, Maryland; Edward Krause, Notre Dame; Forrest Sale, Kentucky; Les Witte, Wyoming; John Wooden, Purdue.

1930–31: Max Collings, Missouri; James Lindy Hood, Alabama; Max Posnak, St. John's; Joseph Rieff, Northwestern; John Wooden, Purdue (College Humor).

1929–30: Charles Hyatt, Pittsburgh; Morris Johnson, North Carolina State; Charles Murphy, Loyola (Chicago); Frank Ward, Montana State; John Wooden, Purdue (College Humor).

1928–29: Thomas Churchill, Oklahoma; Verne Corbin, California; Frank Dougherty, Fordham; Charles Hyatt, Pittsburgh; Charles (Stretch) Murphy, Purdue; Joseph Schaaf, Pennsylvania.

NATIONAL INVITATION TOURNAMENT

Madison Square Garden's NIT, started by the New York City basketball writers but now run by the Eastern Collegiate Athletic Conference, was once a rival to the NCAA Tournament. These days it is usually a gathering of runners-up, despite the equal or superior play it gets in the New York newspapers. Nevertheless, it is a colorful event with good teams staged in the best basketball town in the world.

YEAR	TEAM	COACH	RUNNER-UP	FINAL SCORE
1970	Marquette	Al McGuire	St. John's	65–53
1969	Temple	Harry Litwack	Boston College	89–76
1968	Dayton	Don (Mickey) Donoher	Kansas	61–48
1967	Southern Illinois	Jack Hartman	Marquette	71–56
1966	Brigham Young	Stan Watts	NYU	97–84
1965	St. John's	Joe Lapchick	Villanova	55–51
1964	Bradley	Chuck Orsborn	New Mexico	86–54
1963	Providence	Joe Mullaney	Canisius	81–66
1962	Dayton	Tom Blackburn	St. John's	73–67
1961	Providence	Joe Mullaney	St. Louis	62–59
1960	Bradley	Chuck Orsborn	Providence	88–72
1959	St. John's	Joe Lapchick	Bradley	76–71
1958	Xavier (O.)	Jim McCafferty	Dayton	78–74
1957	Bradley	Chuck Orsborn	Memphis State	84–83
1956	Louisville	"Peck" Hickman	Dayton	93–80
1955	Duquesne	"Dudey" Moore	Dayton	70–58
1954	Holy Cross	"Buster" Sheary	Duquesne	71–62
1953	Seton Hall	John (Honey) Russell	St. John's	58–46
1952	LaSalle	Ken Loeffler	Dayton	75–64
1951	Brigham Young	Stan Watts	Dayton	62–43
1950	CCNY	Nat Holman	Bradley	69–61
1949	San Francisco	Pete Newell	Loyola (Chi.)	48–47
1948	St. Louis	Ed Hickey	NYU	65–52
1947	Utah	Vadal Peterson	Kentucky	49–45
1946	Kentucky	Adolph Rupp	Rhode Island	46–45
1945	DePaul	Ray Meyer	Bowling Green	71–54
1944	St. John's	Joe Lapchick	DePaul	47–39
1943	St. John's	Joe Lapchick	Toledo	48–27
1942	West Virginia	Dyke Raese	Western Kentucky	47–45
1941	Long Island U.	Clair Bee	Ohio U.	56–42
1940	Colorado	"Frosty" Cox	Duquesne	51–40
1939	Long Island U.	Clair Bee	Loyola (Chi.)	44–32
1938	Temple	James Usilton	Colorado	60–36

NATIONAL INVITATION TOURNAMENT MOST VALUABLE PLAYERS

YEAR	PLAYER	SCHOOL
1970	Dean Meminger	Marquette
1969	Terry Driscoll	Boston College
1968	Don May	Dayton
1967	Walt Frazier	Southern Illinois
1966	Bill Melchionni	Villanova
1965	Ken McIntyre	St. John's
1964	Levern Tart	Bradley
1963	Ray Flynn	Providence
1962	Bill Chmielewski	Dayton
1961	Vin Ernst	Providence
1960	Len Wilkens	Providence
1959	Tony Jackson	St. John's
1958	Hank Stein	Xavier
1957	Win Wilfong	Memphis State
1956	Charlie Tyra	Louisville
1955	Maurice Stokes	St. Francis (Pa.)
1954	Togo Palazzi	Holy Cross
1953	Walter Dukes	Seton Hall
1952	Tom Gola and Norm Grekin	LaSalle
1951	Roland Minson	Brigham Young

YEAR	PLAYER	SCHOOL
1950	Ed Warner	CCNY
1949	Don Lofgran	San Francisco
1948	Ed Macauley	St. Louis U.
1947	Vern Gardner	Utah
1946	Ernie Calverley	Rhode Island
1945	George Mikan	DePaul
1944	Bill Kotsores	St. John's
1943	Harry Boykoff	St. John's
1942	Rudy Baric	West Virginia
1941	Frank Baumholtz	Ohio U.
1940	Bob Doll	Colorado
1939	Bill Lloyd	St. John's
1938	Don Shields	Temple

MAJOR-COLLEGE SCORING LEADERS

Just so you can keep your initials straight, National Collegiate Sports Services in New York City, directed by Larry Klein, keeps track of records and statistics for the National Collegiate Athletic Association (NCAA), headquartered in Kansas City, Missouri. NCAA "major colleges" should not be confused with schools in the NCAA's college division (Pacific Lutheran, Clarion State, Rochester Tech) or the National Association of Intercollegiate Athletics (NAIA). Unfortunately, national records and statistics were not kept, according to Klein's office, until the 1947–48 season.

SEASON	PLAYER	SCHOOL	POINTS	AVERAGE
1969–70	Pete Maravich	LSU	1381*	44.5*
1968–69	Pete Maravich	LSU	1148	44.2
1967–68	Pete Maravich	LSU	1138	43.8
1966–67	Jimmy Walker	Providence	851	30.4
1965–66	Dave Schellhase	Purdue	781	32.5
1964–65	Rick Barry	Miami (Fla.)	973	37.4
1963–64	Howard Komives	Bowling Green	844	36.7
1962–63	Nick Werkman	Seton Hall	650	29.5
1961–62	Billy McGill	Utah	1009	38.8
1960–61	Frank Burgess	Gonzaga	842	32.4
1959–60	Oscar Robertson	Cincinnati	1011	33.7
1958–59	Oscar Robertson	Cincinnati	978	32.6
1957–58	Oscar Robertson	Cincinnati	984	35.1
1956–57	Grady Wallace	South Carolina	906	31.2
1955–56	Darrell Floyd	Furman	946	33.8
1954–55	Darrell Floyd	Furman	897	35.9
1953–54	Frank Selvy	Furman	1209	41.7
1952–53	Frank Selvy	Furman	738	29.5
1951–52	Clyde Lovellette	Kansas	795	28.4
1950–51	Bill Mlkvy	Temple	731	29.2
1949–50	Paul Arizin	Villanova	735	25.3
1948–49	Tony Lavelli	Yale	671	22.4
1947–48	Murray Wier	Iowa	399	21.0

* Indicates record

MAJOR-COLLEGE FIELD GOAL PERCENTAGE LEADERS

SEASON	PLAYER	SCHOOL	FIELD GOALS	PERCENTAGE
1969–70	Willie Williams	Florida State	185	.636
1968–69	Lew Alcindor	UCLA	303	.635
1967–68	Joe Allen	Bradley	258	.655
1966–67	Lew Alcindor	UCLA	346	.667*
1965–66	Julian Hammond	Tulsa	172	.659
1964–65	Tim Kehoe	St. Peter's	138	.660
1963–64	Terry Holland	Davidson	135	.631
1962–63	Lyle Harger	Houston	193	.656
1961–62	Jerry Lucas	Ohio State	237	.611

SEASON	PLAYER	SCHOOL	FIELD GOALS	PERCENTAGE
1960–61	Jerry Lucas	Ohio State	256	.623
1959–60	Jerry Lucas	Ohio State	283	.637
1958–59	Ralph Crosthwaite	Western Kentucky	191	.645
1957–58	Ralph Crosthwaite	Western Kentucky	202	.610
1956–57	Bailey Howell	Mississippi State	217	.568
1955–56	Joe Holup	George Washington	200	.647
1954–55	Ed O'Connor	Manhattan	147	.605
1953–54	Joe Holup	George Washington	179	.572
1952–53	Vernon Stokes	St. Francis (N.Y.)	147	.595
1951–52	Art Spoelstra	Western Kentucky	178	.516
1950–51	Don Meineke	Dayton	240	.512
1949–50	Jim Moran	Niagara	98	.530
1948–49	Ed Macauley	St. Louis	144	.524
1947–48	Alex Petersen	Oregon State	89	.476

* Indicates record

MAJOR-COLLEGE FREE THROW PERCENTAGE LEADERS

SEASON	PLAYER	SCHOOL	FREE THROWS	PERCENTAGE
1969–70	Steve Kaplan	Rutgers	102	.927
1968–69	Bill Justus	Tennessee	133	.905
1967–68	Joe Heiser	Princeton	117	.900
1966–67	Bob Lloyd	Rutgers	255	.921
1965–66	Bill Blair	Providence	101	.902
1964–65	Bill Bradley	Princeton	273	.886
1963–64	Rick Park	Tulsa	121	.903
1962–63	Tommy Boyer	Arkansas	147	.913
1961–62	Tommy Boyer	Arkansas	125	.933*
1960–61	Stew Sherard	Army	135	.877
1959–60	Jack Waters	Mississippi	103	.873
1958–59	Arlen Clark	Oklahoma State	201	.852
1957–58	Semi Mintz	Davidson	105	.882
1956–57	Ernie Wiggins	Wake Forest	93	.877
1955–56	Bill Von Weyhe	Rhode Island	180	.865
1954–55	Jim Scott	West Texas State	153	.895
1953–54	Dick Daugherty	Arizona State	75	.872
1952–53	John Weber	Yale	117	.830
1951–52	Sy Chadroff	Miami (Fla.)	99	.805
1950–51	Jay Handlan	Washington & Lee	148	.860
1949–50	Sam Urzetta	St. Bonaventure	54	.885
1948–49	Bill Schroer	Valparaiso	59	.868
1947–48	Sam Urzetta	St. Bonaventure	59	.922

* Indicates record

MAJOR-COLLEGE REBOUNDING LEADERS

SEASON	PLAYER	SCHOOL	REBOUNDS	AVERAGE
1969–70	Artis Gilmore	Jacksonville	621	22.2
1968–69	Spencer Haywood	Detroit	472	21.5
1967–68	Neal Walk	Florida	494	19.8
1966–67	Dick Cunningham	Murray State	479	21.8
1965–66	Jim Ware	Oklahoma City	607	20.9
1964–65	Toby Kimball	Connecticut	483	21.0
1963–64	Bob Pelkington	Xavier	567	21.8
1962–63	Paul Silas	Creighton	557	20.6
1961–62	Jerry Lucas	Ohio State	499	.211†
1960–61	Jerry Lucas	Ohio State	470	.198
1959–60	Leroy Wright	Pacific	380	.234
1958–59	Leroy Wright	Pacific	652	.238
1957–58	Alex Ellis	Niagara	536	.262
1956–57	Elgin Baylor	Seattle	508	.235
1955–56	Joe Holup	George Washington	604	.256

SEASON	PLAYER	SCHOOL	REBOUNDS	AVERAGE
1954–55	Charlie Slack	Marshall	538	25.6*
1953–54	Art Quimby	Connecticut	588	22.6
1952–53	Ed Conlin	Fordham	612	23.5
1951–52	Bill Hannon	Army	355	20.9
1950–51	Ernie Beck	Pennsylvania	556	20.6

† From 1955–56 through 1961–62, championship was determined on highest individual recoveries out of total by both teams in all games
* Indicates record

MAJOR-COLLEGE INDIVIDUAL RECORDS

Most points scored, one game: 100, Frank Selvy, Furman, versus Newberry, 2/13/54 (41 field goals, 18 free throws).

Most points scored, season: 1381, Pete Maravich, LSU, '69–70.

Most points scored, career: 3667, Pete Maravich, LSU, '67–68 through '69–70.

Highest scoring average per game, one season: 44.5, Pete Maravich, LSU, '69–70.

Highest scoring average per game, career: 44.2, Pete Maravich, LSU, '67–68 through '69–70.

Most games scoring 50 points or more, season: 10, Pete Maravich, LSU, '69–70.

Most games scoring 50 points or more, career: 28, Pete Maravich, LSU, '67–68 through '69–70.

Most field goals, one game: 41, Frank Selvy, Furman, versus Newberry, 2/13/54.

Most field goals, season: 522, Pete Maravich, LSU, '69–70.

Most field goals, career: 1387, Pete Maravich, LSU, '67–68 through '69–70.

Most field goals attempted, one game: 71, Jay Handlan, Washington & Lee, versus Furman, 2/17/51 (he made 30).

Most field goals attempted, season: 1168, Pete Maravich, LSU, '69–70.

Most field goals attempted, career: 3166, Pete Maravich, LSU, '67–68 through '69–70.

Highest field-goal percentage, season: 66.7%, Lew Alcindor, UCLA, '66–67.

Highest field-goal percentage, career: 63.9%, Lew Alcindor, UCLA, '66–67 through '68–69.

Most free throws, one game: 30, Pete Maravich, LSU, versus Oregon State, 12/22/69. (He had 31 attempts.)

Most free throws, season: 355, Frank Selvy, Furman, '53–54.

Most free throws, four-year career: 905, Dickie Hemric, Wake Forest, '51–52 through '54–55.

Most free throws, three-year career: 893, Pete Maravich, LSU, '67–68 through '69–70.

Most consecutive free throws, one game: 24, Arlen Clark, Oklahoma State, versus Colorado, 3/7/59. (He was 24 for 24 for the game.)

Most consecutive free throws, season: 60, Bob Lloyd, Rutgers, '66–67 (during six games).

Most free throws attempted, one game: 36, Ed Tooley, Brown, versus Amherst, 12/4/54 (he made 23).

Most free throws attempted, season: 444, Frank Selvy, Furman, '53–54.

Most free throws attempted, four-year career: 1359, Dickie Hemric, Wake Forest, '51–52 through '54–55.

Most free throws attempted, three-year career: 1152, Pete Maravich, LSU, '67–68 through '69–70.

Highest free-throw percentage, season: 93.3%, Tommy Boyer, Arkansas, '61–62.

Highest free-throw percentage, career: 89.8%, Bob Lloyd, Rutgers, '64–65 through '66–67.

Most rebounds, one game: 51, Bill Chambers, William & Mary, versus Virginia, 2/14/53.

Most rebounds, season: 734, Walter Dukes, Seton Hall, '52–53.

Most rebounds, four-year career: 2201, Tom Gola, LaSalle, '51–52 through '54–55.

Most rebounds, three-year career: 1704, Tom Gola, LaSalle, '52–53 through '54–55.

Highest rebounding average per game, season: 25.6, Charlie Slack, Marshall, '54–55.

Highest rebounding average per game, career (minimum of 800 rebounds): 21.8, Charlie Slack, Marshall, '52–53 through '55–56.

MAJOR-COLLEGE TEAM RECORDS

Most points scored, one game: 158, Houston, versus Valparaiso, 2/24/68. (Surprisingly, Houston made only 10 free throws.)

Most points scored, season: 3226, Houston, '67–68 (33 games).

Most points scored, one game, both teams: 260, Houston (152) and Texas Wesleyan (108), 2/22/66.

Fewest points scored, one game (since 1938): 9, Penn State, versus Pittsburgh, 3/1/52; 9, Western Kentucky, versus Wichita State, 12/13/41.

Widest margin of victory: 91, LSU over Southwestern, Tenn. 124–33, 12/8/52.

Highest scoring average per game: 100.3, Jacksonville, '69–70 (28 games).

Most games scoring 100 points or more: 18, Jacksonville, '69–70; 18, Houston, '67–68.

Most consecutive games scoring 100 or more points: 11, Houston, '67–68.

Lowest scoring average per game allowed opponents: 32.5, Oklahoma State, '47–48 (1006 in 31 games).

Highest average scoring margin over opponents: 27.2, Kentucky, '53–54 (87.5 versus 60.3).

Most field goals, one game: 74, Houston, versus Valparaiso, 2/24/68.

Most field goals, season: 1352, Houston, '67–68.

Most field-goal attempts, one game: 126, Louisville, versus Hanover, 12/11/46.

Most field-goal attempts, season: 2925, Kentucky, '47–48.

Fewest field goals, one game (since 1938): 2, Duke, versus North Carolina, 3/8/68; 2, Arkansas State, versus Kentucky, 1/8/45.

Fewest field-goal attempts, one game: 9, Pittsburgh, versus Penn State, 3/1/52.

Highest field-goal percentage, one game: 72.3%, Minnesota, versus Iowa, 1/25/60.

Highest field-goal percentage, season: 54.4%, Ohio State, '69–70.

Most field goals scored per game, season: 41.0, Houston, '67–68.

Most free throws, one game: 53, Morehead State, versus Cincinnati, 2/11/56.

Most free throws, season: 865, Bradley, '53–54.

Most free-throw attempts, one game: 79, Northern Arizona, versus Arizona, 1/26/53.

Most free-throw attempts, season: 1263, Bradley, '53–54.

Most free-throw attempts, one game, both teams: 130, Northern Arizona (79) and Arizona (51), 1/26/53.

Most free throws, one game, both teams: 78, Northern Arizona (46) and Arizona (32), 1/26/53.

Highest free-throw percentage, one game (minimum of 20 made): 1000%, Murray State, versus Austin Peay, 2/1/66.

Highest free-throw percentage, season: 80.9%, Ohio State, '69–70.

Most rebounds, one game: 100, William & Mary, versus Virginia, 2/14/51.

Most rebounds, season: 2074, Houston, '67–68.

Highest rebound average per game, season: 70.0, Connecticut, '54–55.

Most personal fouls, one game: 50, Arizona, versus Northern Arizona, 1/26/53.

Most players disqualified, one game: 7, Weber State, versus Los Angeles State, 12/6/63; 7, Eastern Kentucky, versus Morehead State, 12/16/53.

Most personal fouls, season: 806, St. Louis, '51–52.

Most personal fouls per game, season: 29.3, Indiana, '51–52.

Fewest personal fouls, season: 253, Air Force, '61–62.

Fewest personal fouls per game, season: 11.0, Air Force, '61–62.

Fewest players disqualified, season (since 1951): 2, Connecticut, '54–55; tied by Lafayette, '55–56; Ohio State, '60–61; Ohio State, '61–62; Navy, '62–63.

Most overtime periods, one game: 6, Minnesota (59) at Purdue (56), 1/29/55; 6, Niagara (88) at Siena (81), 2/21/53.

Most overtime games, season: 6, Cincinnati, '66–67 (won 5, lost 1); 6, Georgia Tech, '62–63 (won 5, lost 1); 6, Alabama, '62–63 (won 1, lost 5).

Most consecutive victories: 60, San Francisco, 12/7/55 to 12/17/57 (Illinois ended the Dons' streak).

Most consecutive wins, season: 31, North Carolina, '56–57 (this was the great Tar Heel team that beat Kansas and Wilt Chamberlain in the NCAA final).

Most wins, season: 36, Kentucky, '47–48 (the Wildcats' record that season was 36 and 3).

Most consecutive losses: 37, The Citadel, 1/16/54 to 12/12/55.

Most consecutive losses, season: 26, Dartmouth, '17–18 (the hapless Indians played only 26 games that season or it could have been worse).

NBA CHAMPIONS

SEASON	TEAM	COACH	RUNNER-UP	FINAL SERIES SCORE
1969–70	New York Knickerbockers	William (Red) Holzman	Los Angeles Lakers	4–3
1968–69	Boston Celtics	Bill Russell	Los Angeles Lakers	4–3
1967–68	Boston Celtics	Bill Russell	Los Angeles Lakers	4–2
1966–67	Philadelphia 76ers	Alex Hannum	San Francisco Warriors	4–2
1965–66	Boston Celtics	Arnold (Red) Auerbach	Los Angeles Lakers	4–3
1964–65	Boston Celtics	Arnold (Red) Auerbach	Los Angeles Lakers	4–1
1963–64	Boston Celtics	Arnold (Red) Auerbach	San Francisco Warriors	4–1
1962–63	Boston Celtics	Arnold (Red) Auerbach	Los Angeles Lakers	4–2
1961–62	Boston Celtics	Arnold (Red) Auerbach	Los Angeles Lakers	4–3
1960–61	Boston Celtics	Arnold (Red) Auerbach	St. Louis Hawks	4–1
1959–60	Boston Celtics	Arnold (Red) Auerbach	St. Louis Hawks	4–3
1958–59	Boston Celtics	Arnold (Red) Auerbach	Minneapolis Lakers	4–0
1957–58	St. Louis Hawks	Alex Hannum	Boston Celtics	4–2
1956–57	Boston Celtics	Arnold (Red) Auerbach	St. Louis Hawks	4–3
1955–56	Philadelphia Warriors	George Senesky	Ft. Wayne Pistons	4–1
1954–55	Syracuse Nationals	Al Cervi	Ft. Wayne Pistons	4–3
1953–54	Minneapolis Lakers	John Kundla	Syracuse Nationals	4–3
1952–53	Minneapolis Lakers	John Kundla	New York Knickerbockers	4–1
1951–52	Minneapolis Lakers	John Kundla	New York Knickerbockers	4–3
1950–51	Rochester Royals	Les Harrison	New York Knickerbockers	4–3
1949–50	Minneapolis Lakers	John Kundla	Syracuse Nationals	4–2
1948–49	Minneapolis Lakers	John Kundla	Washington Capitols	4–2
1947–48	Baltimore Bullets	Buddy Jeannette	Philadelphia Warriors	4–2
1946–47	Philadelphia Warriors	Eddie Gottlieb	Chicago Stags	4–1

NBA MOST VALUABLE PLAYERS

The Podoloff Cup, named for the league's first commissioner, Maurice Podoloff, annually goes to the most valuable player, picked by the NBA players. There were no selections prior to 1955–56.

SEASON	PLAYER	TEAM	RUNNER-UP
1969–70	Willis Reed	New York Knickerbockers	Jerry West
1968–69	Westley Unseld	Baltimore Bullets	Willis Reed
1967–68	Wilt Chamberlain	Philadelphia 76ers	Lennie Wilkens
1966–67	Wilt Chamberlain	Philadelphia 76ers	Nate Thurmond
1965–66	Wilt Chamberlain	Philadelphia 76ers	Jerry West
1964–65	Bill Russell	Boston Celtics	Oscar Robertson
1963–64	Oscar Robertson	Cincinnati Royals	Wilt Chamberlain
1962–63	Bill Russell	Boston Celtics	Elgin Baylor
1961–62	Bill Russell	Boston Celtics	Wilt Chamberlain
1960–61	Bill Russell	Boston Celtics	Bob Pettit
1959–60	Wilt Chamberlain	Philadelphia Warriors	Bill Russell
1958–59	Bob Pettit	St. Louis Hawks	Bill Russell
1957–58	Bill Russell	Boston Celtics	Dolph Schayes

SEASON	PLAYER	TEAM	RUNNER-UP
1956–57	Bob Cousy	Boston Celtics	Bob Pettit
1955–56	Bob Pettit	St. Louis Hawks	Paul Arizin

NBA ROOKIES OF THE YEAR

SEASON	PLAYER	TEAM
1969–70	Lew Alcindor	Milwaukee Bucks
1968–69	Westley Unseld	Baltimore Bullets
1967–68	Earl Monroe	Baltimore Bullets
1966–67	Dave Bing	Detroit Pistons
1965–66	Rick Barry	San Francisco Warriors
1964–65	Willis Reed	New York Knickerbockers
1963–64	Jerry Lucas	Cincinnati Royals
1962–63	Terry Dischinger	Chicago Zephyrs
1961–62	Walt Bellamy	Chicago Packers
1960–61	Oscar Robertson	Cincinnati Royals
1959–60	Wilt Chamberlain	Philadelphia Warriors
1958–59	Elgin Baylor	Minneapolis Lakers
1957–58	Woody Sauldsberry	Philadelphia Warriors
1956–57	Tom Heinsohn	Boston Celtics
1955–56	Maurice Stokes	Rochester Royals
1954–55	Bob Pettit	Milwaukee Hawks
1953–54	Ray Felix	Baltimore Bullets
1952–53	Don Meineke	Fort Wayne Pistons
1951–52	no selection	
1950–51	no selection	
1949–50	no selection	
1948–49	no selection	
1947–48	no selection	
1946–47	no selection	

NBA ALL-STAR GAME

Walter Brown, respected owner of the Boston Celtics and one of the pioneer organizers of the NBA, convinced the other owners that the league should have an all-star game to showcase its talent. Brown, who died in 1964, hosted the first event at his Boston Garden. Joe Lapchick of the Knicks was the first East coach, John Kundla of Minneapolis the first West coach. Red Auerbach of the Celtics coached the East Squad 11 times. The East held a 14 to 6 series edge through 1970.

YEAR	SITE	RESULT	MOST VALUABLE PLAYER
1970	Philadelphia	East 142, West 135	Willis Reed, New York Knickerbockers
1969	Baltimore	East 123, West 112	Oscar Robertson, Cincinnati Royals
1968	New York City	East 144, West 124	Hal Greer, Philadelphia 76ers
1967	San Francisco	West 135, East 120	Rick Barry, San Francisco Warriors
1966	Cincinnati	East 137, West 94	Adrian Smith, Cincinnati Royals
1965	St. Louis	East 124, West 123	Jerry Lucas, Cincinnati Royals
1964	Boston	East 111, West 107	Oscar Robertson, Cincinnati Royals
1963	Los Angeles	East 115, West 108	Bill Russell, Boston Celtics
1962	St. Louis	West 150, East 130	Bob Pettit, St. Louis Hawks
1961	Syracuse	West 153, East 131	Oscar Robertson, Cincinnati Royals
1960	Philadelphia	East 125, West 115	Wilt Chamberlain, Philadelphia Warriors
1959	Detroit	West 124, East 108	Bob Pettit, St. Louis Hawks Elgin Baylor, Los Angeles Lakers
1958	St. Louis	East 130, West 118	Bob Pettit, St. Louis Hawks
1957	Boston	East 109, West 97	Bob Cousy, Boston Celtics
1956	Rochester	West 108, East 94	Bob Pettit, St. Louis Hawks
1955	New York City	East 100, West 91	Bill Sharman, Boston Celtics
1954	New York City	East 98, West 93	Bob Cousy, Boston Celtics

YEAR	SITE	RESULT	MOST VALUABLE PLAYER
1953	Fort Wayne	West 79, East 75	George Mikan, Minneapolis Lakers
1952	Boston	East 108, West 91	*Paul Arizin, Philadelphia Warriors
1951	Boston	East 111, West 94	*Ed Macauley, Boston Celtics

* Not officially picked but generally hailed as top performers

NBA ALL-STAR GAME RECORDS

Most points, one game: 42, Wilt Chamberlain, Philadelphia Warriors, 1962.
Most field goals, one game: 17, Wilt Chamberlain, Philadelphia Warriors, 1962.
Most field-goal attempts, one game: 27, Rick Barry, San Francisco Warriors, 1967.
Most free throws, one game: 12, Elgin Baylor, Los Angeles Lakers, 1962; 12, Oscar Robertson, Cincinnati Royals, 1965.
Most free-throw attempts, one game: 16, Wilt Chamberlain, Philadelphia Warriors, 1962.
Most rebounds, one game: 27, Bob Pettit, St. Louis Hawks, 1962.
Most assists, one game: 14, Oscar Robertson, Cincinnati Royals, 1961.
Most personal fouls, one game: 6, held by 11 different players.
Most minutes played, one game: 42, Oscar Robertson, Cincinnati Royals, 1964; 42, Bill Russell, Boston Celtics, 1964; 42, Jerry West, Los Angeles Lakers, 1964; 42, Nate Thurmond, San Francisco Warriors, 1967.
Most games picked: 13, Bob Cousy, Boston Celtics (Dolph Schayes of Syracuse and Bill Russell of Boston were picked 12 times).
Most minutes played, all time: 368, Bob Cousy, Boston Celtics.
Most points, all time: 230, Oscar Robertson, Cincinnati Royals.
Most field goals, all time: 83, Oscar Robertson, Cincinnati Royals.
Most field-goal attempts, all time: 193, Bob Pettit, St. Louis Hawks.
Best field-goal percentage, all time (minimum 15 made): .578, Wilt Chamberlain, Philadelphia Warriors etc.
Most free throws, all time: 78, Elgin Baylor, Los Angeles Lakers.
Most free-throw attempts, all time: 98, Elgin Baylor, Los Angeles Lakers.
Best free-throw percentage, all time (minimum 10 made): .938, Larry Foust, Fort Wayne Pistons.
Most rebounds, all time: 178, Bob Pettit, St. Louis Hawks.
Most assists, all time: 86, Bob Cousy, Boston Celtics.
Most personal fouls, all time: 37, Bill Russell, Boston Celtics.

NBA SCORING AVERAGE LEADERS

SEASON	PLAYER	TEAM	POINTS	AVERAGE
1969–70	Jerry West	Los Angeles Lakers	2309	31.2
1968–69	Elvin Hayes	San Diego Rockets	2327	28.4
1967–68	Dave Bing	Detroit Pistons	2142	27.1
1966–67	Rick Barry	San Francisco Warriors	2775	35.6
1965–66	Wilt Chamberlain	Philadelphia 76ers	2649	33.5
1964–65	Wilt Chamberlain	San Francisco Warriors-Philadelphia 76ers	2534	34.7
1963–64	Wilt Chamberlain	San Francisco Warriors	2948	36.9
1962–63	Wilt Chamberlain	San Francisco Warriors	3586	44.8
1961–62	Wilt Chamberlain	Philadelphia Warriors	4029	50.4
1960–61	Wilt Chamberlain	Philadelphia Warriors	3033	38.4
1959–60	Wilt Chamberlain	Philadelphia Warriors	2707	37.6
1958–59	Bob Pettit	St. Louis Hawks	2105	29.2
1957–58	George Yardley	Detroit Pistons	2001	27.8
1956–57	Paul Arizin	Philadelphia Warriors	1817	25.6
1955–56	Bob Pettit	St. Louis Hawks	1849	25.7
1954–55	Neil Johnston	Philadelphia Warriors	1631	22.7
1953–54	Neil Johnston	Philadelphia Warriors	1759	24.4
1952–53	Neil Johnston	Philadelphia Warriors	1564	22.3
1951–52	Paul Arizin	Philadelphia Warriors	1674	25.4
1950–51	George Mikan	Minneapolis Lakers	1932	28.4
1949–50	George Mikan	Minneapolis Lakers	1865	27.4
1948–49	George Mikan	Minneapolis Lakers	1698	28.3
1947–48	Joe Fulks	Philadelphia Warriors	949	22.1
1946–47	Joe Fulks	Philadelphia Warriors	1389	23.2

NBA FIELD GOAL PERCENTAGE LEADERS

SEASON	PLAYER	TEAM	FIELD GOALS	PERCENTAGE
1969–70	John Green	Cincinnati Royals	481	.559
1968–69	Wilt Chamberlain	Los Angeles Lakers	1099	.583
1967–68	Wilt Chamberlain	Philadelphia 76ers	1377	.595
1966–67	Wilt Chamberlain	Philadelphia 76ers	785	.683
1965–66	Wilt Chamberlain	Philadelphia 76ers	1074	.540
1964–65	Wilt Chamberlain	San Francisco Warriors-Philadelphia 76ers	1063	.510
1963–64	Jerry Lucas	Cincinnati Royals	545	.527
1962–63	Wilt Chamberlain	San Francisco Warriors	1463	.528
1961–62	Walt Bellamy	Chicago Packers	973	.513
1960–61	Wilt Chamberlain	Philadelphia Warriors	1251	.505
1959–60	Ken Sears	New York Knickerbockers	412	.477
1958–59	Ken Sears	New York Knickerbockers	491	.490
1957–58	Jack Twyman	Cincinnati Royals	465	.452
1956–57	Neil Johnston	Philadelphia Warriors	520	.447
1955–56	Neil Johnston	Philadelphia Warriors	499	.457
1954–55	Larry Foust	Fort Wayne Pistons	398	.487
1953–54	Ed Macauley	Boston Celtics	462	.486
1952–53	Neil Johnston	Philadelphia Warriors	504	.4524*
1951–52	Paul Arizin	Philadelphia Warriors	548	.448
1950–51	Alex Groza	Indianapolis Olympians	492	.470
1949–50	Alex Groza	Indianapolis Olympians	521	.478
1948–49	Arnie Risen	Rochester Royals	345	.423
1947–48	Bob Feerick	Washington Capitols	293	.340
1946–47	Bob Feerick	Washington Capitols	364	.401

* Ed Macauley of Boston had .4523

NBA FREE THROW PERCENTAGE LEADERS

SEASON	PLAYER	TEAM	FREE THROWS	PERCENTAGE
1969–70	Flynn Robinson	Milwaukee Bucks	439	.898
1968–69	Larry Siegfried	Boston Celtics	336	.864
1967–68	Oscar Robertson	Cincinnati Royals	576	.873
1966–67	Adrian Smith	Cincinnati Royals	343	.903
1965–66	Larry Siegfried	Boston Celtics	274	.881
1964–65	Larry Costello	Philadelphia 76ers	243	.877
1963–64	Oscar Robertson	Cincinnati Royals	800	.853
1962–63	Larry Costello	Syracuse Nationals	288	.881
1961–62	Dolph Schayes	Syracuse Nationals	286	.896
1960–61	Bill Sharman	Boston Celtics	210	.921
1959–60	Dolph Schayes	Syracuse Nationals	533	.892
1958–59	Bill Sharman	Boston Celtics	342	.932
1957–58	Dolph Schayes	Syracuse Nationals	629	.904
1956–57	Bill Sharman	Boston Celtics	381	.9050*
1955–56	Bill Sharman	Boston Celtics	358	.867
1954–55	Bill Sharman	Boston Celtics	347	.897
1953–54	Bill Sharman	Boston Celtics	331	.844
1952–53	Bill Sharman	Boston Celtics	341	.850
1951–52	Bob Wanzer	Rochester Royals	377	.904
1950–51	Joe Fulks	Philadelphia Warriors	378	.855
1949–50	Max Zaslofsky	Chicago Stags	321	.843
1948–49	Bob Feerick	Washington Capitols	256	.859
1947–48	Bob Feerick	Washington Capitols	189	.788
1946–47	Fred Scolari	Washington Capitols	146	.811

* Dolph Schayes of Syracuse had .9045

NBA REBOUNDING LEADERS

Despite the importance of rebounds in winning basketball games, the NBA, for some reason, did not keep official rebounding statistics for the first four years of its existence.

SEASON	PLAYER	TEAM	REBOUNDS	AVERAGE
1969–70	Elvin Hayes	San Diego Rockets	1386	16.9
1968–69	Wilt Chamberlain	Los Angeles Lakers	1712	21.1
1967–68	Wilt Chamberlain	Philadelphia 76ers	1952	23.8
1966–67	Wilt Chamberlain	Philadelphia 76ers	1957	24.2
1965–66	Wilt Chamberlain	Philadelphia 76ers	1943	24.6
1964–65	Bill Russell	Boston Celtics	1878	24.1
1963–64	Bill Russell	Boston Celtics	1930	24.7
1962–63	Wilt Chamberlain	San Francisco Warriors	1946	24.3
1961–62	Wilt Chamberlain	Philadelphia Warriors	2052	25.6
1960–61	Wilt Chamberlain	Philadelphia Warriors	2149	27.2
1959–60	Wilt Chamberlain	Philadelphia Warriors	1941	26.9
1958–59	Bill Russell	Boston Celtics	1612	23.0
1957–58	Bill Russell	Boston Celtics	1564	22.7
1956–57	Maurice Stokes	Rochester Royals	1256	17.4
1955–56	Bob Pettit	St. Louis Hawks	1164	16.2
1954–55	Neil Johnston	Philadelphia Warriors	1085	15.1
1953–54	Harry Gallatin	New York Knickerbockers	1098	15.3
1952–53	George Mikan	Minneapolis Lakers	1007	14.4
1951–52	Larry Foust	Fort Wayne Pistons	880	13.3
	Mel Hutchins	Milwaukee Hawks	880	13.3
1950–51	Dolph Schayes	Syracuse Nationals	1080	16.4

NBA LEADERS IN AVERAGE ASSISTS

SEASON	PLAYER	TEAM	ASSISTS	AVERAGE
1969–70	Len Wilkens	Seattle SuperSonics	683	9.1
1968–69	Oscar Robertson	Cincinnati Royals	772	9.8
1967–68	Wilt Chamberlain	Philadelphia 76ers	702	8.6
1966–67	Guy Rodgers	Chicago Bulls	908	11.2
1965–66	Oscar Robertson	Cincinnati Royals	847	11.1
1964–65	Oscar Robertson	Cincinnati Royals	861	11.5
1963–64	Oscar Robertson	Cincinnati Royals	868	11.0
1962–63	Guy Rodgers	San Francisco Warriors	825	10.6
1961–62	Oscar Robertson	Cincinnati Royals	899	11.4
1960–61	Oscar Robertson	Cincinnati Royals	690	9.7
1959–60	Bob Cousy	Boston Celtics	715	9.5
1958–59	Bob Cousy	Boston Celtics	557	8.6
1957–58	Bob Cousy	Boston Celtics	463	7.1
1956–57	Bob Cousy	Boston Celtics	478	7.5
1955–56	Bob Cousy	Boston Celtics	642	8.9
1954–55	Bob Cousy	Boston Celtics	557	7.8
1953–54	Bob Cousy	Boston Celtics	518	7.2
1952–53	Bob Cousy	Boston Celtics	547	7.7
1951–52	Andy Phillip	Philadelphia Warriors	539	8.2
1950–51	Andy Phillip	Philadelphia Warriors	414	6.3
1949–50	Andy Phillip	Chicago Stags	377	5.8
1948–49	Bob Davies	Rochester Royals	321	5.4
1947–48	Howie Dallmar	Philadelphia Warriors	120	2.5
1946–47	Ernie Calverley	Providence Steamrollers	202	3.4

NBA ARENAS

Professional basketball has come a long way since the days when the Philadelphia Sphas played their home games in a hotel ballroom, or when players risked tetanus when they cut themselves on the rusty wire cages which enclosed some courts to keep the ball in play. Today most of the buildings are too grand to be called gymnasiums or halls and the courts are spacious and well-lighted. There are exceptions. Chicago Stadium is a sooty relic in a rough part of town. The floor at Georgia Tech's arena, used by Atlanta, has little or no spring and is bad for players' legs, possibly shortening their careers.

TEAM	ARENA	CAPACITY
Atlanta Hawks	Alexander Memorial Coliseum	6,996
Baltimore Bullets	Civic Center	12,289
Boston Celtics	Boston Garden	15,128
Buffalo Braves	Memorial Auditorium	10,683
Chicago Bulls	Chicago Stadium	17,374
Cincinnati Royals	Cincinnati Garden	11,650
Cleveland Cavaliers	Cleveland Arena	11,000
Detroit Pistons	Cobo Arena	10,053
Los Angeles Lakers	The Forum	17,509
Milwaukee Bucks	Milwaukee Arena	10,746
New York Knickerbockers	Madison Square Garden	19,500
Philadelphia 76ers	The Spectrum	15,244
Phoenix Suns	Veterans Memorial Coliseum	12,295
Portland Trail Blazers	Memorial Coliseum	13,000
San Diego Rockets	San Diego International Sports Arena	14,000
San Francisco Warriors	Cow Palace	14,500
	Civic Auditorium	7,000
	Oakland Coliseum Arena	14,000
Seattle SuperSonics	Seattle Coliseum	12,382

NBA INDIVIDUAL RECORDS

Most points, one game: 100, Wilt Chamberlain, Philadelphia Warriors, versus New York, 3/2/62.

Most points, playoff game: 61, Elgin Baylor, Los Angeles Lakers, versus Boston, 4/14/62.

Most points, season: 4029, Wilt Chamberlain, Philadelphia Warriors, '61–62.

Most field goals, one game: 36, Wilt Chamberlain, Philadelphia Warriors, versus New York, 3/2/62.

Most field goals, playoff game: 34, Bob Pettit, St. Louis Hawks, versus Boston, 4/13/57 (two overtimes).

Most field goals, season: 1597, Wilt Chamberlain, Philadelphia Warriors, '61–62.

Most points in playoffs: 562, Jerry West, Los Angeles Lakers, '70.

Most career points in playoffs: 3708, Jerry West, Los Angeles Lakers, '61–70.

Most seasons with more than 1,000 points: 13, Bob Cousy, Boston Celtics, '49–50 through '62–63.

Most games 50 or more points, season: 45, Wilt Chamberlain, Philadelphia Warriors, '61–62.

Most consecutive points without missing: 32, Larry Costello, Syracuse Nationals, 12/8/61.

Most field-goal attempts, one game: 63, Wilt Chamberlain, Philadelphia Warriors, versus New York, 3/2/62.

Most field-goal attempts, playoff game: 48, Wilt Chamberlain, Philadelphia Warriors, versus Syracuse, 3/22/62.

Most field-goal attempts, season: 3159, Wilt Chamberlain, Philadelphia Warriors, '61–62.

Most free throws, one game: 28, Wilt Chamberlain, Philadelphia Warriors, versus New York, 3/2/62.

Most free throws, playoff game: 30, Bob Cousy, Boston Celtics, versus Syracuse, 3/21/53 (four overtimes).

Most free throws, season: 840, Jerry West, Los Angeles Lakers, '65–66.

Most free throws, playoffs: 137, Jerry West, Los Angeles Lakers, '65.

Most free-throw attempts, one game: 34, Wilt Chamberlain, Philadelphia Warriors, versus St. Louis, 2/22/62.

Most free-throw attempts, playoff game: 32, Bob Cousy, Boston Celtics, versus Syracuse, 3/21/53 (four overtimes).

Most free-throw attempts, season: 1363, Wilt Chamberlain, Philadelphia Warriors, '61–62.

Most consecutive field goals without a miss, one game: 18, Wilt Chamberlain, San Francisco Warriors, versus New York, 11/27/63.

Highest scoring average per game, playoffs: 40.6, Jerry West, Los Angeles Lakers, '65.

Highest scoring average per game, season: 50.4, Wilt Chamberlain, Philadelphia Warriors, '61–62.

Highest field-goal percentage, season: .683, Wilt Chamberlain, Philadelphia 76ers, '66–67.

Most rebounds, one game: 55, Wilt Chamberlain, Philadelphia Warriors, versus Boston, 11/24/60.

Most rebounds, playoff game: 41, Wilt Chamberlain, Philadelphia 76ers, versus Boston, 4/5/67 (Bill Russell of Boston twice had 40 in final-series playoff games).

Most rebounds, season: 2149, Wilt Chamberlain, Philadelphia Warriors, '60–61.

Highest rebounding average per game, season: 27.2, Wilt Chamberlain, Philadelphia Warriors, '60–61.

Most assists, one game: 28, Bob Cousy, Boston Celtics, versus Minneapolis, 2/27/59; 28, Guy Rodgers, San Francisco Warriors, versus St. Louis, 3/14/63.

Most assists, playoff game: 19, Bob Cousy, Boston Celtics, versus St. Louis, 4/9/58; tied by Cousy himself, versus Minneapolis, 4/7/59; Wilt Chamberlain, Philadelphia 76ers, versus Cincinnati, 3/24/67; Walt Frazier, New York Knickerbockers, versus Los Angeles, 5/8/70.

Most assists, season: 908, Guy Rodgers, Chicago Bulls, '66–67.

Most personal fouls, one game: 8, Don Otten, Tri-Cities Blackhawks, versus Sheboygan, 11/24/49.

Most personal fouls, season: 366, Bill Bridges, St. Louis Hawks, '67–68.

Most assists by a center: 702, Wilt Chamberlain, Philadelphia 76ers, '67–68.

Highest assist average, season: 11.5, Oscar Robertson, Cincinnati Royals, '64–65.

Most disqualifications, season: 26, Don Meineke, Fort Wayne Pistons, '52–53.

Most consecutive games, no disqualifications: 799, Wilt Chamberlain, 10/24/59 through 3/24/69.

Most minutes played, season: 3882, Wilt Chamberlain, Philadelphia Warriors, '61–62.

Most minutes per game, average: 48.5, Wilt Chamberlain, Philadelphia Warriors, '61–62.

Most consecutive minutes played: 2193, Wilt Chamberlain, Philadelphia Warriors, '60–61.

Most consecutive complete games: 47, Wilt Chamberlain, Philadelphia Warriors, '61–62.

Most complete games, season: 79, Wilt Chamberlain, Philadelphia Warriors, '61–62.

NBA TEAM RECORDS

Most points, one game: 173, Boston Celtics, versus Minneapolis, 2/27/59.

Most points, playoff game: 156, Milwaukee Bucks, versus Philadelphia 76ers, 3/3/70.

Most points, season: 10,143, Philadelphia 76ers, '66–67.

Most field goals, one game: 72, Boston Celtics, versus Minneapolis, 2/27/59.

Most field goals, playoff game: 67, Milwaukee Bucks, versus Philadelphia 76ers, 3/3/70.

Most field goals, season: 3965, Philadelphia 76ers, '67–68.

Most field-goal attempts, one game: 153, Philadelphia Warriors, versus Los Angeles, 12/8/61 (three overtimes).

Most field-goal attempts, playoff game: 140, San Francisco Warriors, versus Philadelphia 76ers, 4/14/67 (one overtime); 140, Boston Celtics versus Syracuse Nationals, 3/18/59.

Most field-goal attempts, season: 9295, Boston Celtics, '60–61.

Highest field-goal average, season: .488, Milwaukee Bucks, '69–70.

Most free throws, one game: 59, Anderson Packers, versus Syracuse, 11/24/49 (five overtimes).

Most free throws, playoff game: 57, Boston Celtics, versus Syracuse, 3/21/53 (four overtimes).

Most free throws, season: 2434, Phoenix Suns, '69–70.

Most free-throw attempts, one game: 86, Syracuse Nationals, versus Anderson, 11/24/49 (five overtimes; Chicago had 71 versus Phoenix, 1/8/70, no overtimes).

Most free-throw attempts, playoff game: 66, Philadelphia 76ers, versus New York, 3/30/68.

Most free-throw attempts, season: 3411, Philadelphia 76ers, '66–67.

Highest free-throw average, season: .794, Syracuse Nationals, '56–57.
Most rebounds, one game: 112, Philadelphia Warriors, versus Cincinnati, 11/8/59; 112, Boston Celtics, versus Detroit, 12/24/60.
Most rebounds, playoff game: 107, Boston Celtics, versus Philadelphia, 3/19/60.
Most rebounds, season: 6131, Boston Celtics, '60–61.
Most assists, one game: 60, Syracuse Nationals, versus Baltimore, 11/15/52 (one overtime).
Most assists, playoff game: 46, Milwaukee Bucks, versus Philadelphia, 3/3/70.
Most assists, season: 2214, Seattle SuperSonics, '69–70.
Most personal fouls, one game: 66, Anderson Packers, versus Syracuse, 11/24/49 (five overtimes).
Most personal fouls, playoff game: 55, Syracuse Nationals, versus Boston, 3/21/53 (three overtimes).
Most disqualifications, one game: 8, Syracuse Nationals, versus Baltimore, 11/15/52 (one overtime).
Most games won, season: 68, Philadelphia 76ers, '66–67.
Most games lost, season: 67, San Diego Rockets, '67–68.
Highest winning percentage, season: .840, Philadelphia 76ers, '66–67.
Lowest winning percentage, season: .125, Providence Steamrollers, '47–48.
Most games won at home: 33, Rochester Royals, '49–50.
Most games lost at home: 29, San Francisco Warriors, '64–65.
Longest winning streak: 18, New York Knickerbockers, 10/24/69 to 11/28/69.
Longest winning streak at start of season: 15, Washington Capitols, 11/3/48 to 12/4/48.
Longest winning streak at end of season: 11, Philadelphia 76ers, 3/3/66 to 3/20/66.
Longest winning streak at home: 29, Minneapolis Lakers, 1/30/49 through 11/19/50.
Longest losing streak: 17, San Francisco Warriors, 12/20/64 to 1/26/65; 17, San Diego Rockets, 1/21/68 to 2/16/68.
Longest losing streak at start of season: 15, Denver Nuggets, 10/29/49 through 12/25/49.
Longest winning streak in playoffs: 7, Los Angeles Lakers, 4/5/70 to 4/19/70.
Most points scored against, season: 10,261, Seattle SuperSonics, '67–68.
Highest average points per game: 125.4, Philadelphia Warriors, '61–62.
Highest average points against: 125.1, Seattle SuperSonics, '67–68.
Highest average per home game: 128.6, Boston Celtics, '59–60.
Highest average per away game: 122.4, Boston Celtics, '59–60.
Most games, 100 points: 80, Philadelphia 76ers, New York Knickerbockers and San Francisco Warriors, '66–67; 80, Baltimore Bullets, Boston Celtics, '67–68.
Most consecutive 100-point games: 77, New York Knickerbockers, '66–67.
Biggest winning margin: 62, Syracuse Nationals (162), versus New York (100), 12/25/60.

AMERICAN BASKETBALL ASSOCIATION CHAMPIONS

SEASON	TEAM	COACH	RUNNER-UP	FINAL SERIES SCORE
1969–70	Indiana Pacers	Bob Leonard	Los Angeles Stars	4 to 2
1968–69	Oakland Oaks	Alex Hannum	Indiana Pacers	4 to 1
1967–68	Pittsburgh Pipers	Vince Cazzetta	New Orleans Buccaneers	4 to 3

ABA MOST VALUABLE PLAYERS

SEASON	PLAYER	TEAM
1969–70	Spencer Haywood	Denver Rockets
1968–69	Mel Daniels	Indiana Pacers
1967–68	Connie Hawkins	Pittsburgh Pipers

ABA ROOKIES OF THE YEAR

SEASON	PLAYER	TEAM
1969–70	Spencer Haywood	Denver Rockets
1968–69	Warren Armstrong	Oakland Oaks
1967–68	Mel Daniels	Minnesota Muskies

ABA ALL-STAR GAME

YEAR	SITE	RESULT	MOST VALUABLE PLAYER
1970	Indianapolis	East 128, West 98	Spencer Haywood, Denver Rockets
1969	Louisville	West 133, East 127	John Beasley, Dallas Chaparrals
1968	Indianapolis	East 126, West 120	Larry Brown, New Orleans Buccaneers

ABA ALL-STAR GAME RECORDS

Most points, one game: 30, Larry Jones, Denver Rockets, 1970.
Most two-point field goals, one game: 10, Larry Jones, Denver Rockets, 1970; 10, Spencer Haywood, Denver Rockets, 1970.
Most two-point field-goal attempts, one game: 19, Spencer Haywood, Denver Rockets, 1970.
Most three-point field goals, one game: 2, Larry Brown, New Orleans Buccaneers, 1968; 2, Charles Vaughn, Pittsburgh Pipers, 1968; 2, Glen Combs, Dallas Chaparrals, 1970.
Most three-point field-goal attempts, one game: 6, Louie Dampier, Kentucky Colonels, 1970.
Most free throws, one game: 10, Larry Jones, Denver Rockets, 1970.
Most free-throw attempts, one game: 13, Larry Jones, Denver Rockets, 1970.
Most rebounds, one game: 19, Spencer Haywood, Denver Rockets, 1970.
Most assists, one game: 9, Larry Jones, Denver Rockets, 1969.
Most errors, one game: 7, Larry Brown, Oakland Oaks, 1969.
Most personal fouls, one game: 6, Don Freeman, Miami Floridians, 1969.
Best percentage two-point field goals (minimum 10 attempts): .727 (8 of 11), Walt Simon, New York Nets, 1969.
Best percentage three-point field goals (minimum two attempts): 1.000 (2 of 2), Larry Brown, New Orleans Buccaneers, 1968; 1.000 (2 of 2), Charles Vaughn, Pittsburgh Pipers, 1968.
Best percentage free throws (minimum seven attempts): 1.000 (7 of 7), Don Freeman, Miami Floridians, 1969.
Most minutes played, one game: 39, Spencer Haywood, Denver Rockets, 1970.

ABA SCORING AVERAGE LEADERS

SEASON	PLAYER	TEAM	POINTS	AVERAGE
1969–70	Spencer Haywood	Denver Rockets	2519	29.9
1968–69	Rick Barry	Oakland Oaks	1190	34.0
1967–68	Connie Hawkins	Pittsburgh Pipers	1875	26.8

ABA FIELD GOAL PERCENTAGE LEADERS (TWO-POINT SHOTS)

SEASON	PLAYER	TEAM	FIELD GOALS	PERCENTAGE
1969–70	Frank Card	Washington Capitols	350	.530
1968–69	Bill McGill	Denver Rockets	411	.552
1967–68	Tom Washington	Pittsburgh Pipers	310	.522

ABA FIELD GOAL PERCENTAGE LEADERS
(THREE-POINT SHOTS)

ABA rules provide that "a goal from the field counts 2 points if shot from inside the 25-foot zone, and counts 3 points if shot from any other place on the floor." In the 1967–68 season, Wes Bialosuknia of the Oakland Oaks made nine of these mortar shots in a row over five games.

SEASON	PLAYER	TEAM	FIELD GOALS	PER- CENTAGE
1969–70	Darel Carrier	Kentucky Colonels	105	.375
1968–69	Darel Carrier	Kentucky Colonels	125	.379
1967–68	Darel Carrier	Kentucky Colonels	84	.357

ABA FREE THROW PERCENTAGE LEADERS

SEASON	PLAYER	TEAM	FREE THROWS	PER- CENTAGE
1969–70	Darel Carrier	Kentucky Colonels	454	.892
1968–69	Rick Barry	Oakland Oaks	403	.888
1967–68	Charles Beasley	Dallas Chaparrals	285	.872

ABA REBOUNDING LEADERS

SEASON	PLAYER	TEAM	RE- BOUNDS	AVERAGE
1969–70	Spencer Haywood	Denver Rockets	1637	19.5
1968–69	Mel Daniels	Indiana Pacers	1256	16.5
1967–68	Mel Daniels	Minnesota Muskies	1213	15.6

ABA LEADERS IN AVERAGE ASSISTS

SEASON	PLAYER	TEAM	ASSISTS	AVERAGE
1969–70	Larry Brown	Washington Capitols	580	7.07
1968–69	Larry Brown	Oakland Oaks	544	7.1
1967–68	Larry Brown	New Orleans Buccaneers	506	6.5

ABA ARENAS

Because of the ABA's constant franchise shuffling (which was also common in the NBA in its early years), some fine arenas have been left behind, e.g. the Los Angeles Sports Arena, Anaheim Convention Center and Oakland Coliseum. The ones in use at this writing are generally good, and if the league lasts there are some new auditoriums being planned and built, most notably the 14,000-seat Nassau Coliseum on Long Island and the 10,745-seat Scope in Norfolk, Virginia. In most cases, the seating capacities listed here were taken from press guides and yearbooks of ABA clubs.

TEAM	ARENA	CAPACITY
Carolina Cougars	Greensboro Coliseum	15,500
	Dorton Arena, Raleigh	7,500
	Charlotte Coliseum	11,666
Denver Rockets	Auditorium-Arena	6,841
	Coliseum	10,000
Floridians	Miami Beach Convention Hall, north hall	9,000
	Miami Beach Convention Hall, south hall	6,700
	Curtis Hixon Hall, Tampa	6,000
	Jacksonville Coliseum	8,500
	West Palm Beach Auditorium	5,500
Indiana Pacers	Fairgrounds Coliseum	9,147
Kentucky Colonels	Freedom Hall	16,933
	Convention Center	5,733
Memphis Pros	Mid-South Coliseum	10,753
New York Nets	Island Gardens	5,000
Pittsburgh Condors	Civic Arena	13,500
Texas Chaparrals	Moody Coliseum, Dallas	9,000
	Tarrant County Convention Center, Fort Worth	13,500
	Lubbock Municipal Coliseum	10,400
Utah Stars	Salt Palace	12,224
Virginia Squires	Old Dominion U., Norfolk	5,200
	Hampton Roads Coliseum, Hampton	10,000
	Roanoke Civic Center	10,010
	Richmond Arena	6,000

ABA INDIVIDUAL RECORDS

Most points, one game: 59, Spencer Haywood, Denver Rockets, versus Los Angeles, 4/15/70.

Most points, playoff game: 53, Roger Brown, Indiana Pacers, versus Los Angeles, 5/19/70.

Most points, season: 2519, Spencer Haywood, Denver Rockets, '69–70.

Most two-point field goals, one game: 25, Mel Daniels, Indiana Pacers, versus New York, 3/18/69.

Most two-point field goals, playoff game: 19, James Jones, New Orleans Buccaneers, versus Dallas, 4/7/69; 19, Levern Tart, New York Nets, versus Kentucky, 4/17/70; 19, Spencer Haywood, Denver Rockets, versus Washington, 4/19/70.

Most two-point field goals, season: 986, Spencer Haywood, Denver Rockets, '69–70.

Best percentage two-point field goals: .552, Billy McGill, Denver Rockets, '68–69.

Most three-point field goals, one game: 10, Les Selvage, Anaheim Amigos, versus Denver, 2/15/68.

Most three-point field goals, playoff game: 7, Roger Brown, Indiana Pacers, versus Los Angeles, 5/25/70.

Most three-point field goals, season: 199, Louie Dampier, Kentucky, '68–69.

Best percentage three-point field goals: .379, Darel Carrier, Kentucky Colonels, '68–69.

Most two-point field-goal attempts, one game: 45, Spencer Haywood, Denver Rockets, versus Los Angeles, 4/15/70.

Most two-point field-goal attempts, playoff game: 39, Connie Hawkins, Minnesota Muskies, versus Miami, 4/15/69; 39, Spencer Haywood, Denver Rockets, versus Washington, 4/19/70.

Most two-point field-goal attempts, season: 1987, Spencer Haywood, Denver Rockets, '69–70.

Most three-point field-goal attempts, one game: 26, Les Selvage, Anaheim Amigos, versus Denver, 2/15/68.

Most three-point field-goal attempts, playoff game: 15, Charles Vaughn, Pittsburgh Pipers, versus New Orleans, 4/20/68.

Most three-point field-goal attempts, season: 552, Louie Dampier, Kentucky Colonels, '68–69.

Highest scoring average, season: 34.0, Rick Barry, Oakland Oaks, '68–69.

Most free throws, one game: 24, Tony Jackson, New Jersey Americans, versus Kentucky, 11/27/67.

Most free throws, playoff game: 17, Doug Moe, New Orleans Buccaneers, versus Pittsburgh, 4/27/68; 17, James Jones, New Orleans, versus Oakland, 4/21/69; 17, Fred Lewis, Indiana Pacers, versus Kentucky, 5/3/70.

Most free throws, season: 626, Don Freeman, Miami Floridians, '69–70.

Best percentage free throws: .892, Darel Carrier, Kentucky Colonels, '69–70.

Most rebounds, one game: 33, Mel Daniels, Indiana Pacers, versus Miami, 3/6/70.

Most rebounds, playoff game: 35, Tom Washington, Pittsburgh Pipers, versus Minnesota, 4/6/68.

Most rebounds, season: 1637, Spencer Haywood, Denver Rockets, '69–70.

Best rebounding average: 19.49, Spencer Haywood, Denver Rockets, '69–70.

Most assists, one game: 22, Steve Chubin, Anaheim Amigos, versus Dallas, 1/14/68.

Most assists, playoff game: 16, Mack Calvin, Los Angeles Stars, versus Dallas, 4/22/70.

Most assists, season: 580, Larry Brown, Washington Capitols, '69–70.

Most errors, one game: 14, Steve Chubin, Anaheim Amigos, versus Denver, 11/6/67.

Most errors, playoff game: 9, Warren Armstrong, Oakland Oaks, versus New Orleans, 4/21/69.

Most errors, season: 506, Larry Brown, New Orleans Buccaneers, '67–68.
Most personal fouls, season: 382, Gene Moore, Kentucky Colonels, '69–70.
Most games disqualified on personal fouls: 25, Gene Moore, Kentucky Colonels, '69–70.
Most minutes played, season: 3808, Spencer Haywood, Denver Rockets, '69–70.

ABA TEAM RECORDS

Most points, one game: 177, Indiana Pacers, versus Pittsburgh, 4/12/70.
Most points, playoff game: 150, Indiana Pacers, versus Oakland, 5/2/69.
Most points, season: 10,079, Dallas Chaparrals, '69–70.
Least points, one game: 75, Kentucky Colonels, versus Minnesota, 11–14–67; 75, Pittsburgh Pipers, versus Minnesota, 11/24/67.
Least points, playoff game: 86, Minnesota Muskies, versus Kentucky, 3/29/68.
Most two-point field goals, one game: 65, Oakland Oaks, versus New York, 4/1/69.
Most two-point field goals, playoff game: 56, Denver Rockets, versus Washington, 4/18/70; 56, Denver Rockets, versus Washington, 4/28/70.
Most two-point field goals, season: 3601, Washington Capitols, '69–70.
Most three-point field goals, one game: 12, Kentucky Colonels, versus Miami, 3/1/69.
Most three-point field goals, playoff game: 13, Minnesota Pipers, versus Miami, 4/19/69.
Most three-point field goals, season: 335, Kentucky Colonels, '68–69.
Most two-point field-goal attempts, one game: 131, Miami Floridians, versus Dallas, 2/10/70; 131, Minnesota Muskies, versus New Orleans, 12/6/67 (overtime).
Most two-point field-goal attempts, playoff game: 120, Indiana Pacers, versus Oakland, 5/3/69.
Most two-point field-goal attempts, season: 8003, Miami Floridians, '69–70.
Most three-point field-goal attempts, one game: 32, Anaheim Amigos, versus Denver, 2/15/68.
Most three-point field-goal attempts, playoff game: 26, Minnesota Pipers, versus Miami, 4/19/69.
Most three-point field-goal attempts, season: 1006, Minnesota Pipers, '68–69.
Highest scoring average: 126.49, Oakland Oaks, '68–69.
Most free throws, one game: 60, Indiana Pacers, versus Los Angeles, 2/1/69.
Most free throws, playoff game: 46, Oakland Oaks, versus New Orleans, 4/19/69.
Most free throws, season: 2607, Oakland Oaks, '68–69.
Most free-throw attempts, one game: 73, Miami Floridians, versus New York, 11/20/68.
Most free-throw attempts, playoff game: 58, Indiana Pacers, versus Oakland, 5/2/69.
Most free-throw attempts, season: 3434, Oakland Oaks, '68–69.
Most rebounds, one game: 93, Denver Rockets, versus Dallas, 4/8/70.
Most rebounds, playoff game: 77, New Orleans Buccaneers, versus Oakland, 4/23/69.
Most rebounds, season: 4845, Denver Rockets, '69–70.
Highest rebounding average: 61.90, Minnesota Muskies, '67–68.
Most assists, one game: 43, Indiana Pacers, versus Pittsburgh Pipers, 4/12/70.
Most assists, playoff game: 37, Los Angeles Stars, versus Dallas, 4/22/70.
Most assists, season: 1961, Washington Capitols, '69–70.
Most errors, one game: 40, Oakland Oaks, versus Kentucky, 11/29/68.
Most errors, playoff game: 31, Oakland Oaks, versus Denver, 4/6/69.
Most errors, season: 1991, Washington Capitols, '69–70.
Most personal fouls, one game: 46, New York Nets, versus Washington, 12/26/69.
Most personal fouls, playoff game: 38, Oakland Oaks, versus Indiana, 5/2/69.
Most personal fouls, season: 2409, Kentucky Colonels, '69–70.
Most players disqualified on personal fouls, one game: 5, Indiana Pacers, versus Oakland, 1/30/69; 5, Los Angeles Stars, versus Indiana, 2/1/69.
Most players disqualified on personal fouls, playoff game: 3, Indiana Pacers, versus Oakland, 5/7/69; 3, Dallas Chaparrals, versus New Orleans, 4/9/68; 3, Kentucky Colonels, versus New York, 4/17/70.
Most players disqualified on personal fouls, season: 76, New York Nets, '69–70.
Most minutes played, season: 20,435, New Orleans Buccaneers, '69–70.

PRO BASKETBALL QUIZ

You qualify as an unadulterated, A-1 basketball nut if you can match 40 or more of these nicknames with the proper cities, areas or states. The names are from past and present franchises in the National Basketball Association, American Basketball Association and American Basketball League, with a few clubs from older leagues thrown in just to be mean. For the wordophiles, a chaparral is a growth of stubby oaks, a muskie is a game fish, a zephyr is a gentle breeze and a Kautsky is a particular basketball-loving Hoosier. And yes, Chicago has had at least six different teams over the years.

Anaheim	Minneapolis	All Stars	Nationals
Anderson	Minnesota	Americans	Nets
Atlanta	Minnesota	Amigos	Nuggets
Baltimore	New Jersey	Blackhawks	Oaks
Boston	New Orleans	Bombers	Olympians
Brooklyn	New York	Braves	Pacers
Buffalo	New York	Bruins	Packers
Carolina	New York	Buccaneers	Palace Five
Chicago	Oakland	Bucks	Pipers
Chicago	Oshkosh	Bullets	Pipers
Chicago	Philadelphia	Bulls	Pipers
Chicago	Philadelphia	Capitols	Pistons
Chicago	Philadelphia	Cavaliers	Pistons
Chicago	Phoenix	Celtics	Pros
Cincinnati	Pittsburgh	Celtics	Rebels
Cleveland	Pittsburgh	Chaparrals	Redskins
Cleveland	Pittsburgh	Chiefs	Rens
Cleveland	Pittsburgh	Colonels	Rockets
Cleveland	Portland	Condors	Rockets
Denver	Providence	Cougars	Rosenblums
Denver	Rochester	Falcons	Royals
Detroit	St. Louis	Floridians	Royals
Detroit	St. Louis	Gears	Saints
Fort Wayne	San Diego	Hawks	76ers
Hawaii	San Francisco	Hawks	Sphas
Indiana	San Francisco	Hawks	Squires
Indianapolis	Seattle	Hawks	Stags
Indianapolis	Sheboygan	Huskies	Stars
Indianapolis	Syracuse	Ironmen	Stars
Kansas City	Texas	Jets	Steamrollers
Kentucky	Toronto	Jets	Steers
Los Angeles	Tri-Cities	Jewels	Suns
Los Angeles	Utah	Kautskys	SuperSonics
Los Angeles	Virginia	Knickerbockers	Trail Blazers
Memphis	Washington	Lakers	Warriors
Miami	Washington	Lakers	Warriors
Milwaukee	Waterloo	Majors	Zephyrs
Milwaukee		Muskies	

ANSWERS: Anaheim Amigos, Anderson Packers, Atlanta Hawks, Baltimore Bullets, Boston Celtics, Brooklyn Jewels, Buffalo Braves, Carolina Cougars, Chicago Bruins, Chicago Bulls, Chicago Gears, Chicago Majors, Chicago Stags, Chicago Zephyrs, Cincinnati Royals, Cleveland Cavaliers, Cleveland Pipers, Cleveland Rebels, Cleveland Rosenblums, Denver Nuggets, Denver Rockets, Detroit Falcons, Detroit Pistons, Fort Wayne Pistons, Hawaii Chiefs, Indiana Pacers, Indianapolis Jets, Indianapolis Kautskys, Indianapolis Olympians, Kansas City Steers, Kentucky Colonels, Los Angeles Jets, Los Angeles Lakers, Los Angeles Stars, Memphis Pros, Miami Floridians, Milwaukee Bucks, Milwaukee Hawks, Minneapolis Lakers, Minnesota Muskies, Minnesota Pipers, New Jersey Americans, New Orleans Buccaneers, New York Celtics, New York Knickerbockers, New York Nets, Oakland Oaks, Oshkosh All Stars, Philadelphia 76ers, Philadelphia Sphas, Philadelphia Warriors, Phoenix Suns, Pittsburgh Condors, Pittsburgh Ironmen, Pittsburgh Pipers, Pittsburgh Rens, Portland Trail Blazers, Providence Steamrollers, Rochester Royals, St. Louis Bombers, St. Louis Hawks, San Diego Rockets, San Francisco Saints, San Francisco Warriors, Seattle SuperSonics, Sheboygan Redskins, Syracuse Nationals, Texas Chaparrals, Toronto Huskies, Tri-Cities Blackhawks, Utah Stars, Virginia Squires, Washington Capitols (the NBA, ABA and ABL all fielded teams under this name), Washington Palace Five, Waterloo Hawks.

Bibliography

AUERBACH, ARNOLD RED, *Basketball for the Player, the Fan, and the Coach.* Pocket Books, 1971 (paperback).

AUERBACH, ARNOLD RED, and SANN, PAUL, *Red Auerbach, Winning the Hard Way.* Little Brown, 1966.

BONTEMPS, ARNA, *Famous Negro Athletes.* Dodd, Mead, 1964.

DANZIG, ALLISON, and BRANDWEIN, PETER, *Sport's Golden Age, A Close-up of the Fabulous Twenties.* Harper & Bros., 1948.

FRAZIER, WALT, and JARES, JOE, *Clyde.* Rutledge Books/Holt, Rinehart & Winston, 1970.

HEPBURN, ANDREW, *Complete Guide to New York City.* Doubleday, 1964 (paperback).

HIRSCHBERG, AL, *Bill Russell of the Boston Celtics.* Messner, 1963.

HOBSON, HOWARD A., *Scientific Basketball.* Prentice-Hall, 1955.

HOLLANDER, ZANDER, *The Modern Encyclopedia of Basketball.* Four Winds Press, 1969.

HOLMAN, NAT, *Holman on Basketball.* Crown, 1950.

KOPPETT, LEONARD, *Championship NBA.* Dial Press, 1970 (paperback).

KOPPETT, LEONARD, *24 Seconds to Shoot, An Informal History of the National Basketball Association.* Macmillan, 1968.

LECHENPERG, HARALD, *Olympic Games 1960.* A. S. Barnes, 1960.

MALONEY, BUD, *The Official History of the National AAU Basketball Tournament in Denver.* Bud Maloney, 1960 (paperback).

MOKRAY, WILLIAM G., *Ronald Encyclopedia of Basketball.* Ronald Press, 1963.

NAISMITH, JAMES, *Basketball, Its Origin and Development.* International Committee of Young Men's Christian Associations, 1941.

OLIVER, NEWT, *One Basketball and Glory.* Newt Oliver, 1969 (paperback).

PADWE, SANDY, *Basketball's Hall of Fame.* Prentice-Hall, 1970.

PAXTON, HARRY T., *Sport U.S.A.* Nelson, 1961.

RAIBORN, MITCHELL H., *Financial Analysis of Intercollegiate Athletics.* NCAA, 1970 (paperback).

SMITH, RED, *Out of the Red.* Knopf, 1946.

TUNIS, JOHN R., *The American Way in Sports.* Duell, Sloan & Pearce, 1958.

WEYAND, ALEXANDER M., *The Cavalcade of Basketball.* Macmillan, 1960.

WOODEN, JOHN R., *Practical Modern Basketball.* Ronald Press, 1966.

———— *Yesterday in Sport.* Time-Life, 1968.

PERIODICALS: *Sports Illustrated, Sport, The Sporting News, Time, The Rotarian, Saturday Evening Post, The New York Times, New York Post, Los Angeles Times, Washington Post & Times-Herald, San Francisco Examiner, Chicago Tribune.*